HIGH & DRY

For John — Doing what I do wouldn't have been possible without your help all these years and it's appreciated, old friend — Best always, [signature] 12/12

High & Dry

by S.M. Park

This book published by University of Hell Press.
www.universityofhellpress.com

© 2012 Stephen M. Park

Book Design by Vince Norris
www.norrisportfolio.com

Cover Coloring by McHank
www.McHank.com

All Illustrations and Cover Art by the author.

Published in the United States of America.
ISBN 978-1-938753-05-3

Table of Contents

For Lois "Sweet Pea" Griffin
(1962 – 2009)

"The golden moments in the stream of life rush past us, and we see nothing but sand; the angels come to visit us, and we only know them when they are gone."

– George Eliot

I stood at the picture window in the front of my house this morning, watching the world go to work. There's a furniture cleaning plant across the street that reminds me of the dumps I've slaved in. Not just the building, but the poor bastards who work there. I watch them park their old cars in the neighborhood, then straggle up the street at 7:58 in the morning. Sucking the last cigarette, giving their assholes a good scratch, looking like breakfast was a Colt 45 and Beer Nuts.

That'd be me if it weren't for marijuana. I had over fifty full-time jobs in a twenty-year span and most of them were as dead-end as that plant. It was only towards the end, when I was word processing for attorneys, that the jobs themselves became vaguely tolerable.

But by then *I'd* lost it. I was doing three 12-hour days a week for a Bay Area firm, hoping that being off more than I was on would make the idea of work more palatable. It was the best I could manage but hardly good enough – I spent my off hours desperately searching for a way to move to Boregon and grow pot full-time.

Then one February morning the firm's senior partner called me into his office. He was a venerable old San Francisco icon, Bohemian Club and all that (I imagined him gardening in a silk vest and tie), and I vividly recalled our last conversation.

"Wilson," he'd said then, "I've noticed that you're a real grumpy bastard in the morning."

"Well … yeah."

"But come noon – when you've just returned from lunch – you're like a new person. Still hardworking and all, but friendly, even outgoing and helpful to your coworkers."

The old fox paid more attention than I thought.

"So whatever it is you puff at lunch," he said.

"Huh?"

"Smoke it before you get here in the morning."

I just stared at him.

"That'll be all, Wilson."

It's one of the things I liked about working for attorneys, the unspoken parameter of *I don't care what you're on, asshole, just get the work done.*

So now I'm back in the boss' office and the big guy looks diminished somehow, sad and kind of forlorn. I'm thinking it's just old age, he's gotta be crowding eighty. Then he starts a long speech about what a stellar worker I've been and my many contributions to the firm and – little by little, against all hope – I realize he's laying me off (something about the firm needing another secretary as opposed to a word processor). What's stranger yet … the poor bastard actually feels *bad* about it!

I jumped up, reached across the table, took his right hand in mine and pumped it. "Thank you!" I exclaimed. "I was beginning to think this would never happen!"

"But … I don't understand," he said. "I thought you'd be upset."

"Upset!?" I laughed. "After waiting twenty years for someone … ANYONE … to lay me off a job!"

"Why would you want a layoff?"

"Unemployment benefits, of course!"

The old guy shook his head. Balled up the notes he was reading from and tossed them into the wastebasket. "You always were a weird one, Wilson," he sighed. "When would you like your last day to be?"

"How's today sound?"

Six months later, as the benefits ran out, my first crop came in.

I found myself in a *Safeway* checkout line at 11:00 a.m. this morning. Normally I shop before seven in a ritzy grocery up the road so I don't have to be around Boregonians. Their excessive thriftiness drives me crazy; I'm an ugly American spendthrift, I'll admit that right off the top, and what I want for my dollar is no misers in sight.

Only the *Safeway* bakery, though, makes the twelve-grain bread I like. So there I was, elbow-to-elbow with the penny savers, waiting on forever. One cash register over an old man had the floor, leaning on the counter to challenge every item the cashier rang up. *Oh that coupon couldn't have expired ... Are you sure that's the full twenty percent? ... I thought those were 38 cents, not 39.*

Then, when he'd finally paid and his order was bagged, he stood at the end of the counter and carefully removed each item to check it against his receipt. I was finally at the front of my line when he raised his fist in exaltation, took one step towards the cashier.

"You overcharged me two cents!" he gasped ... and dropped dead on the spot. You know the look? You don't have to have seen people die before to know that when the light goes out ... that's it. The old guy fell backwards, bounced once and lay still.

"Oh my God!" moaned my cashier. "Does anybody here know CPR?"

"Forget it," I said, lifting my bags of bread. "He died the way he lived ... like a cheap bastard."

The woman beside me turned to the woman behind her, then motioned back at me.

"Californian," she said.

Except for a three-year layoff in the late seventies I've been smoking dope for forty-five years. Cigarettes, booze, smack, coke, meth, downers and psychedelics (most in copious quantities) have all come and gone in the interim, but marijuana? I'll snatch away the oxygen mask for one last hit.

Even as the best thing about the drug is that I didn't smoke it until after high school. This was less a matter of discipline than timing. Weed wasn't readily available in Portland, Boregon in 1965 and I was one of the few guys in my high school who'd even read about it. I carried around a paperback of Terry Southern's *Red Dirt Marihuana,* in fact, fantasizing about the day I could visit Tijuana and try out some "reefer."

I underestimated my baby boomer brethren, though: by late '65, when the first stirrings of drugs and unrest were filtering north from Berkeley, there were plenty of us looking for new experiences. The first time I smoked weed I was attending Portland State University. The campus was downtown and I'd registered late, ending up with mostly upper division courses even as – like many of my classmates – my sole objective was avoiding the draft. I was walking through the crowded hallways on the first day of school when I ran into Jake McDuff, an old buddy from high school. We bullshitted a little, then he asked me where I was living.

"At home," I said. "At least until I save some money."

"How about moving in with me?" he said. "I just rented a studio apartment on 6th Avenue."

"Yeah? How much is the rent?"

"Well, I got the place for ten dollars a month, so your share would be five."

I just stared at him. "Five dollars a *month*? How bad a dump is it?"

"It's basically a whorehouse, High. There's six other studios in the place and – far as I can tell – hookers rent all of 'em."

"Count me in, man."

There I was, a reasonably hardworking, Most Likely to Succeed type kid from a good family – a kind of poor preppie, actually – but the moment Jake described that seedy studio I knew I'd run away from home to live in it. It's the part of my nature I've given up trying to explain. Somehow there's a shiftless, wino drifter at the very core of my being. This is confirmed by drawings I did as an adolescent and pre-teen. You'll find an unshaved, bindle-stiff bum in all of them. Even the Christmas cards. I could be drawing all six of my family in various cartoon poses and when you take a good look at the Santa in the background he doesn't have a sack but a stick with a kerchiefed bundle on it or, worse, is obviously a drunken tramp who's stolen the suit.

And it went beyond my subconscious speaking through my art. I was nine when Disneyland opened and my parents took my brothers and I for a visit. Walt Disney still roamed the grounds then and when my mother spotted him she dragged me over to meet him.

"Mr. Disney," she said, "this is my son, Wilson. He's quite a cartoonist himself."

"Is that right?" he said, leaning over to shake my hand. I was in shock … this man was pretty much *God* to me. "Maybe someday you can come to work for me, Wilson."

"Gee, thanks, Mr. Disney," I stammered, "but … I'm gonna be a bum."

It's a story my mother told often afterwards – "The exact moment I realized something was slightly *bent* in Wilson" – and now I had to tell her I wanted to trade our wonderful home for a whorehouse.

Well, not in so many words, of course. I actually had a rather elaborate speech prepared when I approached her the morning after my meeting with Jake. She had her back to me and was washing the breakfast dishes in the sink.

"Mom," I said, "Jake McDuff is renting an apartment downtown and asked if I'd like to move in with him. Now I …"

"That's fine, Wilson," she said, not so much as turning around. "And you can still do your laundry here if you wish."

That was it. Eighteen years of her queenly reign and she lets me go like that. That's when parents trusted their kids (whether they should have or not). I gave her a big hug from behind, scrambled downstairs to pack my bag.

Jake had not exaggerated about 160 SW 6th Avenue. There were a couple "studios" downstairs and another four on the floor above, where ours was the corner suite next to the only bathroom on the floor.

Once inside you stepped into a narrow, shabby kitchen area, then took a quick left into a 10' by 10' room with a single window. It was sort of a jail cell with a kitchen attached, if you discounted the faint odor of smoke and the scorched southern wall. Jake hadn't told me about that part.

"It's a special feature," he said. "The winos that lived here got cold last winter and decided to build a fireplace."

At the base of the wall … in the part that hadn't burned away … I could see a blackened mound of bricks.

"So they hack a hole in the wall with an axe," says Jake, "actually mortar a bunch of bricks in there and start a fire … *but they forgot to add a chimney!* It's a miracle the whole place didn't burn down!"

It cracked us up that day and many times thereafter. Invariably we'd be sitting around and somebody new would come around and ask what happened to the wall. For awhile we made up tales but none of them outstripped the truth. The fact that Jake knew that, that like me he thought that nasty little studio was a great place to live, is one of the reasons the first roommate I ever had was pretty much the best one.

He was definitely a smooth, unflappable bastard (he went on to run some of the toughest card clubs in Gardena and Los Angeles in the eighties and nineties) and that was reasonably helpful around that dump. The other rooms *were* rented by whores and they dragged their johns in throughout the night. Usually the early a.m. hours, of course, when the men would be too shithoused to get a good look at what they were paying for.

When buyer's remorse set in there were lots of loud skirmishes in the hallway. Worse yet were the half-lit characters who pounded on *our* door, insisting that this or that hooker lived there and he wanted to see her right now; or the ones who pissed or puked on the bathroom walls, then passed out with their pants down.

It was quite an adventure for a kid from a home so painfully neat it would pass military inspection. As an added bonus, one that has reverberated through the years, my mother and father actually came to visit me one morning.

They meant to surprise me with my laundry. I'd been down at campus and ran into them as they descended the steps afterwards. My father began to speak but my mother held up her hand, walked over and stared at me with what I called her "harp mouth," lips pursed so tight they vibrated.

"I want you to know, Wilson," she said, "that I can't believe a son of mine would live in a place like that."

"Well, I ..."

"Wait a minute, I'm not finished." She paused, leaned in closer. "You've always been a slob, Wilson, and evidently, despite the best efforts of your father and myself, you plan to remain one."

"Well, I ..."

"So you're eighteen now. It's your life and where and how you live it is your business." She paused and took a deep breath. "But I want no part of it. As long as I live I'll never visit a place where you live again!"

Then the two of them slipped into the family station wagon and drove off. I stood there awhile, calmly assessing what had just been said, and finally thought, *Damn! that worked out pretty well*. (And it has. Decades later my mother, true to her word, regularly visits my three brothers' homes, but has never been *near* mine.)

Anyway, that 6th Avenue apartment saw plenty of parties and if there'd been anything but cigarettes around my buddies and I would have smoked it. Four of us were sitting on the roll-up beds in the front room during Christmas '65 when McDuff returned from a trip to Tijuana. He was deeply tanned with a big, shit-eating grin and motioned for quiet as he stood in the doorway. "Amigos," he said, reaching into the pocket of his shirt and pulling out a twisted, hand-rolled cigarette that he stuck in front of our noses, "I bring you the gift of *mari – ju – wana*."

10

Now understand: not only had none of us ever smoked dope before, but other than alcohol and caffeine we'd never used a drug. Did we hesitate? Did even one of us sit back and think, *Man, do I really want to introduce a mind-altering substance into my body?*

Fuck no ... we were baby boomers, we were entitled, we were there for the sensations! The four of us leaped for the joint at the same time, banging our heads and crumpling to the floor like the Four Stooges.

I flew home from Utah recently after visiting Zion National Park with a friend. When I grabbed a cab at the airport the driver was an immigrant who had little idea where he was going, much less where the hell he was. He was a giant, hulking character with a bullet head and strong, thick neck. Some kind of Russian, I think, because after storing my bag in the trunk he turned from the front seat and, using a series of hand gestures, shrugs and Slavic phrases, made it clear he didn't speak English and I'd have to show him where to go.

So I leaned forward and guided him the fifteen miles from the airport to my home by pointing at the appropriate streets. Judging by the way he drove (chin on top of the steering wheel, eyes bugging out as we wove across the yellow line), it was clear he hadn't been doing that long, either. This was substantiated by the snapshot of his family on the dashboard (there was a wife and two sturdy daughters, and they appeared to be praying).

When we finally pulled up to my place the fare was $25.00. I handed him a fifty and told him to keep the change.

He began a vague protest but I waved him off. "Listen, pal," I said, "you can't understand a word I'm saying, but what you're doing … well, it's like me flying into Moscow, stealing a cab, then driving around picking up fares. You're one audacious, desperate sonofabitch! You belong in America!"

He flashed a toothless grin for all of us.

I was president of my senior class in high school but that was mostly a fluke. I was fifteen when my father moved our family to Portland from the Bay Area and I spent my last two-and-half years at McKinley High. It was one of the best schools in the state at the time and also one of the largest, with over 700 students in my class alone.

The high school I'd gone to in California was basically *Grease* without the music, so when my brother Joe and I first stepped into McKinley I looked around at all the neatly dressed, fresh-faced kids and found myself grinning from ear to ear.

"Goddamn!" I exclaimed. "This must be where Wally Cleaver went to school!"

Joe did a mock gag in response ... he hated changing schools as much as I loved it. Part of the difference, I think, was our heights: his was normal but I'd been the tallest guy in class all my life, so I had a niche carved out the moment I showed up.

Plus I was a cartoonist. It seems like all high schools have at least one, and being able to draw made it easy to meet other kids.

It was near the end of my junior year when I found myself outside the principal's office with my best friend Jim Cable. There was a list of students running for class president and I waved them off with a laugh.

"Same old bunch of losers," I said.

"Is that right?" said Jim. "Why don't you run then?"

"Oh I'd win easily, Cable."

"That's ridiculous, High. I'll bet you five bucks you can't do it."

I grinned. "You want me to run for Senior Class President on a *bet?*"

"Why not? You chicken?"

I thought about it. That Class of '65 was so huge that two years after moving to Portland I was still *seeing* people in it for the first time, much less meeting them.

I, on the other hand, was the starting center on the basketball team, so maybe *they'd* seen me. (And was that a good or bad thing? I was pretty lazy, after all, and known to smoke three packs of *Galaxy* cigarettes a day (they came with coupons and I needed 18,000 for a St. Bernard).)

The longer I thought about it, though, the more I liked the sheer implausibility of the idea. When I reached out to shake Jim's hand I was conscious, for the first time in my young life, of not just appreciating absurdity ... but embracing it. It was a very intoxicating sensation.

"You're on, pal," I said. "Five bucks says I can win the class presidency."

There were five other candidates and we gave our speeches to the class a week later. I was fortunate and drew the shortest lot, choosing to speak last. While the others droned on I sat on the stage behind them and squirmed with anticipation. I was always nervous about public speaking until I actually got up there, at which point I suffered a kind of reverse stage fright and couldn't wait to perform.

I was a ham, in other words, not to mention a smart-ass Bay Area kid who was so cocky he hadn't even prepared a speech. When it was finally my turn I stepped to the podium and motioned to the other candidates:

"Recognize these characters?" I asked. "You should ... you see

15

'em every year at this time, running for one office or another so they can add another 'Student Activity' to their Princeton application.

"Me? I'm only here because I made a five dollar bet with Cable that I could win this thing!"

The auditorium erupted in laughter and it was straight downhill from there: I received 80% of the vote and found myself McKinley High's Senior Class President.

Which was pretty much the last thing I wanted to be, then or now. It's forty years later and when I see old high school buddies they still introduce me to strangers as "our Senior Class President." Just writing about it makes me cringe. Not only because the whole episode was a joke to begin with, but because I'm still responsible for organizing the annual reunions.

I've tried to hide, but Cable tracks me down.

I glance out my picture window a lot during the day because I do all my reading, thinking and drawing (hell, much of my *living* at this age) in a corner of the old couch that's wedged in front of it. This is partly self-protection – the lock on the front door has been broken for years – but there's also the fact I'm an inveterate people watcher and I've plenty to keep me entertained in this neighborhood, particularly since the lesbian coffee shop opened on the corner.

It's the porn theater crowd that's interesting, though. You know that creepy feeling you get when you're walking into one kind of porn shop or another, the sense that somebody's watching you? Well, they are. After twenty-five years (and three couches), I'm confident that I could watch 100 males walk up the street and tell you *exactly* which ones are headed for the jerk joint.

Of course, they're all at least sixty-five years old. It mystified me at first – *Get a DVD player, Pops*, I thought – but gradually it dawned on me that these must be guys whose wives never leave the house. They can't just slip a *Supersuckers* or *Fuck Sluts* in the machine without her knowing about it, and they either don't have computers or don't know what to do with them so they're stuck jacking off with the other chicken-necked croakers. All of them gasping and groaning and pounding beneath the ten-foot tall pussies on the screen.

Or so I imagine … I'm sixty-four with a DVD player and cable, so I've never been in the place myself. I know I'll never forget the night a bunch of fundamentalist Christians showed up to picket the theater. Their mournful chant from down the street? Right as I slipped between the legs of a woman I'd met through a personals ad? "HEY MISTER! GET OFF MY SISTER! HEY MISTER! GET OFF MY SISTER!"

I got it working and the louder they chanted, the better it got.

I've been struck over the years by the number of friends who can't imagine me having a family. It's a reasonable perspective, I suppose, given that I see my mother and three brothers (my father died 18 years ago) so seldom they might as well be imaginary. And after I wrote about that incident at the Portland State apartment, when my mother vowed to never set foot in a place I inhabited again, I was half-congratulating myself before I realized my brothers have never visited, either. In my four decades as an adult, in the many places I've lived all over the west coast – even being in the same house here the last twenty-five years – only once has one of them dropped by. That was brother Ben in 1982, when I lived in Bolinas with a woman named Karen. We didn't have any chairs in the shack, of course, but he and his wife seemed comfortable enough on the front steps. (Well, for the hour they stayed, anyway.)

I was taken aback when I considered this. I wasn't sure which was more offensive to me … the fact my siblings had never come to see me, or the realization I hadn't thought about it before. And weren't those the same things, really?

But I was always the strange one in the group. It began at birth, when I emerged as a 22-inch, 12-pound porker, and continued through the first two years of my life. According to my parents I cried constantly, the victim (if you could believe my spinning eyeballs) of vicious migraine headaches. Then about the time brother Ben was born – with Joe in between, both of them as normal-sized as my older brother Ray – whatever was squeezing my skull disappeared.

Or at least found a new outlet. "It was cartoons," my mother says. "You shut up the moment you started drawing them."

I'll have to trust her in that regard. I do remember that, as I grew up, life seemed pretty damned good to me. Like my brothers I made friends easily but, unlike them I preferred my own company. Give me my quiet room with its *Hardy Boy* novels, plastic models and art supplies and I never wanted to leave; no day was long enough for all the things I enjoyed doing by myself.

My siblings were just the opposite. Like most boys before TV and video games they only came inside when they had to and Joe and Ben, in particular, were superbly coordinated kids whose lives revolved around physical activity.

I was going to be like them whether I liked it or not. My mother's daily mantra, as she dragged me screaming from my room, was that she had no intention of raising a "bookworm" or a "lounge lizard." Then she'd shove me out the front door and lock it behind me, leaving me to confront the competitive little brothers from hell.

They were jock jackals, intense *win or die* lunatics. It didn't matter (and it wouldn't now) whether it was the ski slope, the basketball court or the baseball diamond, they attacked sports as if every game were their last. Joe was the slightly better athlete, Ben the more determined psycho. To be part of their whirlwind was a life-altering experience, not only for me but every kid in the neighborhood. The grade school we went to was a block away and anybody who was interested in a game knew the High boys would be there waiting for them. They chose the teams, settled the squabbles and kept the action moving, even when we played with older kids.

Me? I was along for the ride like everybody else. I enjoyed sports, and by dint of my mother's lockouts had learned to play them as well as my gangly body allowed, but I was too moody and daydreamy to care the way my brothers did. I wanted to be someplace where I could hang out in the right side of my brain without a pass hitting me in the face or a baseball skidding between my legs.

But it wasn't going to happen. Not only was I limited in the hours I could spend alone during the week, but we went away as a family virtually every weekend. My father had a large plumbing firm then (he'd lost it through alcoholism and a series of financial misadventures by the time the 60s came around) and it did well enough that when we weren't at resorts or cabins for the skiing, swimming or fishing, we were using our season tickets for the local pro teams. (Even *women's roller derby* for chrissakes!)

When we weren't playing sports, in other words, we were watching or talking about them. I think about that and wonder who I'd have been if my mother let me be the recluse I wanted to be, then remember that my parents hardly ignored my artistic bent. If there was a figure drawing or oil painting or pottery class around they'd rearrange the whole family's schedule to get me there, and my father, right up to the day he died, could sit for an hour studying something I'd drawn.

So what am I complaining about? Well, nothing, actually. The truth is that I've very few complaints about my childhood. I thought at the time it was like any other kid's but in fact it was pretty idyllic. My parents adored each other and us, we lived in a beautiful old section of San Mateo, my brothers and I learned early on when to leave each other alone and Ray, who was older than me by five years and the kindest one of the bunch, was our babysitter when my parents weren't around. Even my father's surreptitious drinking and the later downfall of his business barely pierced our awareness. If it had we wouldn't have absorbed his constant litany like gospel, the notion that nothing was more important than personal integrity. (Which he knew something about, having done thirty-five B-24 missions in WWII as a ball turret gunner without once mentioning it afterwards.)

Plus he was the nicest man I ever met. I said it at his memorial and I still believe it. My favorite story about him was right after we moved to Portland in October of 1962. He was selling mutual funds at the time and had found a house to rent in the city's best school district. He'd also spent his last dime getting new carpet laid on the floors. I was a high school sophomore at the time and on our third night in the place I went to bed in my room and, right before turning out the light, opened a letter an old friend had sent me from the Bay Area. He'd just been laid for the first time and explained the event in such graphic detail that I knew I'd have to destroy the letter (my mother read *anything* with print on it). I could have shoved it in a textbook and thrown it away at school the next morning but no, that would have meant getting out of bed. Instead I pulled some matches from the bed stand (ostensibly there to mask the smell of farts, but really around for midnight cigarettes), clumped the pages of the letter together and lit them. I had this odd idea that they would flare, burn quickly, then dissolve to ash by the time the flames reached my fingers. At which point I'd simply blow them out. Still more evidence of why I was the strange one in the family because, of course, the pages flared up all right but didn't go out when I shook and blew on them, falling to the bedspread instead. I had to swat them onto the floor to keep the fabric from igniting, only to watch the smoldering pieces melt holes in the carpet. The new, just-laid carpet that was so important to my father.

That's what got to me ... I really hated to disappoint the guy; if he had a trace of meanness anywhere in him I'd never seen it. Fortunately this fear of letting him down had made me very resourceful over the years. I was in potential trouble *a lot* and if I didn't want it brought home I had to be sure I got away with it. (Which I'm still doing now, I suppose.)

Anyway the rug had four melted patches now. I was an artist with glue and scissors. I would simply cut a stiff fiber from one section of the rug – where its loss would not be discernible – and glue it to the top of a melted patch. I began at ten in the evening and when my mother knocked on the door at 7:00 a.m. I'd just finished up. I rose to my feet, looked down at my handiwork and it was good. Hell, it was better than good, it was magnificent. Unless you knew there was no way to tell the burnt patches even existed.

I changed my clothes and strolled to the breakfast table, groggy but triumphant. My mother had made some *Eggo* waffles and bacon and I sat down at one end of the table with Ben and Joe on either side of me and my mom on the far end. I reached my right hand out and pointed to the plate of waffles.

"Mom," I said, "would you please pass the waffles?"

She reached out and lifted up the plate, started to hand it to me and gasped. "OH MY GOD!" she wailed. "WHAT'D YOU DO TO YOUR HAND!?"

Huh? I looked at my outstretched palm and fingers and they were black with soot: I'd been so busy congratulating myself that I forgot to wash my hands. Christ, I was dead now. There was no explanation for their condition other than the truth and suddenly the preposterous nature of what I'd done – and how humiliating it was going to be to explain it – sunk in.

I looked over at Joe and he grinned. "Oh, I can't wait to hear this one," he said.

He and Ben would have laughed themselves sick if the family gathering in my room hadn't been so grim. When I was done describing

23

what had happened, and how I'd been up all night trying to rectify it, my father was speechless and my mother furious.

"But mom," I protested finally, "consider the artwork. You can't really see where I glued the stuff in."

"Oh yeah? And what happens the first time I vacuum? You think that *Elmer's Glue* is going to hold?"

As usual, I hadn't factored in the cleaning part.

"Well," said my mother, turning to my dad, "how are we going to punish him?"

It was time for the man of the house to pass judgment. My father looked at me while I stared at my smug brothers in the hall, the two of them all but wringing their hands in anticipation. Finally, after due deliberation, dad handed down his sentence:

"Wilson," he said, looking as grim as he could muster, "you're going to have to *walk* to school today!"

What? Was that possible? Had I heard him right?

The expressions on my brothers' and mother's faces confirmed I had. "So, I've got to walk to McKinley?" I asked. "Three whole miles?"

"That's right," said my father, "so you better get started."

I'd walked home from school the day before … I could do three miles in my sleep. This was a whole new twist on my father's sweet nature.

I'd strolled about a mile through the neighborhoods when he drove by in his Buick, my two brothers beside him in the front seat. Joe was in the middle and couldn't do anything, but Ben leaned against the passenger window, gave me the finger and snickered. My father went another block, pulled over and stopped, then swung the car around and headed back my way. Did still another U-turn and pulled up beside me. Ben rolled down the window.

"Well," said my dad, leaning over the steering wheel, "have you learned your lesson, Wilson?"

"Oh absolutely," I said.

"Well hop in back then, it looks like it's going to rain."

I slid into the back seat, cradled my books in my lap and hung my head.

"Oh … and Wilson?" said my father.

"Yeah?"

"You're a goddamned buffoon!"

The four of us had a good long laugh over that. I miss my dad. He could beat the Nazis and the booze but cigarettes kicked his ass. He just couldn't quit them. My older brother has emphysema now and he's the same damn way.

Ben was the only one at the hospital when my father died of pneumonia in '94. He was so weak he could barely raise a finger but he motioned my brother over, indicated that he wanted his oxygen mask removed. When Ben did so my father whispered his last words:

"Coffee … cigarettes."

So if I hadn't got the Irish from my mother's side I'd figure my penchant for addiction came from my dad.

My mother herself? She has one drink a day and wouldn't get near a cigarette. (I think she bitched every time my father ever lit one.) What's more she's ninety-four years old now and has never – to her sons' or late husband's or extended family's knowledge – been ill. All the childhood viruses we dragged home one after another? My father would catch them but not her. The flu? Every year when a new bug arrives she nurses other old people who've caught it without once manifesting a symptom herself. She was felled by heatstroke when we were kids and my brothers and I still talk about it because it's the only time we ever saw her incapacitated, much less in bed. (She had an older sister who was much the same way. Never a thing wrong with her until she was ninety-five, when she complained of a slight stomach ache one afternoon, laid down for a nap and was gone ten minutes later.)

Last year mom tripped and fell on a downtown sidewalk. Because she had packages in her arms she couldn't get her hands up to protect herself and landed face first on the concrete. She broke her nose and the orbs around both eyes while tearing loose her upper lip.

She was rushed by ambulance to the Mills Hospital emergency room and after bandaging her cheeks and nose as best they could (and reattaching her lip with Gorilla Glue), the doctor told her she had a severe concussion and would have to be hospitalized overnight.

"Sure, sure," my mom said, and as soon as he and the nurses left the room she jumped off the surgical table, grabbed her purse and walked the two miles back to her apartment.

"Ed was due to phone," she told me later, "and I didn't want to miss his call."

Ed's her lover. He's eighty and thinks she's eighty-five.

I've always said I became a basketball player in a vain attempt to fuck a cheerleader and – though that was certainly the core motivation, the fantasy that kept me practicing when the other rationalizations dropped away – there were obviously other factors involved.

First, of course, was my height. I grew up playing whatever sport was in season with my brothers and friends but the older I got the more apparent it became that my tall, skinny frame would best serve me on the basketball court. In the short term this posed at least two problems: (1) it was the sport I liked the least; and (2) the same growth spurts that destined me for the game made it difficult for me to play. I was such a weak, spindly beanpole by the time I reached junior high, for instance, that I couldn't walk and dribble a ball at the same time.

Yet I tried out for both the 7th and 8th grade teams because I was the tallest kid in the school and that had to count for *something*, didn't it?

Not to Mr. Gomez, the P.E. instructor, coach and third reason I became a basketball player. Each year during tryouts I was the first kid he'd cut. Before he did, however, he'd make a point of humiliating me in front of my classmates. I'm not sure why this was ... I don't remember him being that cruel to anybody else and there was certainly nothing subtle about the approach he took with me. He'd enter our scrimmages, a thirty-five-year-old man playing with children, and knock me down under the boards or block my puny shots with a sneer of triumph. "Look at you, High, ..." he'd say. "There's not a muscle in your body! You play like a baby!"

I didn't take it as badly as some kids might have (at least not outwardly), because I'd always had an uneasy relationship with authority. When I was elected student body president at my grade school, for instance, the principal called me and my parents into his office and said he wished he could cancel the election. And when my high school career was over my coach (who'd sent me to two different psychiatrists during the season) told my mother that should he be walking anywhere in the world and spot me coming towards him he'd cross the street to avoid me, "Even if it meant being killed in traffic."

What a thing to say to somebody's mother. Though now that I think about it ... when that same coach gave me the team Most Valuable Player award at a student assembly later, everybody in attendance booed me. (My girlfriend, Kathy – a non-cheerleader – led the loudest chorus of jeers.) So there had to be *something* about my attitude that irked people.

That said there's no excuse for demeaning and abusing a thirteen-year-old boy the way Gomez did; I know it left scars I was barely aware of. I went on to play on the "C" team as a freshman in high school, then the junior varsity the next year before finally starting on the varsity as a junior. In the interim I spent thousands of hours lifting weights, running, going to summer basketball camps and shooting baskets by myself. I'd have sworn it was the nude cheerleader fantasies that kept me lifting off that blacktop, but in December of my senior year I hitchhiked to the Bay Area over Christmas break. I had nothing in mind but hanging out with old buddies and one Saturday a bunch of us met up at the junior high gym for a pickup game.

And there was Gomez. I'd rarely thought of him in the intervening years but suddenly the mere sight of the guy made my blood boil. He was strutting around like a peacock, the way he always had, and insisting we let him play in the game.

That was fine by me. I made sure I was on the opposing team and can honestly say (though it isn't saying much) that I was never so focused in a game. Gomez was eight inches shorter than I was and every time he shot I blocked it. It was so easy that in each instance I tried to smash the ball back into his face, and – even if I usually missed (slamming it off his head or shoulders or the floor) – everyone in the gym was perfectly clear about my intentions. When it came time to rebound I'd let him position himself in front of me, then elbow him in the neck or chest when the ball came off the rim. I wanted him to turn around and challenge me. I wanted him to take a swing at me or mock me the way he used to so I could beat him senseless with my fists.

Instead he begged off after fifteen minutes and limped quietly away. I remember it like it was yesterday, how I was so livid my lips were trembling and I had to snort air through my nose. *You little bastard,* I thought, *you cowardly piece of shit scumbag. Who plays like a baby now!!???*

Then years later my mother sent me his obituary from the paper and I quickly scanned to the bottom of it, hoping he was buried somewhere so I could piss on his grave. It was only then that I realized he might have known what he was doing all along, that abuse was the only way to motivate a smug kid like me.

Had trying to prove him wrong made me the player I was? Was my entire basketball career the result of that sonofabitch goading me?

Naaahhhh. I squeezed the obit into a ball, shot it at the nearest waste basket.

It missed by a mile.

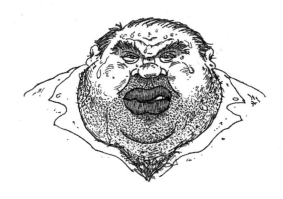

My long stretch as a factotum began even as my high school basketball days were ending. I'd been working as a bag boy in a grocery store since my junior year, but it was only part-time and I was looking for full-time work that would help me pay for college. I didn't know I'd end up in a $5-a-month whorehouse at the time, or even that I'd be enrolling at Portland State. I had my eye on Trinidad State instead, a junior college in the "four corner" area of Colorado that was the only school to offer me a full ride in basketball. I'd been recruited by local alumni and had never met the coach, but I'd have done damn near anything to get out of Boregon.

Then they sent me their brochure for the coming year, the photos inside culled from newspaper photos of the 12 frosh prospects. It was eleven giant black guys and me, all of them soaring high above the hoop to dunk. Wilson High? The white guy with the blackest name of the bunch? I was doing what I usually did, i.e., shooting a long, lazy hook shot that was difficult to block and required a minimum of effort.

All of a sudden Boregon looked a hell of a lot better to me. I wrote the coach and told him I'd reconsidered, that you could tell by looking at those pictures that the rest of his recruits were serious athletes and basketball, oddly enough, was just a game to me.

In more ways than I let on, actually. I was reminded of this as I watched a basketball tournament in Portland a few years ago. I was still dazed from a load of 'shrooms the night before and the *Drizzle Stick* I'd smoked for breakfast hadn't helped much.

So it was easy to ignore the fact that the guy in the seat next to me kept looking my way. When a time-out was whistled on the floor he leaned over and tapped my arm.

"Excuse me," he said, "but I'd swear I know you from somewhere. Did you play in the PIL way back when?"

"McKinley High," I said. "'64 and '65."

"Yeah? Same years as me. I played for Grant."

"Great." I didn't ask him his name, not out of rudeness, particularly, but because I was still coming back down to earth. Another quarter passed before he reached over and nudged me again. This time he woke me up.

"Hey!" he said, "I finally got it! I remember who you are!"

"Yeah?" I yawned.

"Yeah. You're *The Guy Who Never Ran!*"

Now it might have been the *Drizzle Stick* and the lack of sleep ... the arena did seem a little wavy ... but I was moved by this.

"You ... you remember that?" I said.

"Are you kidding me? You were a *legend* to the guys on our bench, man, you managed to play whole games without even *jogging* fast. How'd you get away with that?"

I sat up straight, cleared my throat and beamed – it wasn't often that the lazy guy gets his due. "Well I'll tell you," I said, "you had to be a choreographer, not a hustler blah blah blah ..."

Anyway, I'm sure I saved myself and that Trinidad State coach a lot of grief. (Though it was too late afterwards to enroll anywhere but Portland State.) And it wasn't like I was getting financial help from home, not with my dad selling light bulbs door to door at the time.

So I needed a decent job. Instead I ended up at Betty's Ice Cream Parlor. It was a new place opening at a local mall and working around calories all day appealed to me. I'd been growing like a weed since eighth grade and no amount of face stuffing or weight-lifting had put any meat on me.

I'd been so desperate the year before, in fact, that I even went to a quack naturopath for "protein" shots. Ten bucks a pop once a week.

Three months later I'd lost four pounds.

The owner of Betty's didn't have that problem: he was 5'10" and weighed over 500 pounds. His name was Fat Pat Hansen and not only was he the fattest sonofabitch I'd ever met ... he was the meanest. He figured out I was sensitive about my own weight, for instance, and immediately started insulting me about it. He could be out in front of the parlor and I'd be fifty feet away – scooping ice cream behind the counter – and he'd yell over the heads of the customers: "Hey get up here and clean this table ... *beanpole!*"

Then have himself a good sick laugh over it. My responses were pretty limited under the circumstances: not only was he the boss, but he already called himself "Fat Pat." He figured he'd survived people giving him shit all his life and now it was his turn. Worse yet, those of us who worked there had to do anything he and his weird family demanded. This included his batty wife Betty – who I realize now was so loaded on downers that she smeared her lipstick on with a rag – and his twin sons Rick and Dick.

And I thought those giant black guys at Trinidad State were a reality check. In truth the Hansens were about as weird as it got in 1965 Portland. I'd be working on the grill one minute, scooping cones and bussing tables and stocking supplies the next, while Rick and Dick stole my tips from the tables and their father ordered more sandwiches and sundaes for all of them. A week after the store opened a mother and little boy came in and asked for Butter Brickle cones. I pushed back the freezer cover, went to scoop some out but found the tub had disappeared. That was strange ... I was sure I'd put one in there that morning. I asked the customer to wait and went to the back room, where I found Fat Pat perched atop a freezer. He had his left hand around a tub and was using his right to scoop the ice cream straight into his mouth. It ran down his chin in creamy white rivulets and was – at that point in my life – the most disgusting thing I'd seen.

"Yeah, *beanpole!*" he grunted, spraying little nuts around. "What the fuck is it?"

"Uhhhhh ... Butter Brickle," I said. "That must be the Butter Brickle."

"What of it?"

"Well, I have a customer who wants two cones."

"Are those the cones!?"

I looked down ... I was holding the two sugar cones between my fingers. "Well yeah, but ..."

"Give 'em to me, you *putz!*" I walked over, afraid to get too close to his throbbing, gelatinous pork, and handed him the cones. I knew what he was going to do and wanted to look away but instead stared, fascinated, as he dipped the cones into the sweaty soup of the tub.

"Here," he said, handing them back. The sloppy mounds were already dribbling down the sides. "They'll never know the difference."

I walked around the corner, threw the cones in a wastebasket. Stepped back out front to the mother and son. "Well," I said, "how about some Cherry Ripple instead?"

Six weeks after the parlor opened I was the only original employee left (I'd watched another dozen kids come and go in the meanwhile). Fat Pat's creepy appearance and disgusting habits – he and the twins (burgeoning porkers themselves) liked to have belching contests in the corner while Betty chain smoked – had reduced business to a crawl. It was as if the guy had opened the parlor just to prove he could eat everything in it. I didn't understand that kind of bitterness then and I still don't. I stuck around because (1) I needed the money; and (2) I was openly amazed that a family like that even existed.

I tolerated their shit right up to the day Fat Pat accused me of stealing.

"I just looked at yesterday's receipts," he said one afternoon in July, "and we're twenty bucks short."

"So?" I was washing a group of sundae dishes in the sink behind the counter.

"So you were on the cash register yesterday and I think you mighta helped yourself to some cash, *Bones!*"

I stood up, grabbed a dish towel and dried my soapy hands. Walked around the counter to where Fat Pat stood frowning. "Are you calling me a thief?" I asked, my voice trembling.

"That's right, *Beanpole*. I've suspected you for awhile now ... this isn't the first time we've been short around here."

"Well look no further than your own children then ... they're on the register as often as I am."

"You're calling Rick and Dick *thieves?!*" he gasped, bellying up to me with that giant gut of his.

"They steal my goddamned tips," I said. "Why wouldn't they steal from the register?"

"I oughta break your skinny neck!" growled Fat Pat. "I been *carrying* your worthless ass since I hired you!"

I like to think it was right at that moment that I snapped into my adult life. "HEY FUCK YOU, PORKY!" I screamed, spraying all the spit and venom I'd stored for months straight into his face. "YOU CAN SHOVE THIS JOB UP YOUR ASS!"

Now understand that this transpired at 2:00 p.m. on a hot weekday afternoon, and there were three mothers with children at the parlor tables. They were already drawing the kids closer, encouraging them to gulp down their ice cream, as the confrontation between Fat Pat and myself escalated.

But none of us were prepared for what happened next. Suddenly

Fat Pat roared like a wounded bear, giving me time to pinwheel out of the way as he charged. I slipped out of his sweaty grasp, dodged behind a couple of tables as he tried first to chase me – grunting, snorting and trembling with such fury that his porky body actually *shook* – then, amazingly, jerked a heavy, bottom-loaded table over his head.

At this point the mothers began scrambling and screaming behind me even as the first bread roll bounced off my head. Rick and Dick had a bag of them and were firing at me from behind the counter while their father lumbered forward to crush me and Betty chain smoked and cackled in the background.

It was a freeze frame I'll take to my grave and – just for an instant – I soaked it in like a supplicant.

Then I spun on my heels, dodged those customers clamoring for the exit and ran for my life.

Later I decided Fat Pat had staged the whole affair because it was payday. He owed me two weeks in wages but refused to send it to me and I finally had to go to the State Labor Board to get him to fork over.

They strong-armed him into compliance but he wouldn't mail me the check, insisting instead that I come to the parlor and get it, "If you've got the balls, beanpole!" I was, I admit, one very terrified kid. The defiant part of me – the attitude that had alternately antagonized and intrigued every coach I'd played for – was actually looking forward to the confrontation. Unfortunately it was a very, very small part; looming larger was me – the skinniest guy in town – having to go another round with the fattest. It was a rematch that didn't bode well for Wilson High.

Still my parents didn't raise their boys to be cowards so the last day of July I made the long walk from my house to the ice cream parlor. I remember hyperventilating a little and my hands going numb as I finally stepped onto the mall parking lot. As I walked across it and drew nearer and nearer to Betty's I heard the drone of a horn and saw Fat Pat's Buick surrounded by a crowd of gawkers.

Now I know people think I make these stories up but really ... whose got that kind of imagination? What's more I've plenty of witnesses to this weird scene. As I walked up to the parlor and tried to peer through the spectators at the car I noticed Ed Fowler, a recent hire and fellow McKinley High grad, standing in the back. He spotted me and hustled over.

"Jesus Christ, High!" he said, grinning from ear to ear. "Do you see what happened?"

"No," I said. "I just got here."

"It's unbelievable. Those little pricks Rick and Dick used the car yesterday? The one with the special seat for Pat that slides all the way back?"

"Yeah?"

"Well, they moved it up a couple notches and when Fat Pat got in this afternoon ... he got *stuck!* I'm serious! Look at him in there! The steering wheel's wedged so deep in his gut he can't move! They've called the fire department to cut him out!"

"Come on," I scoffed. "Life ain't that sweet."

I walked over, pushed through the growing crowd of people until I reached the open door of the Buick. The horn was wailing unmercifully and the only part of the steering wheel still visible was the column protruding from Fat Pat's gut. When he saw me he started pinwheeling his arms and gasping, his beet red face deepening to purple. It took a superhuman effort on his part but he managed to draw in just enough breath and girth that the horn ceased blaring. "I'll never pay you, beanpole," he gasped. "Neverrrrrrrrrrrrrrrrrrr!"

Then he released his breath and the horn started wailing again. I leaned over the top of the door, just out of reach of his hands, and started laughing. I laughed so hard and for so long that I hardly felt Rick and Dick punching me in the back or Betty trying to pull me away.

"Fat Pat!" I yelled, just as the fire truck started across the parking lot, "you can forget about the check, Porky! This is payment enough! This is perfect! This is fantastic! Thank you! Thank you! Ha ha ha ha ha ha ...."

Then Rick got me around the neck and they dragged me down.

When I run into friends from McKinley High who worked at Betty's it's always the first thing we talk about. This is because for most of them it was not only the shortest job they ever had but easily the strangest.

Not for me, though. No, for me it was just the beginning, the first indicator that I was tracking lower than my peers. I would always be the kind of guy who took the first job that came along and its nature didn't matter much. There were things I would come to *prefer* in the workplace – a decent boss, swing shift hours, a bit more than minimum wage – but it's not like I went looking for them.

So when a friend's father offered me a job in the dinette he owned downtown I accepted immediately. It turns out he had a couple of cafes, too, but the dinette was a twelve-stool, one-counter place that bordered the worst section of Portland. The woman who'd run it by herself for thirty years was taking a six-month medical leave and I was her replacement.

Two hours into the first day I knew I was in serious trouble. The place was busy from the time the door opened at 6:00 a.m. until eleven in the morning, when you had a half-hour reprieve before the lunch crowd poured in. Old Elma, the sole employee all those years, did the fry cooking, sandwich making, place setting, dishwashing, counter cleaning, waitressing, soda jerking and cash register work by herself.

Three days later, when my training was "complete" and she was on leave, those became my responsibilities. I'd be lying if I said I remembered anything about the next two weeks but the way I felt at closing. Which is to say light-headed, wrung out and sick. The busy part wasn't even as bad as all the bitching from customers; most of them were regulars and they were used to Elma's brisk efficiency.

Economy of motion was not my strong suit at eighteen. I was more the kind of guy who would knock a jar of pickles into the onion container while trying to spread mustard on a ham sandwich with his right hand and flip a burger with his left. I close my eyes now, take myself back there and all I hear is the clamor and bedlam, all I see is the mess.

Even harder on me, though, was "the customer is always right" maxim and having to bite my tongue when insulted. This was a legacy from my parents' WASP household and the foundation was firm enough to last a couple weeks.

Then the third Monday, at the height of the lunch hour with all the regulars grumbling about this order or that one, my basic nature asserted itself. I took the spatula, flung it against the wall and raised myself to my full height behind the counter, arms waving atop my head.

"ENOUGH!" I yelled. "IF ANY OF YOU ASSHOLES THINKS YOU CAN DO A BETTER JOB THAN I CAN GET YOUR ASS BACK HERE RIGHT NOW OR SHUT THE HELL UP FOREVER!"

I was a skinny kid but I had a voice like a foghorn and for a moment they all quieted. Then Ernie, a whiny little Italian guy who worked in a warehouse, snickered. "Anyone could do a better job than you, kid. You're a joke."

"Oh yeah?" I walked over, retrieved the spatula from the floor. Brought it to Ernie and set it on the counter. "You're always bragging about what a great cook you are, Ernie," I said. "Why don't you come back here and show us your stuff?"

"I can't do that, kid. There's health department regulations ... you can't have just *anybody* behind the counter."

"Does it look like the health department's ever been in this dump, Ernie?"

The other regulars started laughing and cajoling him and the next thing you know old Ernie was back there making noontime meals while I took care of everything else. Tuesday, it was Ann, a secretary, and the day after that Roy, the operations officer at the bank across the street. I thought it was a pretty clever solution and was starting to fancy myself a Tom Sawyer kind of guy when Mr. Kitchen, the owner, walked in at the height of lunch hour.

He took one look at Roy back there – a Big Chief apron he'd brought from home covering his shirt and tie and slacks – and dropped his head in his hands.

"Jesus, Wilson," he said, drawing me aside, "I hired you because you were supposed to be responsible, because you were president of your class ... *and now you have customers cooking for you?*"

"They enjoy it, Mr. Kitchen."

"I could be closed down for this! It's outrageous!"

"Hey! It's not like I'll be telling anyone."

He sighed. "I'll take over, son ... you're fired. Pick up your check on Monday."

I took off my apron, grabbed my coat and left before he changed his mind. Lit a cigarette and started walking through the wino section of town. I swear I hadn't gone two blocks before I heard a commotion in the alleyway to my right. The door at the top of a staircase flew open and a ruddy-faced guy in a white shirt and bow tie stepped out with a bum in tow. He dragged him to the edge of the porch, then shoved him down the stairs.

"AND DON'T COME BACK HERE YOU WINO SONOFABITCH!" he screamed.

Then he took a deep breath and looked at me standing there. "Hey, buddy," he said, "want a job? We just had an opening."

I dragged on my *Galaxy* cigarette, listened to the wino moan as he crawled behind some garbage cans to puke.

"Sure," I said. "Why not?"

Ever since I was writing about my brothers and mentioned Karen's place in Bolinas, California I've been thinking about it. It was the summer of 1981 and she had a primitive cabin on a lot overlooking the ocean. Directly behind the house was a fenced-in pot garden that a friend had planted for her.

She said just looking at it scared the shit out of her. Me? I thought it was the most beautiful thing I'd ever seen. I'd been around marijuana crops before – when I met Karen I'd just returned from a visit to an old friend's crop in Mendocino County – but I'd certainly never grown it myself.

I was a fast learner, though. I was working part-time as a word processor in San Francisco at the time (billing myself as The World's Fastest Typist) and good weed was very expensive; the prospect of having all I could smoke in the year ahead was intoxicating. I devoured every book I could find on the subject – particularly Clarke's *Marijuana Botany* and Rosenthal and Frank's *Grower's Guide* – and spent my spare time tending to the 20 plants. There was a row of tall, tightly bunched sativas in the back and a diverse assortment of indicas in the front, one of which – the one I called "Princess" – would eventually yield two pounds by herself. I know because she was the only plant I harvested.

The night the others were stolen I like to think sex saved my life. I was in the middle of it with Karen – on our bed beside the window facing the garden – when I heard a loud noise out back. I pulled out from between her legs and hobbled over to stand at the window.

"What is it?" she gasped.

"Shhhhh!" I stared out at the garden but there was just enough moonlight that all I could see was my own reflection in the glass, a skinny, bed-headed doofus with a wobbly hard-on and heaving chest. I looked like something R. Crumb had drawn.

"Oh fuck it!" I said, jumping back in the bed and resuming where I left off. "It was probably just the cat."

When I went out in the morning not only were the plants gone but so were the axe and machete that I kept beside the door. If it hadn't been for the *coitus interruptus* I might have dressed and run outside the night before. Would those tools have been used against me? And if the thieves were that conscious of potential weapons, wouldn't they have brought their own? It was a scary prospect and the only counterbalance to the terrible sense of outrage I felt afterwards ... that theft cost Karen and I thousands of dollars and months of work.

So the next year I transformed the grow space into a greenhouse with a padlocked front door and – miracle of miracles – actually harvested the crop. The year after that someone snapped the padlocks and stole everything as we slept. The fury and frustration that followed, the likelihood that the thief was somebody we knew in that small coastal town, seethed in me all winter. When spring came I reinforced the inner walls of the greenhouse with two-by-fours and covered a new front door with locks and a metal crossbar.

The scum might fuck with me again, I thought, *but at least I'd hear them this time!*

So fall came and the crop I'd grown from Dutch seeds was spectacularly beautiful, so vigorous it seemed to vibrate in the warm autumn air. I was torn, as outdoor growers usually are, between harvesting it early and letting it go just a *little* bit longer. But the feds hadn't busted anyone that year and that greenhouse looked like a fortress so I decided to wait a few more days.

What I hadn't counted on was something I was barely aware of at the time, that I was one *sicko* San Francisco 49ers fan. It was a lifelong affliction, I'm afraid, one that I'm barely over now. I went to my first Niner game in 1950 with my father and brothers, watched them lose a big lead and the championship game at Kezar Stadium in 1957, then again at Candlestick in 1971 when Staubach and the hated Cowboys came from thirteen points down in the last two minutes.

But now it was 1984 and after winning the Super Bowl in '81 the Niners had their best team ever and I don't know … my life must have been particularly bereft at the time, because it was hard for me to concentrate on anything else. I read obsessively about the team, listened to awful sports talk shows and spoke about little else. (Poor Karen … I'm sure she wishes she had that year back.)

Anyway, by midseason the Niners are undefeated and playing the Saints on a Sunday afternoon in New Orleans. It was always our toughest road game and I had the old television in the cabin cranked up as loud as Karen would tolerate. She sat on the bed, quietly knitting a wool cap for winter, as I screamed nonsense at the screen like, "BLOCK SOMEBODY, CROSS, YOU FUCKIN' PIECE OF SHIT!" or "JONES IS WIDE OPEN, MONTANA, OPEN YOUR GODDAMN EYES!"

Finally it's late in the game, the Saints are ahead by four points and the Niners are backed up at their goal line. The tension is killing me. I know a loss means nothing in the grand scheme of things, that's it's just a stupid-ass football game, but I'm not a rational man at this point. I'm rubbing my beard, jumping up and down and pacing, stamping the floor in agony when another play fails.

Then Montana rolls into the flat, his receivers clear out the right side of the field and he loops a pass to fullback Earl Cooper, who takes off unimpeded towards the Saints' goal line.

"HOLY SHIT GO COOPER GO!" I screamed. "GET TO THE END ZONE YOU BIGASS SONOFABITCH!"

Somewhere in the background I hear Karen calling to me. "Wilson," she yells. "Wilson! What was that crashing sound!?"

"I DON'T KNOW THE NEIGHBORS YELLING MAYBE GO COOPER GO YOU MOTHERFUCKERRRRRRR!"

"I just heard it again, Wilson!"

"TOUCHDOOOOWWWWWN   FORTY-NINERS   ALL RIGHHHHT BABY WE DID IT AGAIN YEEEEAHHHH!"

"WILSON!"

"Huh?" I was on my hands and knees by then, pounding the floor with my fists. "What? What is it?"

"I heard two loud crashes out back! It sounded like it came from the plants area!"

I stood up, dazed, and wandered over to the back window. Glanced out at the greenhouse, checking to see that the padlocks and crossbar were still secure. "Everything looks great, Karen," I said, then patted her on the shoulder and hurried back to the TV to catch the replays.

Later, when the Niners had won and a beautiful ocean sunset blanketed the horizon, I stepped out on the front porch of the cabin and lit a jumbo joint. *Jesus,* I thought, *what a great guy I am! I'm a winner, my team's a winner, and I've enough pot out back that I won't be working for months!*

Then I strolled behind the cabin, started undoing the various locks on the greenhouse door. I was halfway through before I realized something was wrong.

Where's the smell? I thought. *Where's the stench of skunk?*

I fumbled through the last two locks and flung open the door, nearly falling over in my shock and despair. Not only were all twenty-five plants gone, but to steal them someone had knocked down the whole north wall of the greenhouse IN BROAD DAYLIGHT! There were old fence boards and smashed two-by-fours spread across a ten-foot radius, and I could clearly see tire tracks in the dirt field next to the property. I stumbled out to stare at them as the neighbor across the street – a retired professor – pulled up in his car.

"Jesus," he said, "what happened to your greenhouse?"

"I … I … someone … I …"

"You know," he said, "I noticed a four-wheel drive rig idling in that lot earlier, figured it was some friends of yours."

"Friends of mine? Why?"

"Well, there were two guys in the cab and they were listening to the Niners game."

"The Niners?"

"They sat there for hours, like they were waiting for you to come out or something."

Slowly and sickeningly, piece by pathetic piece, I put it together. Basically I was such a Niners fanatic that someone in town had heard about it, and he and a partner had been crazy enough to sit in that empty lot, in the middle of the afternoon with houses all around, and track the Niners game on the radio, all in anticipation of a play so big I'd start hollering and wouldn't hear them smash into my greenhouse (not once but twice), knock the wall down, toss twenty-five plants in the back of their rig and escape. Hell, they'd been loading up at the very moment I was glancing at the greenhouse door, afraid I'd miss a replay.

How many Sundays had they been out there listening? It's hard to believe they showed up just that once. They might have been in that field every weekend in September for all I knew, hating me more and more as the Niners won laughers. By the time they took the plants they probably figured I owed them something.

Plus, as Karen liked to remind me afterwards, I'd paid more attention to the plants during sex than I had watching the Niner game.

Maybe I wasn't such a great guy after all.

Five years later, long after Karen and I had broken up and I was living in Boregon, she called me one afternoon.

"Remember when our pot was stolen because you were yelling at that stupid 49er game on the television?" she asked.

"Oh yeah," I said.

"Well, I just found out who did it!"

"Come on."

"No, I heard it from this guy who was trying to get in my pants. The thief's name is Jim Whelan and he not only lives in Bolinas, but he made the down payment on his house by selling our pot! Everybody knows about it ... they think it's a big joke!"

"Sounds kind of far-fetched to me, Karen."

"Oh yeah?" she said. "Then how come Whelan's dog is named 'Earl Cooper'!"

I came up off the couch. "Bullshit!" I said. "No way!"

"Oh yeah, that's another thing the guy told me. So Cathy and I walked by this Whelan's yard the other day and his dog was outside. I called to him: 'Earl Cooper, Earl Cooper, come over here, Earl' ... and he trotted right up to me."

I laughed. "You gotta hand it to the guy," I said. "That takes some balls."

"So now you think it's funny, Wilson?"

"Well, come on, Karen. It's been five years."

"Uh huh," she said. "And don't you wonder what kind of dog 'Earl Cooper' is?"

"What do you mean?"

"He's a fat little Chihuahua."

I paused, sat back down. "Well," I said, "that changes everything. We might have to kill this Whelan."

The outdoor crop I grew after leaving Bolinas proved how far I'd go for the sake of pot. I was house-sitting a friend's place in Forest Knolls, California – just up the road from Pt. Reyes in Marin County – and he gave me the go ahead to plant on the steep hillside behind his home.

Probably because he didn't think I could. It was rocky, thinly soiled terrain that was covered with a thick tangle of manzanita bush. I'd have to plant inside that vicious maze if I wanted to conceal the pot from flyovers by the Feds.

So I did. I took my two-week vacation from work and spent the first half of it layered like a mummy in the hot May sun, hacking and sawing paths through the twisting, five-foot high manzanita. When I'd get far enough in to discourage any but the skinniest thief I'd scoop out a 4' by 4' hole, then cut away the mess of stems overhead to let in light.

After seven straight 12-hour days I'd lost eight pounds and dug 20 precarious sites on the hill. This was the good news; the bad was that the easy part was over ... now I had to transport soil to those holes.

It's been twenty years and I still wince thinking about it. I had a ton of mushroom compost delivered to the bottom of the hill and briefly considered a bucket-and-pulley system for transporting it. But that would have been too slow and I had neither the time nor the patience for it. Plus it wouldn't have worked logistically: I used a dry creek bed to climb to the top and the different paths to the holes veered off in branch-like formations. Once I reached them I had to drop to my hands and knees and crawl through the maze.

So the only solution was to move that compost two cubic feet at a time, on my back, in a burlap bag. It was such absurdly hard work that it took all of my addict's determination to pull it off. On top of the crawl after the climbs – and I made about fifty of those a day – there was the stifling, 90-degree heat. I had rags tied around my head and towels hung from trees to mop myself, but was still so slippery from sweat that I kept losing my footing.

These, though, were simply obstacles: the real killer was the Poison Oak. I'd suffered severe outbreaks before so when I was scouting the hill that spring it was the first thing I took care of, hacking the oily plants to the ground before spraying them with *Roundup*. I didn't wipe them out completely, of course – even a fire wouldn't do that – but they did bud feebly and late. I thought I'd be safe as long as I avoided the remnants.

Right. As the dermatologist at Kaiser Hospital told me – when I showed up with a rash from my neck to my toes after five days of hauling dirt – all it takes to contact poison oak in the spring (when the plants are at their ripest) is to pass them with a good sweat going.

I was furious ... I had only two days of vacation left and there was still a lot of dirt to move. Did the dermatologist have a better solution than *Calamine Lotion,* some way I could be around that poison oak without it affecting me?

Oh sure, he said. I could take a poison oak tincture, a homeopathic approach that built up an internal immunity to the oils. He left the office, came back with a series of brown bottles and handed them to me.

"Now understand," he said, "and I say this only as a precaution, but roughly one in a thousand people gets internal poison oak from drinking that stuff."

I didn't like those odds – not with my weird medical history – but what was I to do, the planting season was upon me. I gulped down the first bottle.

I was back in the same hospital twenty-four hours later. A friend had driven me because not only were my eyes swollen shut but the rest of me was as bloated, white and spongy as a Pillsbury Doughboy. I had the poison oak internally, all right, and figured I'd die just from the thought of it.

But a good jolt of steroids reduced the swelling overnight. After that I had to keep taking the Prednisone (ten pills a day) for another month. Every time I'd wean myself to say, seven pills a day, I'd balloon up again. I loathed the stuff: I've rarely been so wired and only slept in short, feverish snatches.

But I dragged the rest of that dirt up the hillside. And after watering the holes with a long hose from the house I planted twenty big females in their beds.

The balance of the summer was easy by comparison. Crawling through that manzanita to water, fertilize and prune the plants was hard on a six-foot-six guy, of course, but I kept the ultimate goal in mind and was satisfied with the plants' progress. (Plus no one was likely to steal them … that manzanita maze would poke your eyes out if you didn't know what you were doing.)

The only problem was where the original seeds came from. It was

1985 and back then dependable seeds were difficult to find (I'd had all the ones I'd created stolen with the Niner crop). Unless you knew a grower who hybridized his own or were able to get something through the mail from the Seed Bank in Holland you were stuck with whatever you scavenged from the bottom of ounce bags. The breeding history those strays represented, their climate preference, quantity and quality potential and flowering time ... these were all a crapshoot. You could blow your summer baby-sitting a bushel of ragweed.

Which is, of course, exactly what I did. I thought I'd beaten the game by collecting my seeds from an ounce of excellent Hawaiian weed. Unfortunately they weren't being grown in Hawaii, with its rich mineral soil and tropical sun, so when they finally matured in late October they were as tasty as old twigs and just about as effective.

But I never got poison oak again.

A friend I hadn't heard from in years called yesterday to say he was moving to Chile to grow asparagus. Was I interested in coming along?

I wasn't, actually, and that probably surprised him. As a kid my parents asked my brothers to stop daring me to do things because I rarely turned down a challenge. As an adult that morphed into a fascination with bad ideas or, at least, an odd indifference to my own well-being.

That cafeteria I worked in after Mr. Kitchen's dinette was a good example. Basically I was part of a gang of six rummies – we were paid minimum wage plus two free meals a day – who did daily food preparation for the buffet-style operation out front. (If the customers had been able to see us they would have tossed their forks and run for it.) It was idiot's work, really, where one wino would select a bowl, the next would put noodles in it, the third would pour on spaghetti sauce and the fourth the mozzarella cheese, etc. As the only able-bodied character in the group I spent most of my time in the storeroom. I'd smoke cigarettes, move the occasional box around, daydream about my next free meal. Now that I was no longer cooking my appetite had returned and I was determined to gain weight.

Then on the fifth morning the preparation boys got behind so I was asked to help out on the salad line. We were making Thousand Island dressing and the first wino plopped mayonnaise in the bowl, the second poured in ketchup, the third a handful of diced pickles.

It was my job to stir the mess up. It went okay for a couple rounds but the character to my left was obviously distressed. He kept moaning and gurgling and nearly fell over once.

"Are you all right, buddy?" I asked, pushing a bowl to the guy on my right.

"Ohhhhh," the third guy groaned, "I'm gonna be sick."

"Well go to the bathroom, man. I'll cover for you."

"Ohhhhhhh." He bent forward and vomited a stream of bile into the ketchup, mayonnaise and pickles.

"Oh Jesus," I said, blanching in horror. "That's *disgusting!*"

The wino finished up with a couple dry heaves, stepped back and wiped his mouth. Shoved the barf bowl down to me.

"Just stir it in, Stretch," he mumbled. "Happens all the time."

"WHAT!?"

"We puke in all the food here," he sighed. "Why do ya' think we don't eat it?"

"Because you're fuckin' *winos!?*"

The others laughed. "No," said the guy next to me, "but that *is* why we're puking."

"Yeah, Stretch," said the ketchup man. "How'd you like those ravioli yesterday? Taste a little sour to you?"

More laughs all around. *To hell with this rathole!* I thought, gagging as my breakfast crawled up my throat. I undid my apron, jerked it over my head and left by the back door. In the alleyway the same wino I'd replaced earlier in the week was sucking on a pint of Muscatel.

"Hey, Stretch!" he croaked, looking me up and down with a shit-eating grin. "How'd you like the ravioli?"

I opted for civilization after that and got a job selling sporting goods in a department store. The money was poor but the hours were flexible and I was able to attend Portland State in the morning, work at night and squeeze in the occasional good times at the apartment in the interim. I was at the store a couple days after Christmas, pretending to rearrange some boxes of golf balls, when Don Taylor, a junior college coach from Longview, Washington who'd watched me play in the PIL, tracked me down to offer me a basketball scholarship.

He was a huge guy, as tall as I was and twice as wide, and what I remembered about his teams is they never stopped running.

"Coach Taylor," I said, "I'm honored but you've definitely got the wrong guy."

"How's that?"

"Come on, you saw me play. I don't like to run. I think basketball should be a slow, choreographed process that concentrates on *execution*. Sort of like a ballet."

He laughed and slapped my back so hard he damn near knocked me over. "Jeez, Wilson!" he roared. "When I heard you weren't playing I went to your old coach and he told me you were a MAJOR wiseacre! Ballet my ass, pal, you'll *run* when you play for me!"

"But I'm not gonna play for you, Coach," I coughed.

"Why not? Whatya got going here?"

I thought about it. I *was* still trying to get out of Boregon and didn't care if I ever saw Portland State again; at least Longview was 50 miles north. But playing *basketball?* The closest I'd come to exercise in the last six months was running from Fat Pat.

"This scholarship?" I asked. "What does it entail exactly?"

"Tuition-and-fee waiver, a work-study job and, in your case, a special bonus."

"What's that?"

"The volunteer fire department outside of town just built a new firehouse and you, Wilson, will be its first and only resident. What do you think of that, eh? Free rent on top of everything else!"

I didn't tell him I was only paying $5-a-month at the time. I didn't say anything for awhile, actually, just let Coach Taylor do his sales pitch until he convinced me that – everything considered – it was simply too weird an opportunity to pass up.

"Okay," I said finally. "I'm in."

"Welcome aboard!" crowed Porter, swallowing my right hand with his own while his left snaked into my pocket and snatched the pack of *Galaxies*.

"You won't be needing these anymore," he said, crushing them.

"Wait!" I said. "Save me the coupon!"

The firehouse … that's what I remember now. The basketball's an ugly blur because Taylor *was* a run-and-gun coach and it exhausted me just watching us play, much less having to participate. I do not pretend to be proud of my athletic career (such as it was), because on balance I should have been out there for better reasons than height and pussy. The fact that I wasn't meant I had to hear about my "bad attitude" from every coach I played for.

It was a reasonably fair exchange, I suppose, especially now that I was getting a college education from the deal. Plus I *could* play the game and was actually a very good defender and rebounder. Taylor wanted more, of course, but that's why he was the coach.

What I longed for was a smoke. I had to sneak them early in the morning – just after midnight – in the field behind the fire station. I didn't dare fire up inside: I'd had Taylor make "surprise inspections" at eleven at night and that firehouse was ten miles east of town in the middle of nowhere. I'd tell myself I was putting something over on him even as I stood out there in 30-degree temperatures, trying to hit my mouth with the cigarette.

The peace and quiet was welcome, anyway. There wasn't much of it when I got home at night. The firehouse had thirty volunteers, all of whom were mill workers, and though I was the only full-time resident the rest of them hung out there as much as possible. It was their home away from home and they liked washing and fondling the big red truck.

Mostly they just sat around hoping for a fire. These happened about three times a month. In the interim they had weekly training sessions where groups of them would take the truck out for practice runs, hanging off the sides as they raced around town popping the siren.

Unfortunately they were all pretty short guys, so when they dragged me along I had to wear one of their uniforms. This consisted of a little fire hat strapped atop my head, a yellow jacket that reached my elbows and pants that stopped mid-calf. I looked and felt like the biggest buffoon in Longview and that was how the volunteers liked it: to them my mechanically disinclined nature and total disinterest in firehouse procedure proved I was a feeble-minded jock. A few of them, in fact, even came to basketball games just to root *against* me.

When an actual fire occurred they'd leave me behind or, if they had to drag me along, tell me to stay out of the way once we got there. "Make yourself scarce, Hormel," they'd say, and run off to fight the blaze.

They called me "Hormel" because that's what I had in the cupboards at the firehouse: *Hormel Chili.* Dozens and dozens of cans of it. There was nothing in the refrigerator and no condiments or staples or other canned goods on the shelves … just the chili. I suppose it was unusual and it was definitely unhealthy – I'm not sure my stomach ever recovered – but after my café-cooking days I tried to keep food and its preparation as simple as possible. So I ate the chili morning, noon and night and pretty soon, whenever a fireman farted, one of the other guys would yell "Hey! Was that a *Hormel* I heard?"

I'm sure the loose bowels and general lack of nutrition contributed to my fatigue. Between fifteen hours of classes, my on-campus janitorial job, the basketball games and practices I was in a daze most of the time. Plus the place was so far out of town that I'd often end up walking home.

So when the basketball season wound down to the final game I was relieved. Coach Taylor gave us Thursday off and I accepted a ride to the firehouse with my friend Carl Elmer. He was a local kid who would go to the junior college for a year or two before heading to the paper mills to work. It seemed to be the pattern in that town: young men wanted mill jobs so they could buy themselves a hot car, which would then rust to dust in the corrosive air of the mill parking lot, and in paying off that vehicle and the one that replaced it they'd be stuck for life.

But who knows? Maybe Carl got out, maybe he's an accountant in Ohio somewhere. If so I bet he remembers that day at the firehouse. We pulled in at 3:00 p.m. and I invited him inside for a bowl of chili. I'd no sooner grabbed the cans from the cupboard, however, when the fire alarm went off.

Carl jumped straight in the air. "Holy shit!" he yelled, covering his ears as the siren blared from the roof overhead. "What the hell's that?"

I set down the chili, ran over to the radio as the address of the fire came across. "It's a fire!" I yelled, scratching down the address. "But don't worry about it! Any second now the volunteers will come running in!"

But a minute passed, then two and no one showed. I stepped out into the parking lot with Carl, waited for the volunteers' trucks to come screaming up the road. Slowly it dawned on me that three o'clock meant a shift change at the paper mills, with day shift quitting and swing shift coming on.

The volunteer firemen were all mill workers on either the day or swing shift ... *ergo* I was fucked. I looked over at the fire truck, then back at Carl.

"Elmer," I said, "do you think you can drive that truck?"

He went around to the front of the garage and peered in at it. "Wow!" he said. "It's huge!"

"Can you drive it?"

"Shit yeah! Can't you?"

"I don't how to use a stick shift."

"Damn, man ... are we going to the fire?"

"I'm afraid so," I said, still hoping a volunteer would drive up and save my ass.

"Cool," he said. "Where's my hat?"

Five minutes after that – Carl had to find a hat that fit just right and he couldn't believe *my* uniform – we pulled out of the garage and headed for the fire. He had his window down and kept checking himself out in the mirror while popping the siren and hooting like a rodeo clown. Before long we had a trail of cars following us as we sped down Road 10.

"You sure you know where this address is?" I said.

He gave me the same patronizing look as the volunteers. "I'm on top of it, man," he said. "I'll get you there and ... then what? You'll fight the fire, huh? I don't have any training."

I wanted to tell him I didn't either but I was having trouble breathing. *This is a bad one,* I thought, *I really fucked up this time. Couldn't I have listened just once when those guys were talking about where to screw in this hose or that one?* I reached in my uniform pocket, fumbled for the pack of cigarettes I'd brought along. Shook one out and lit it.

"Hey what are you doin'?" gasped Carl. "You can't smoke cigarettes ... you're an athlete!"

"Trust me, buddy," I said, "we got way bigger problems than that. Just drive."

He knew where he was going, anyway ... that was something. A left and a couple quick rights and there we were in a cul-de-sac, where the house nearest the street had a chimney fire. There were a dozen people on the lawn and when Carl pulled to the curb I jumped out and ran to the front of the truck.

"Jesus Christ!" yelled the owner. "Where the hell have you been, man?"

"Eh, mechanical problems," I said, holding up my arms to calm everyone down. Except with that tight little jacket on they sort of got stuck up there.

"Hey!" said a woman in the crowd. "You don't look like a fireman! How old are you?"

"And what about the kid in the truck!"

I glanced behind me. Not only had Carl not moved, he was tipping his hat and waving to the neighborhood children. "All right!" I said, "I'm a volunteer fireman and I'm on top of this!" I ran to the side of the truck and, finally coaxing Carl out of the cab, got him to help me pull the ladder off. "Take this to the side of the house," I said. "Then I'll drag the hose over and you can get up there and blast the fire with water!"

"You mean *you'll* get up there, Wilson," he said. "I don't know shit about fighting fires."

"But I'm afraid of *heights*, man!"

He laughed. "And you a tall guy! Real funny, Wilson ... I'm amazed you can joke at a time like this."

I wasn't joking: I did hate heights. I hated the thought of the control box on the other side of the truck even more but ran around there, anyway. Jerked the door open, looked in at two rows of gauges that meant absolutely nothing to me. Decided to count on luck as I twisted this dial and that one, then clamored on top of the truck, grabbed the end of the hose and ran across the lawn to tepid cheers.

At the base of the ladder I looked up, gulped and turned to Carl. "This is your last chance to be a hero, man," I said.

"No way, Wilson," he replied, looking around nervously. "I'm starting to get a little worried here, actually. I mean ... you look ridiculous in that uniform. Are you sure you know what you're doing?"

"Are you nuts, Elmer? I don't have the faintest fuckin' idea what I'm doing!" I started up the ladder, tried to keep my eyes straight ahead as I dragged the hose past the second story onto the roof. The fire was still smoldering around the chimney and by climbing over the steeply pitched shingles (not daring to look down) I managed to shimmy reasonably close.

I looked up at the darkening sky, prayed for the first time since grade school. *Oh Lord,* I pleaded ... *let there be water, Lord!*

I cranked open the lever at the end of the hose, waited for the surge of pressure that would tell me water was coming.

Nothing ... not a drop. I glanced down, shrugged as I tried to pick out the owner in the crowd. "Sorry!" I yelled. "I guess we're out of water!"

"WHAT!? ARE YOU INSANE! WHAT KIND OF FIREMEN ARE YOU?" he screamed.

Then some guy in the back chimed in, "Hey no wonder!" he laughed. "The idiot never attached the hose to a hydrant! He thought the truck was full of water!"

In the end a couple of neighbors put the fire out with a garden hose. When Coach Taylor heard about it my basketball career ended with the ignominy it deserved.

2011 will usher in my thirtieth year as a cannabis cultivator, the last twenty-five of which I've spent in this house. My old high school buddy Dwayne Hammer purchased the place in 1987 and I rented it from him until I bought it myself in 2000. It's a serviceable three-bedroom one-bath property but I don't care much about that ... my focus has always been on the basement. When I first returned to Portland and Dwayne and I were scouting potential grow sites we walked through this house and decided its long concrete basement was too narrow for my purposes. Then we left and were halfway across the lawn when Dwayne stopped and shook his head.

"You know," he said, "there's something wrong here. That house is too big for a basement that small."

So we returned downstairs and discovered that what we'd thought was a wooden wall was actually a partition. We located a crude door on its northern end, stepped through to find ourselves in a 20' by 30' unfinished room.

"What do you think?" said Dwayne. "Would this make a good flowering room?"

61

"Hell yeah," I said, "it's perfect! Especially with that dirt floor."

Dumbest words I ever uttered? Pretty close. I was a novice at indoor growing at the time and didn't realize that the utility those dirt floor and walls afforded me (i.e., I could slop water and fertilizer around with impunity) also meant I couldn't control the room's environment, the single most crucial factor in indoor growing.

So instead of a perfect grow site I was doomed to one that's caused me endless frustration. For openers the temperature and humidity are largely dependent on the climate outside, which makes the room a tomb in winter and a hothouse in summer. Then there's the bugs: they creep from their dirt hiding places in waves, so no matter how many times I spray or bomb I can't kill them all. (I've been in a ferocious war with mites for decades.)

All this might have been surmountable if I'd brought in carpenter friends and transformed the room into a kind of long railcar, but the ceiling is so low now that I move around in a crouch, my head buffeted by a crash helmet. And I don't mean to suggest that the quality of the buds is the issue here ... the highs (as a rule) are superb. The problem is quantity, or bud density. I buy seeds on the Internet, grow them out and I'm lucky to realize an ounce per plant. I give clones of the same varieties to growers with controllable, insulated rooms and they achieve weights two to three times better than mine.

Yet I've hardly given up. I brought those six years of outdoor/greenhouse cultivation experience to Portland and I've tried everything I could think of in the interim: experimenting with smaller and larger pots, switching organic soils, leaving the plants in the vegetative state longer, buying newer, ever more exotic hybrids, changing bulbs more frequently, substituting new hoods, increasing the carbon dioxide levels, stapling white plastic instead of Mylar to the ceiling and walls, using every organic supplement from bat guano to fish fertilizer ... and have rarely made a dent in the production problems.

Fortunately I'm in it for the highs. It'd be nice to be rich by now, and I could have used fewer blows to my grower's pride over the years, but even with a million in the bank I'd be searching for newer and weirder stones. If you ever visit Amsterdam or Vancouver, Canada, just hang around a cannabis seed shop for awhile and listen to what most Americans ask for. Chances are it'll be some variation on, "What do ya got that'll produce the biggest, strongest buds in the shortest amount of time." I call this the "Ant Approach" to growing (no imagination required). You find yourself a fast-growing, industrial strength, female indica, then turn it into a factory (endlessly reproducing clones from a series of mother plants). Not only is this the easiest way to produce marijuana, it's also the most lucrative. In British Colombia, for instance, where the thousands of indoor growers have access to the best seeds on the planet, all the emphasis is on yield over diversity so virtually every commercial cultivator grows the same thing (Big Bud a few years ago, then Hash Plant and now, last I heard, some kind of bland Jamaican). This "B.C. Bud" is bought by Americans until they tire of it, at which point the Canadians switch to another easy cloning, fast producing hybrid.

Talk about boring ... who wants to look at the same plant everyday, much less smoke it? I'm such a slave to diversity that I grow up to fifteen varieties at once (which, along with the dirt room, doesn't help production much either). Right now I've all the following in flower:

APOLLO 13
RED DRAGON
OG KUSH
KEVORKIAN
GRAPEGOD
ROYAL HAZE
BLUE DREAM
PINEAPPLE EXPRESS
CHOCOLATE CHUNK

MR. SHIVERS
GIGABUD
TANGERINE DREAM
MIDNIGHT KUSH
HANGTOWN
L.A. CONFIDENTIAL
AK-47
PURPLE HAZE
STRAWBERRY COUGH

With a rash of new varieties waiting in the wings. When any given harvest is complete and the buds from the different plants are properly cured I mix them together to create an indica/sativa smorgasbord. (There are likely to be eight to ten different kinds of buds in an ounce bag; not only have my customers been exposed to a multiplicity of smells, stones and tastes over the years, but they've tried over three hundred different varieties of marijuana.)

Before I do that, though, I select the best buds from the best plants for my personal stash. My weed's great but except for some Thai Stick in 1972 and some Maui Wowee in 1975 I've never smoked anything that I was eager to burn all day. I might light a little *Mr. Shivers* in the morning, for instance, then some *Purple Haze* and *OG Kush* during the afternoon, before finishing off with *Strawberry Cough* or *Red Dragon* at bedtime.

Sixty-four and the living is easy.

There's more to the Ant Approach than just monocropping, though, and it includes having the good sense to keep a regular job while you're growing. This allays the suspicions of others even as it allows you to sock away large amounts of cash.

I'm more in the "grasshopper" mold myself. Hell, other than the highs the "no jobs" part is the main reason I grow. I've spent a quarter century doing exactly what I please everyday and I remind myself of that constantly so years from now – when I'm sitting in jail or waiting outside a homeless shelter for my mush – I won't get caught up wondering about what might have been.

There's no ant in Wilson High.

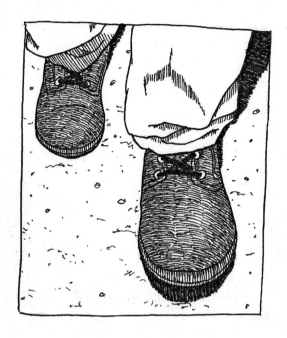

I've always been a walker. It could be genetic – my mother still takes long walks everyday – but if so it's a gene that skipped my brothers. I can say with reasonable certainty that none of them has ever gone for a stroll in his life. They'll head out for a run or a bike ride, or lug a heavy bag around a golf course, maybe even *hike* a distance if it's steep enough … but just walk? With no objective in mind but the act itself? It's hard to imagine.

So I like to think my ambulatory nature was sparked by being too uncoordinated to ride a bike. I know my father couldn't take it. He was a famously patient guy but after I wobbled and crashed every time he let go of the handle bars he gave up and consigned me to a life of training wheels. It was only the intercession of my step-grandfather

– my favorite person when I was a kid – that saved me from total humiliation. Every afternoon he'd stand in the driveway and coach me on gravity until finally, desperately, I could make it up and down the street without falling on my head.

At which point I lost interest in bikes forever. What I liked best was to walk. It didn't matter if it was two blocks or two miles, those long stork legs – that went all the wrong ways otherwise – were perfect for walking. Plus I could see what was going on around me when I strolled and, even better, there was all that time to *think*. By the time I was in high school I'd convinced myself there was no problem so big I couldn't walk it off.

Because walking is a meditation. If you enjoy your own company and you can handle (even prefer) being alone, then you're probably a walker by nature. You don't need an iPod or headphones or some grisly Spandex costume, much less a baby carriage or a cell phone. You just open the door and go out for a stroll.

It's what I've done everyday for the last twenty-five years. Rain, sun, snow or sleet I walk at least five miles a day and sometimes as many as ten or fifteen. In the old days, up until 1995 or so, this just made me eccentric. Now there's all this media hoopla about the benefits of walking so suddenly I'm hoofing it for health purposes.

But no, that's what the clowns in Spandex are doing. Or the fat squirrels on the treadmills and "walking machines." It makes me think of my favorite American moment in Europe, when I was selling T-shirts at an Ostrich Convention in Belgium. It was a weekend event at a mountain resort and come the end of the day the attendees had to hike a steep, half-mile hill to their lodgings. You could stand at the bottom and see whole European families – grandma, mom and dad, grandkids – pound up the sidewalk without hesitation. The Americans? Oh, they were easy to pick out:

"Where's the tram? I can't believe there's no tram!"

"What about a bus! There must be a shuttle bus!"

"Go get the car, Jim. You can drive us up, then walk back."

"It's so farrrrrr, mom!"

If I sound bitter it's because – whether I walk for exercise or not – I'm sterling proof that the health claims attendant to walking have merit. I've tempted death too many times to contemplate, abused this body with untold substances and been living on luck so long I feel like a coin flip. Yet every five years I go in for a physical and the results are always the same. My height, weight, blood pressure and cholesterol are identical to what they were in my thirties. I feel like a high school kid, I haven't had a cold or flu bug since Reagan was President and I eat whatever I want whenever I want.

A shining stoner beacon, in other words, a ghost made whole by strolls. (I even make care decisions based on geography: my physician, dentist, naturopath and masseuse ... all are within walking distance.) So do you think, after years of proselytizing, that I've convinced even *one* other person to get off his or her ass and walk everyday?

Nahhhh. I think being alone with your thoughts, even if it's only a half hour a day, is too much to ask of most Americans.

I write about being born to a bindle-stiff mentality, but at eighteen I was trying to convince myself that there was a philosophy professor in me. Some clown in a corduroy jacket with elbow patches, maybe a briar pipe and dark wood office, my rumpled hair in a halo around my head as I wandered the World of Ideas. This wasn't a dream of mine but a fantasy, what I thought I might want if I actually had the ambition to achieve something in life. So I tried to keep the image close as I started the spring term at Lower Columbia College.

Because my main objective, of course, was continuing to avoid the draft. (Even though I wasn't as concerned about military service as most of my peers: I was 6'6", after all, and could type 100 words a minute, so there was a *chance* the army wouldn't put me on the front lines.) What's more I'd always enjoyed school and had managed straight A's winter term in spite of distractions like being suspended from that last game and all the kids at the junior college – once the story of the fire truck incident had spread through the town – calling me "Hormel."

Fortunately my tuition-and-fee waiver and work-study job covered spring term and after leaving the firehouse I rented a $25-a-month room atop a fabric store on Commerce Street. It was a quiet place and I enjoyed living alone. The first three weeks of the term were so uneventful, in fact, with me doing little more with my free time than writing letters to Kathy, my old high school girlfriend, that I thought my increasing restlessness was a simple case of boredom.

Then one Friday afternoon Tom Fallon, my Creative Writing 101 professor, asked us to write a short story based on a real incident in our lives. When we came back on Monday he had each of us read our efforts aloud.

I wish I still had what I wrote because it's hard to describe what happened when I read it. I know it was a yarn about a black handyman who'd fallen off the roof of the house next door when I was nine years old, and what that death had taught me about the fragility of life. I'd added a bit of levity to counteract the sappiness, of course, but remember imagining the story as a kind of gently humorous, *Reader's Digest* type of piece.

Imagine my shock when – after just three or four paragraphs – I had to shout to make myself heard: my classmates were literally shrieking with laughter. Convulsive, hiccupy stuff that only got worse the further I read.

I couldn't understand it … were these kids racist? Was my fly open? Was it some kind of *Hormel* hangover, them associating the handyman on the roof with me and the chimney fire? I was the last to read that day and when Professor Fallon pulled me aside after class I wasn't the least surprised.

The first thing he did was offer me one of the nasty little *Roi-Tan* cigars he liked. I lit it up, sucked the oily gray smoke into my lungs and coughed.

"Damn!" I gasped. "You *inhale* these things?"

"Yeah," he said. "Can't you tell?"

He did have a gravelly voice. Hell, he looked more like a longshoreman than a professor, as if he dressed in the dark in the morning, then figured a shave was too much trouble. We sat there for a moment at his desk, both of us working our *Roi-Tans*, and he finally shook his head and laughed.

"Don't tell me," I said. "You saw me play basketball, or heard the firehouse yarns."

"Well both, as a matter of fact," he said, "but I was thinking about that story you wrote. You were surprised at everybody laughing like that, weren't you?"

"Yeah. I mean it wasn't exactly a humorous subject."

"It's your *tone*, High. Plus you're a born storyteller on top of it. I knew guys like you in the Navy – guys of Irish descent, usually – who could make anything humorous just by describing it."

"The Irish I've got," I said, thinking about my mother's County Cork ancestors. "But what about the story I wrote? What'd *you* think of it?"

Fallon laughed. "Christ, Wilson," he said, "I've waited a long time to say this to a student but ... you're a *writer*, kid, you've got a real gift with words."

"Come on."

"I mean it. I knew it from the first piece you wrote in here – all you need now is something to write *about*. And I'll tell you something else. I think you should drop out of school, go have yourself some adventures while you're still young enough to appreciate them."

I almost forgot to breathe. Here was a professor I'd respected but barely spoken to before, telling me what seemed – subconsciously, at least – the very thing I'd waited my whole life to hear: *You're a writer, kid. You should drop out of school, go have yourself some adventures while you're still young.*

How could this be? What was so earthshaking about it? And why hadn't I thought of it myself?

Then I remembered the catch:

"What about the draft?" I said.

"What about it, High? You're probably too tall to pass the physical, and if not ... hell, the army's where real adventures begin."

That was probably true ... if you lived. I stood up, shaky and dazed, and walked over to the window that overlooked the campus. Took a good pull on that *Roi-Tan* and pretended to think about what Fallon had said. I say *pretended* because in the dozen steps it took to get from his desk to the window I'd already made up my mind. I was an all-or-nothing kind of guy and dropping out of college, just playing my future like a pair of dice, not only excited me but seemed exactly the right thing to do.

There was some brief consideration of what my parents would think, of course, and, more urgently, Kathy at her high-end Southern California college, but it was fleeting. Whatever the immediate heartache for any of us, the wisdom of my decision would be made clear eventually. I was sure of that.

In the meanwhile it was the *road* for me, baby, it was time to set the inner bindle stiff free!

"You know what they call me around here?" I asked Fallon.

"'Hormel'?"

"Yeah," I said. "I won't miss that."

Thirty years is a long time to grow without being busted, though I've had my share of close calls along the way. I raise my plants in dirt and that soil has to be dragged in and out of the house in plastic bags. This would be easy enough if I had a garage that attached to the house but, unfortunately, I don't. Instead I have to fill my camper truck with bags from the nursery, then wait until nightfall to sneak them inside.

Getting rid of the used soil is the same process in reverse. It was vaguely challenging in my forties, but at sixty-four skulking around in the dark is just plain embarrassing. My neighbor to the south is a rabbit-eared character (if I've fooled him all these years I should have been a spy), so every creak of the truck or rustle of a bag has me looking for his silhouette in a window.

Anyway, one morning in 1999 I returned from the nursery with the usual load of dirt. I swung a left in front of my house, threw the old Ford in reverse and was backing up my driveway when I saw a cop car parked there. It was unmarked, but there was no mistaking that dark blue, featureless Plymouth, so I braked the truck, drove up the street and pulled to the curb.

The first thing I thought of is the Thomas Fuller quote I adopted as my grower's mantra way back in the Eighties: "He who is afraid of every nettle should not piss in the grass."

Because particularly back then (before the Medical Marijuana era) you had to be defiant to do what I do. It's not a macho thing, just a fact that the pot business – like any drug enterprise – is no place for pussies. You're hunted twenty-four hours a day by cops who'll jail you for what you do and thieves who'll kill you for it. What's more you have to be ready for the day either of them arrives because if you stay in this business long enough they will (like cockroaches) appear.

And now it was my turn. I felt surprisingly calm, even resigned, as I grabbed a bag of groceries from the seat and started up the street. It looked like there was only one cop in the car, sitting in the passenger side, and when he saw me he hopped out and walked towards me.

He was a plain clothes guy with the obligatory mustache and sports coat and nearly as tall as I was. We met in the middle of the lawn and I found myself worrying about my friend Elaine. She'd been staying with me for awhile and was inside the house with strict orders not to open the door to anyone.

"You the owner of this house?" asked the cop.

"Yeah," I said. We were ten feet from my front porch and with a crop due the next day it smelled like skunks fucking under there.

Fortunately the cop looked like a smoker ... he probably couldn't smell his own farts.

"Detective Haney," he said, sticking out his hand.

I shook it. "Wilson High," I said.

He looked at me like I might be pulling his leg, then motioned towards the porch. "Let's go up there to talk," he said, keeping his voice low.

I glanced around. Other than a wino pushing a shopping cart up the street we were alone. "No, no," I said, "this is fine right here. What's going on, Officer?"

"Well," he muttered, "I knocked on your door a few times and didn't get an answer, so I figured you were gone for the day."

"And ...?"

"I went ahead and parked in your driveway. I'm part of a drug surveillance team."

What could I say to that? Suddenly I wished I still smoked cigarettes.

"We're watching that tavern over there," he said.

I followed his gaze to the One Stop Lounge at the end of the street. I nearly burst out laughing in my sudden, overwhelming relief. He wasn't there to bust me ... he wanted to spy on the biker bar.

"So?" he said.

"Huh? So what?"

"Can I use your driveway for awhile?"

If he stayed he might smell the pot, but if I told him no he might get suspicious. Either way I wasn't sticking around to find out. "Sure," I said. "But I've got a friend inside – she's real sick, so that's why she didn't answer the door when you knocked – and I have to take her to the doctor."

"That's fine," said Haney. "I'll probably be gone by the time you return." He stuck out his hand again. "Thanks, Mr. ... High. You're a good citizen."

"Oh yeah," I laughed, "the best." I took the porch steps three at a time, unlocked the door and nearly knocked Elaine over when I stepped inside.

"Oh my God," she gasped, "are we going to jail!?"

"No, no," I said, pushing by her and shoving perishable items into the refrigerator. "But grab your coat! There's no sense hanging around with a cop in the driveway."

We left through the front door and when we reached the lawn I turned to wave at the cop but he was already slouched low in the front seat. We jumped into my Pimpmobile (an '84 Lincoln Town Car) and drove off. Came back hours later to an empty driveway.

Two days later the headline in The Boregonian read, "GIANT HEROIN BUST IN SE PORTLAND TAVERN."

Which only corroborated my other grower's mantra, i.e., better lucky than good.

So ... did the cop realize I was growing and shine it on, or did he somehow overlook the obvious? I'll never know for sure. It's like my neighborhood. It has a rather seedy patina – with a porn theater and lesbian coffee shop bordering the biker bar – but I've always been comfortable here.

A lot more than Dwayne was. When he first considered buying the place the location worried him.

"Why?" I asked.

"Come on! There's a biker bar, a porn theater, a leather shop and a cleaning plant with a couple dozen employees. It's much too conspicuous around there."

"Actually," I said, "it's just about right."

"What do you mean."

"You'd have to be nuts to grow in a place like that, Dwayne ... it's the perfect camouflage."

And it has been ... so far. Like the cop I don't know if the neighbors are on to me or not. My approach has been to act like they aren't and assume they are, which creates a delicate balance between friendliness and outright bribery. I had a T-shirt design business a few years ago, for instance, and when the older people around here died off and young couples bought their homes I was sure to pass out kid shirts to the expectant parents. (Pot-bellied pig shirts, appropriately enough. I have a bunch of them left in my attic. It was easy to peddle adult tees to pot-bellied pig owners, but I never sold them a single kid shirt because, they said, they didn't have kids ... they had pigs.)

This helps establish my poor artist pose. I live in a small house with a rusty truck and an old car in the driveway, and try to be just distant enough that the neighbors pass me off as the requisite weird bachelor.

Dealing with the mailman is easier. I've had the same one for years now, and inasmuch as he has to step on my porch to deliver the mail he knows I either: (a) keep skunks for pets or (b) cultivate a basement jungle.

So every Christmas I give him a 60-buck bottle of Glenlivet Scotch. The first year it was Crown Royal and it was still in a paper bag when I offered it to him.

"Here," I said. "Merry Christmas!"

"Oh no," he said. "President Clinton has given us strict orders not to accept gifts."

"Well, it's a bottle of Crown Royal ..."

Whifffff ... he had it out of my hand and into his bag before I knew it was gone. When he reached the bottom of the stairs he took a good sniff, then turned around and gave me a sheepish grin.

"Actually," he said, "I'm kind of partial to scotch."

"You got it ... pal."

Our government. Viet Nam. Staring down the barrel in the summer of '66. After I dropped out of junior college I went to work in a Longview paper mill, pulling newly printed boxes off conveyor belts and tying strings around them. It was my first experience with a dull, faceless assembly line job – unless you counted my week with the winos in the cafeteria – and I found it more tolerable than I thought. Mentally and physically it required next to nothing of me, and left my mind free to consider weightier matters.

With my uncertain future at the top of the list. If I passed the draft physical, I was a soldier. If I didn't, I could do whatever I chose with my life (starting with a move back to the Bay Area). The second option was preferable, of course, but I could live with the first if the army would just get on with it.

So I was actually relieved when the notice for the physical arrived in early July. I'd been hearing fantastical stories about the schemes kids were concocting to flunk so I thought, *What the hell, I should check with my family doctor in Portland, see if anything in my past will get me a deferment.*

His name was Dr. Culp and he was a tough little bastard I'd been going to since I was sixteen years old. The last time he'd seen me I couldn't breathe and thought I'd suffered a heart attack. Instead it was hyper-ventilation from my "Regular Guy Year," trying to play basketball, be the art editor of the paper, run the senior class activities, draw cartoons, earn a 4.0 and work two jobs ... all at once. He told me to breathe into a paper bag and gave me a bottle of tranquilizers. (They were "reds": I took just one of them before my mother, horrified at my slurred speech and slovenly antics, flushed the balance down the toilet.)

So the week before the physical I made an appointment and rode a bus to Portland to see him. I wasn't expecting much and got right to the point once we sat down, "Listen, Doc, I have my draft physical next week. You know my medical history: is there anything in it that'll get me out of the Service?"

He sighed and shook his head. "Damn," he said, "what the hell's wrong with your generation? Do you know how many boys your age I have coming through here now, looking for me to write something ... *anything* ... to get them out of the draft? To change their measles to rheumatic fever maybe, or their bruised knee to a ligament tear? It terrifies me, Wilson! Where's the *patriot* in you kids!?"

"Hey hey," I said. "It was worth a try."

Culp laughed, drew up his clipboard and started scribbling on it. "You don't understand, Wilson," he said. "You I *will* write a note for. I can't imagine a worse soldier."

What did he mean by that? Did I even care? I must have because when I got back to my Longview apartment I steamed open the sealed envelope he'd given me (he told me to carry it to the physical and he'd send another copy to the draft board). There was a paragraph or two of puffery, then came the gist of the matter:

Wilson is an incorrigible risk taker who refuses to follow

orders. As a taxpayer I don't want to pay for the two years this boy will spend in the stockade. Please excuse him from his military obligation.

Respectfully,
Dr. L. Culp

Huh? I kept turning the note over and opening and closing the envelope. There had to be more to it than that. Surely Culp didn't think something that silly would get me out of McNamara's War?

But no, that was it. I was disgusted. I crumpled the note up and threw it in a wastebasket, only retrieving it a week later on my way out the door to the physical. By then the prospect of army service had me nervously hedging my bets. I smoothed it out on the bus ride to Portland, hoped Culp knew something I didn't.

It didn't seem likely once I arrived at the exam site. Virtually all of the males from my McKinley High class – nearly 350 of them – were also in attendance, and none of us could find anyone who wasn't desperate to avoid military service. The schemes ranged from pennies under the armpits (to raise blood pressure), to eating hard-boiled eggs for weeks on end (to increase albumen in the urine), to a mix of exaggerated sports injuries, psychiatric maladies, hives, headaches, homosexuality, hay fever, … hell, we had the whole alphabet in there and everyone thought my note was the most pathetic by far.

The Sergeant I sat down with at the end of the physical agreed. (He was my last chance as the guy measuring me had pounded on my head until he could get a 6'5"-7/8ths on the scale, just enough to pass me.) He read the note I handed him, laughed out loud before pinning it to the bulletin board behind him.

"You don't mind if I keep that, do you?" he asked. "Every week we have a contest for most ridiculous excuse and, High, … that baby's a winner!"

"No problem," I sighed. "But the doctor sent you another one, I can see it in my folder there."

The Sergeant tore it open, read through it quickly, mumbling that it was more of the same crap. Then he came to the end, peered a little closer and set the note down.

"Well, Wilson," he shrugged, "when the Russians land in Portland and all the women and children are gone, we'll consider your ass."

"Huh?"

"You're out, pal. You're a Permanent 1-Y. No Viet Nam for you."

"But I don't get it … what did Culp write in that note that wasn't in the first one?"

"Just these initials down here," said the Sergeant, turning the note around and pointing to the doctor's signature.

"What do they mean?"

"That Culp's an active Major in the Marine Medical Corps. He could tell me to excuse you for a big nose and I'd have to do it. So long, Mr. High … we *won't* be in touch."

Jesus. I *floated* out of there, wafting down the hallway with my head in the clouds. Somewhere a guy with one arm was yelling about getting a Permanent 1-Y instead of a 4-F (he was shoving his stub in the doctor's face, screaming, "You think it'll grow back, asshole?!") but what neither of us realized then is that of the 400 boys processed that day, we were the only two who failed. All my buddies with all their excuses had passed with flying colors. When the physical was over the army gave you a cookie and a carton of milk and had you wait in an auditorium until everyone else was done. That's where my ex-classmates were sitting when I emerged onto the stage in front of them.

"Hey High!" yelled my old buddy Cable. "What'd they think of that note of yours?"

There was a loud chorus of laughter from my ex-classmates. I waited until it died down, then jerked my arms in the air like Winston

Churchill.

"I fuckin' did it, boys!" I yelled. "I flunked! I'm out! I'm Permanent 1-Y!"

You could have heard a pin drop in there. Finally some guy I didn't even know managed a feeble clap. "Way to go, Stretch!" he yelled.

But my ex-classmates weren't buying it. Hell, they'd had *legitimate* excuses and were *still* gonna die for nothing? While Wilson High? The jerk-off with the joke note? The horse's ass class president? The Guy Who Never Ran ... he was getting a free pass!?

The first milk carton bounced off the curtain behind me. After that they poured through the air.

And all the while I'm up there hooting and hollering and hopping around, thinking *California, here I come ...*

The World's Fastest Typist. As innocuous as that sounds now it seems even sillier that I made my living that way. Not because I didn't think I was (I truly never met, heard or read of anybody who could type as fast as I did for as long as I could on any kind of keyboard – be it a teletype, a typewriter or a computer), but because speed typing was a natural for me, a perfect confluence of the monk and monkey in my head.

Once I learned to touch type, anyway. The summer after eighth grade my mother got this idea in her head that I should learn to use a typewriter. This would not be such an unusual notion now, not when kids start using keyboards as adolescents, but in 1961 I couldn't imagine a fourteen-year-old girl with typing skills, much less a boy my age. In retrospect it seemed very prescient of mom to even make me try. When I complimented her on this once she simply laughed. "I wanted you out of the house in the morning," she told me, "and after seventh grade I enrolled you in that summer reading class. Do you remember that?"

"No."

"I'm not surprised. You had a whole long list of books to read and you read them all the first week. Even finished your little reports on

83

them. Then there I was ... stuck with you again."

"So the typing ...?"

"You were so uncoordinated I was sure it'd take you all summer to learn."

And she wonders where I get *my* attitude.

So there I was at the local high school for five mornings a week, not only the only kid under fifteen in my typing and English classes, but also the tallest and skinniest. (I'd grown nine inches in the past year, stretching from 5'4" to 6'1" with no discernible increase in weight.)

My self-consciousness abated somewhat the first time the teacher walked in. He was a 6'9" 260-pound giant who had played professional basketball for the St. Louis Hawks in the early 50s and was now teaching typing in summer school. He stopped in front of his desk, peeled off his tacky sports coat to reveal arms as big around as my body.

"I'm Mr. Taylor," he rumbled. "But you can call me 'Big Joe.'"

I literally gulped. I can't speak for the other 50 students in the room, virtually all of whom were girls of varying ages, but it's safe to say Big Joe's voice was scarier than his size and he was the biggest sonofabitch I'd ever seen. Then, to prove he could type too, he rolled over a little Olympic portable on a stand, set up something in the textbook to read, hit the timer and started pounding. I remember it like it was yesterday: how was it possible for fingers that big to manipulate a keyboard that small?

When he was done he corrected his work and he'd typed 70 words a minute for three minutes straight with one error. He slid the typewriter stand aside, stepped toward us and extended his hands. "If I can type that well with mitts like these," he said, "imagine what you can do with those scrawny little paws of yours!"

He had me convinced. Unfortunately I'd done some hunting and pecking on my older brother's typewriter over the past month or so (it was a graduation gift from my parents and he barely looked at it before passing it on to me) so even though the keyboards in class were blank I remembered where the letters were and looked down as I typed.

It was the morning of the third day when a giant shadow crept over me. I twisted my head and saw Big Joe standing there.

"You like to look, don't you, High?" he said.

"Well," I said, "maybe once in awhile."

I was in the far left corner of the room – the same place I always sat if I had a choice – and Big Joe pulled up a chair and sat down next to me. He drew a handkerchief from his back pocket and slowly unfolded it in front of me.

"You see this kerchief?" he asked.

"Uh huh."

"I'm going to blindfold you with it."

"What!?" I had visions of him wanting to cover my eyes before he reached over, popped my head like a grape.

"I'm going to blindfold you so you can't look at the keyboard or anything else. Then I'm going to read the lesson aloud and you'll type along to what I'm reading."

I'd been doing 20 words a minute as a hunt-and-pecker … I didn't think I could do 5 if he blindfolded me. "I don't know, Big Joe," I said.

"I do," he replied, and wrapped the hankie around my eyes. For the next three mornings, until I learned exactly where each letter was simply by touch, Big Joe read to me while I fumbled around in the dark, trying to keep up. He never did it for anyone else in the class, even though, before I was blindfolded, it seemed to me that everybody in there was cheating. Did he recognize my hidden talent as a typist? (Does such a thing even exist?) Or did he simply feel sorry for me because he'd been a tall, awkward, skinny kid himself?

I'll never know and I suppose it doesn't matter. What's important is the impression he made on me, the way being taught to type by a huge, rugged bastard like that mediated my own misgivings about "being good at a girl's job."

And I would have missed so much if I hadn't learned to type … it has (along with walking) been the great meditation of my life. By the end of that summer, when I was hammering out eighty words a minute with no errors, I pretty much had the formula down, i.e., the faster I typed, the more my right brain kicked in and the more far away and serene I felt.

Drugs would help in that regard later, of course – marijuana *is* a performance-enhancing drug when it comes to speed typing – but back in that summer of '61 there was another incident that cinched my typist future. This was my English teacher pulling my maiden typewritten paper from the messy pile of book reports on his desk. From where I sat I could almost *feel* his relief as he leafed through those crisp, neat, typewritten sheets, then set them down with a sigh and scrawled a grade on top.

When I saw it was a big, fat "A" I knew I was in there: unless it was an in-class assignment I never submitted a handwritten paper again. It's why I either carried a portable typer with me during the wino years or bought a used one as soon as I could afford it. I worked in typing pools through college and when word processing became popular in the late 70s I out adrenalined those rush-job attorneys.

Not that it matters anymore: scanners replaced me and voice commands will, eventually, replace them. The other day I got an actual typed letter from the ten-year-old daughter of a friend of mine, thanking me for a gift I'd given her. This is what she wrote:

> "It is s%o hard to wr#$% t= on a tYpwriter. IT is some&*
> kind of machi+#$ne from the old da&$ys & you can*('t
> Erase! Tha*n&nk G^od for Compute%rs!"

Amen, kid.

I would have had a legitimate "out" from the army if near-death experiences counted for anything. In the fall of 1957, when I was a skinny but otherwise healthy ten-year-old, I mysteriously contracted spinal meningitis. As infectious as the disease is none of my brothers or friends caught it from me and there were, in fact, few other cases in San Mateo County that year. All I remember are flu-like symptoms and a splitting headache: if it hadn't been for the quick action of my mother I would have died at home. She recognized the rash on my neck and cheeks as a meningitis indicator (again, something she'd read), so she rushed me to the emergency room at Mills Hospital, where a spinal tap confirmed the diagnosis.

I spent the next three weeks in an isolation ward, moving in and out of comas. The doctors told my parents I was unlikely to survive and, even if I did, there was no telling what that long-term inflammation of the brain would mean. The only memory I have now is the furnace behind my face. And so many shots in the ass that my butt wasn't black and blue ... it was just black. And those moments when I was vaguely conscious and there'd be a crowd of family in sanitary masks at my bedside, treating me with the sort of overt tenderness that's usually sublimated in WASP families. (I remember basking in it and believe it's the reason why I'm comfortable in hospital settings even today, a *major* advantage in the years to come.)

And gradually, against all odds, I got better and better and was finally fully conscious for two days straight. When I could eat solid foods and my temperature was normal my parents brought me home.

I was stable for a week. Then my temperature began rising even as the crippling headaches returned, accompanied this go round by vicious stomach cramps. A week after I'd left the first hospital I was back in a second one. This time the diagnosis was *encephalitis, a worse* inflammation of the brain than the *meningitis!* The doctors warned my parents that not only was there no record of anyone having contracted those rare viruses one after the other, but in my already weakened condition the chances of my surviving (much less coming back with my mental faculties intact) were in the slim to none range.

They were right, but not in the way they imagined or I understand even today. I went through another two weeks of comas, my brain boiling like an egg and my stick body shivering with spasms, as if the little boy with the seamless life had suddenly been shoved in a toaster oven.

And then, as suddenly as it had come, the second fever passed, the virus ran its course and I woke. I'm sure there were cognitive tests, and one curious physician after another shining penlights in my eyes and having me follow this finger or that one, but what I kept wondering was, *What's with Slug World? Why is everyone around me a beat slow?*

Because the fevers had burned a racetrack in my brain, stamped my psyche with a permanent starter's gun. As I went back home and gradually recovered my strength I found I couldn't read, write, draw or think fast enough, and patience of any kind was an alien concept. I've talked to dozens of physicians and shrinks about this over the years, but with no similar cases to study their guess is as good as mine. All I'm sure of is I went in a reasonably normal kid and popped out a buzzed adrenaline junkie.

I was nineteen before I discovered the antidote.
It came in bottles and cans.

So there I am. It's July of 1966 and I'm a perfectly healthy nineteen-year-old whose free of college, free of the draft, free of any obligation but earning a meager living. Just the notion of it was so intoxicating that I was giddy on the bus back to Longview. I figured I'd work another couple months at the mill, save enough to buy a decent used car, then return to the Bay Area in style.

It was a good plan but I was too young to factor in my outsized sense of entitlement. By the time I'd reached the box plant the next morning I'd convinced myself that even twenty-four hours was too long to wait. I went over to the mill office and quit, got a last check for three hundred dollars, then walked the four miles back to town. Instead of my apartment I went to the bank first, then Derek Hayden's place. He was a friend who worked the swing shift at the plant and the last time I'd seen him he told me he had a cheap old car for sale. I knocked on his door, asked him about the vehicle when he stepped out.

"Well hell, Wilson," he said, motioning towards the sidewalk, "that's it right over there."

It was a once white, now severely rusted '57 Plymouth. I walked over, took a better look at it with Derek trailing behind. The tires were bald, the muffler hung by a wire, the vinyl seats had springs sticking through and the windshield was spider webbed and cracked. Worse yet, I could see a stick shift on the floor.

"Damn, Derek," I said, whistling under my breath. "Does this thing even run?"

"Sort of," he said. "The brake vial leaks so you have to add fluid all the time. And you don't wanna drive 'er too fast. The alignment's shot and it shakes like hell at speeds above fifty."

"You think it'd make it to California?"

He laughed. "You can't be serious, High ... it scared me just driving it to the mill and back. Speaking of which ... why aren't you at work?"

"I quit. I flunked my draft physical and I'm heading for the Bay Area today. How much do you want for this baby?"

"Well, I'm asking sixty dollars."

"I'll give you fifty ... *if* you teach me how to shift gears. I've never used a clutch before."

He looked at me like I was joking. "You can't operate a stick shift and you want to drive this junker to California!? I can't be involved in something like that ... you'll be killed before you reach Portland!"

"Oh bullshit," I said, counting out fifty dollars and shoving it into his hand. "I've got a *way* with cars."

Way away. In truth I was a mechanically distressed doofus who considered machinery in any form my personal enemy. My ease in ignoring that terror underscored the strength of the sudden, single-minded *urgency* in my mind, the way an idea could take over my beingness and block everything else out. Plus I didn't realize it then (because I barely know it now), but I was the same about cars as I was about jobs, i.e., I'd take the first one that came along and ride 'er 'til she was done.

Which might not be far in that Plymouth, particularly when you factored in my troubles coordinating the clutch and gear shift motions. After we'd lurched around Derek's neighborhood for a half hour I pulled to the curb and killed the engine.

"So let me be sure I've got this right," I said. "Once I get it up to 40 miles an hour and into fourth gear, I don't have to get out of fourth gear as long as I stay above that speed? I mean I could, in theory, drive all the way to the Bay Area without changing gears again?"

"Well yeah," said Derek, "if it weren't for toll booths, buying gas, taking a piss, stopping to eat and having to slow down for other cars."

"Uh huh. Well, that's enough instruction then, I think I'm ready. You can go ahead and sign the pink slip over to me."

"You can't drive this Plymouth to California, High!" he scoffed. "You haven't made it around the *block yet!*"

"This whole shifting thing, Derek. ... I've a feeling I'll get better at it when I *have* to."

I didn't, really. I stalled three times on the way to my apartment, and after collecting my meager belongings I barely made it to the freeway. I lost the throw out bearing before I reached Eugene, Boregon – replacing it left me a grand total of 200 bucks to start my new life with – and I remember the 700-mile drive south like it was yesterday. That Plymouth was exactly what it looked like: a death machine. The brakes failed whenever I went two hundred miles without adding fluid, the engine had a leaky radiator and overheated twice, I blew a front tire in the hundred-degree heat outside Redding, California and the rust pitted cab was so full of holes that it whistled at high speeds.

Those being any in excess of the 50 mph ceiling Derek warned me about. I figured 60 was an absolute minimum on California highways, so it was hard to anticipate the car's other problems when the alignment had me whipping back and forth like a stone in a blender.

But I made it. Twenty hours after I began I wheezed into the driveway of Tom Canby, my old friend from high school. He lived at his grandparents' home in Hillsborough with a pool, bathhouse and tennis courts, and I took such grim satisfaction in seeing the Plymouth in that setting that I gave it a good boot when I stepped out, causing the muffler to tumble onto the driveway. I looked around, made sure no one was watching and kicked it behind some bushes.

I straightened out my T-shirt, ran my fingers through my hair and walked the familiar path to Tom's bedroom at the back of the house. The window was open and I could hear him in there talking to someone, so I let myself in the back door, tiptoed down the hallway to his room and stepped inside.

"Hey!" I exclaimed, throwing my arms over my head so my hands smacked the ceiling, "it's me, Canby … I'm back!"

Tom was flopped on his bed and sitting on the chairs across from him were Chris Taylor and Doug Lunder, another two friends from the old days. They were all drinking beer and stared uncertainly at me until Tom jumped up.

"Goddamn it, Wilson?" he said. "Is that really you?"

"Hell yeah," I said. "Who'd you think it was?"

"Jesus," gasped Taylor. "What's that fuckin' *smell!?*"

"Christ it's awful," chipped in Lunder. "Worse than a skunk!"

Tom came towards me, then backed off with a grimace. "Damn Wilson!" he said, holding his hand up to his face. "It's *you!* It smells like B.O. and some kind of … rotten egg stench."

"Oh," I said, shrugging. "I've been working in a paper mill up north. The sulphur gets in your skin and clothes and reeks when you sweat. Don't worry … you'll get used to it. Where I've been everybody smells like this."

This failed to reassure them. They made me take two showers, in fact – sending me back for a second one after a whiff test – and while I was in there they threw my clothes in the trash, leaving me a T-shirt and a pair of Tom's shorts to wear. When I finally stepped from the bathroom I found them staring out the window at the Plymouth. They'd take a long look at it, then over at me, then back at the Plymouth.

"You really drove that piece of shit seven hundred miles to get here?" said Canby.

"Yeah."

"I don't believe it," said Lunder. "Look at the fluid that's drained out already ... there's crap all over the driveway!"

"Yeah," said Taylor. "I bet you hitchhiked, then bought that thing at a wrecking yard nearby."

"Oh right," I said, sitting at the end of Canby's bed, "that makes a lot of sense. You losers are drunk and it's only noon."

"You want one?" said Tom, handing me a can of beer.

"No thanks," I demurred, remembering my days in the Portland State whorehouse. "I can't stand the taste of the stuff."

"Then just bottoms it up," said Canby. "Drink the whole can straight down and that way you only taste it once."

It was like the epiphany with Professor Fallon: as I tipped up the 12-ouncer and started gulping I thought, *Why didn't I think of that?*

At AA meetings in the years to come I would describe that beer at Canby's as the demarcation line, the moment when I made the transition from regular guy to alcoholic. In some respects that was true, in other ways nonsensical. I'd always been a moody, overly sensitive guy, for instance, who (at least since the brain inflammations as a kid) was strung a bit too tight. These afflictions not only contradicted my personal image but also the one I liked to project to other people, namely that of a give-a-shit hobo who rolled with the punches and treated life as a weird experiment.

That guy was in there, all right, but he had to deal with the asshole at the controls when I woke up in the morning. My youngest brother suffers the same affliction. Like me, Ben finds that the single most distinguishing feature about his sleep is how pissed he is when it's over. We come to in rages, basically, like a serial killer slapped into consciousness. (When we were kids and it was time to get us up my

94

mother could only tap on our doors with a knuckle (without speaking) or she'd be screamed at.)

Ben's a farmer and to combat his diurnal mood he's spent decades rising at four in the morning to play basketball at a local gym. He's sixty years old now and still banging with guys in their 20s and 30s *before* a full day of work on the farm, trying to exhaust his irritability and rage in a socially acceptable manner.

Me? Well, I've sought a slightly more relaxed strategy. At nineteen, though, the hardest part was simply being aware I *was* in a bad mood, then using my feeble mental and philosophical tools in a vain attempt to improve it. This war between who I was and who I philosophically wanted to be made me the kind of whacko Dr. Culp considered unsuitable for military service. It also inclined me to self-medication and that, in the end, proved very dangerous indeed.

Because as the booze surged through me that day at Tom's I recognized the antidote I'd been reluctant to acknowledge before. It wasn't my first experience with drunkenness: I'd drank twice in high school and on three different occasions at the Portland State apartment, blacking out each time. Later I'd read a pamphlet at the box plant that claimed you were an alkie if you'd had *three* blackouts in a lifetime, much less gone five-for-five as a teenager.

I scoffed at the likelihood of addiction then. But at Canby's, laughing and bullshitting with him and the other guys as I knocked back beer after beer, I realized that booze made me feel the way I wanted to feel *without wasting all the mental energy.* What a great shortcut I thought … why not employ it everyday?

By midnight, even as I vomited whiskey and beer and chips into the same bushes I'd kicked the muffler into, I knew it was the alkie's life for me. Boozers I've met since talk about the decades it took for them to confront their malady but, *Hell!* all I needed was that one night. I mean it was suddenly so goddamned obvious to me: there I was a bright, talented, disaffected guy who loved being high and had no ambition other than a vague notion of writing a book someday. And most writers were drunks to begin with. So instead of hiding from drunkenness, perhaps it was time to pursue it.

The biggest obstacle was the hangovers. I'd forgot that part, the way my head and mouth felt when I woke after a night of drinking. In this instance face down on the couch in Canby's bathhouse. I was sitting on a stool at the bar later, sucking down a *Schlitz* half quart I'd found in the refrigerator, when Tom walked in.

"Holy fuck!" he exclaimed. "Yesterday you're a teetotaler, now you're drinking a beer at *eight in the morning!* Are you kidding me!?"

"Canby," I said, belching, "I've decided I'm alcoholic."

"What do you mean ... 'decided?' It doesn't work like that, High ... it takes years and years of drinking to become an alcoholic."

"And with any luck I'll have those. In the meanwhile, here's the way I figure it. I want to drink and I like how I feel when I drink, but I don't want to stop once I start. So instead of worrying about it, or trying to stay sober, or pretending I'm not that way ... why not just take *advantage* of the urge instead!? Ride that booze cruise until I sober up or die!"

Canby looked at me for a moment, then walked to the other side of the bar and found himself a can of beer. Cracked it open and saluted me with a belch of his own.

"You always were an extreme bastard, Wilson," he said. "I'm glad you're back."

I reminded Tom of all that when I saw him three months ago. After years of heavy drinking he started shooting cocaine in 1978 and continued to do so for another fifteen years. By 2002 his liver was barely functioning and his spleen was gone. Fluids accumulate unabated in his body so when I visited he looked – and probably felt – like a yellow beach ball.

But he didn't complain; no one's ever heard Canby complain. He knows what he did to himself, and why – as an ex-junkie – he's buried deep on the liver transplant list.

"Remember," I asked him, "when you found me drinking a beer in the bathhouse that first morning?"

He laughed. You could tell it hurt. "Damn!" he said. "This must be where the booze cruise ends, High!"

LONESOME LOUIE HOUSTON

A week after I arrived in the Bay Area I was living in that old Plymouth. It happened without much forethought on my part, one morning I woke in the back seat with my feet out the window and the next thing I knew that was my daily routine. I had paperbacks and boxes of crackers on the front seat, empty beer cans on the floorboards in back, brake fluid and water jugs in the trunk. There were plenty of parties to occupy my evenings and when I needed a shower or a real meal I'd drop by Canby's place. I passed an indolent month that way before finally returning to work, first painting houses with a friend in San Bruno, then loading and unloading watermelons from produce trucks before I hooked on with Delta Airlines at the airport.

My hiring was something of an aberration. Delta was based out of Atlanta, Georgia and usually employed only neat, earnest, clean-cut characters to work the tarmac and ticket counters. I, on the other hand, living on fast food and booze as I did and sleeping in my car, had a head start on the grungy hippie look. I wouldn't have made it past the initial interview if I hadn't been given a test. It was one of those deductive reasoning exams popular at the time – 50 questions to answer in twelve minutes – and after I became the first applicant to finish it, much less score higher than 40, I was hired on as a ramp agent.

Which made little sense, of course, because it took about as much brains to load and unload luggage as it had those watermelons. I worked from midnight to eight in the morning (a concession, perhaps, to my disheveled appearance), and though the graveyard hours were the worst part of the job they also meant we had but three planes to service the entire shift.

So there was less supervision and a smaller crew, two of us to load luggage onto a cart and another two to shove it into the belly of the plane. Because I was tall and the bins were only four-and-a-half feet high I spent most of my time at the baggage chutes. My partner was Lonesome Louie Houston.

He'd been nicknamed "Lonesome" because he rarely smiled and seldom spoke. He was twenty-five years old, an average-sized guy from San Angelo, Texas who wore horn-rimmed glasses and worked like a demon. We labored in the labyrinth of chutes beneath the airport, pulling bags off conveyor belts and tossing them onto carts.

Or Lonesome did, anyway. In the time it would take me to bend over, grab a bag and swing it over my shoulder and onto a cart he'd have four of them in there. Then when the carts were full he'd be the one to jump in and drive them to the plane. I worked with him my first two weeks and not only did he rarely speak, he had a permanently bored expression that only lessened when he was doing the work of two people.

So as the nights went by I learned to simply stay out of his way. I'd pull up a chair at the bottom of the chute, chain smoke cigarettes while I waited out the drunk I'd come in on or the one I was getting over. I had certainly not tiptoed into alcoholism. In my haste to take advantage of it, in fact, I'd convinced myself that I should drink whenever I felt like it and simply see what happened.

Sitting there in the noisy, midnight bowels of the airport, slipping in and out of consciousness had been the main result so far. But I didn't begrudge Louie his need to work his ass off and the muteness thing was fine with me ... you couldn't hear yourself think in there, anyway.

Then one night I came in way drunker than usual and Louie found me passed out beneath a chute. When I woke I was standing upright in a black, coffin-like space with my forehead resting against metal. This was vaguely reassuring – if it was a coffin I hadn't been buried yet – but I was woozy and couldn't feel my feet. Then my eyes adjusted to the dark and I realized there were three horizontal slats in front of my nose. I dipped down, peeked through the top one and recognized the employee dressing room.

Which meant I was ... what? Standing inside one of the seven-foot tall lockers? How was that possible? It was a great place to pass out, all right – and I'd surely take advantage of it in the future – but I couldn't remember having the idea myself. Then I heard footsteps and someone tapped gently on the locker door. "Wilson?" said a soft, Southern voice. "Are you awake yet, Wilson?"

Who the hell was that? I peeked through the slats again, saw Lonesome Louie looking up at me. I tried to open the locker door but couldn't manage it from the inside. "Yeah I'm awake, Louie," I said. "Get me out of here, would ya, I gotta piss."

He opened the door and I tried to step out but my feet were asleep and I tripped, pitching forward into Lonesome's arms. He dragged me to the chairs beside the wall and lowered me into one.

Then he laughed. A grin crept across his face (it was like ice cracking), then his mouth opened and out came this odd ack-ack noise.

"Christ!" I said, slipping my shoes off and rubbing my feet. "How the hell did I get in that locker?"

"I put you in there," said Lonesome. "You were so drunk I couldn't wake you and to hide you from the other guys I dragged you over here, stood you up in the locker and shut the door."

I just looked at him. His voice was a soft Texas drawl with very little inflection. A monotone really, even when, like now, he seemed amused.

"Except," he added, "they sure as hell could have *heard* you. Do you know you snore standing up? I had to hustle by every fifteen minutes or so, bang the door hard to wake you."

I held my head: I was still bleary-eyed and tipsy. I'd discovered scotch the night before and it had not been a positive experience. "Why'd you do all that for *me,* Lonesome?" I asked.

"I don't want you to get fired," he said. "I enjoy working with you."

"You're kidding me."

"No, you're a real strange duck, High."

"That's something coming from you. And hell! I come in drunk half the time and don't do anything ... why would you enjoy working with me?"

"Because of that. I like to be so busy I've no time to think. With you around that's pretty much guaranteed."

"And you don't want to think because ..."

"I suffer from suicidal depression."

"You've had it rough, eh?"

"No, I've had it easy. I just haven't enjoyed it."

I laughed, stood up to head for the urinal but stuck out my hand first. "Well thanks, partner," I said, "I appreciate you looking out for me like this."

"Don't mention it," he said, giving my hand a brisk shake. "And while we're on the subject ... is it true what the other guys say? That you actually live in that awful car of yours?"

"Yeah."

101

"Why?"

"It's comfortable enough 'til winter comes and I've no money for an apartment at the moment. I keep drinking it up."

"You can stay at my apartment in Millbrae, High. I've an extra bedroom that no one uses."

"Really? How much a month?"

"Nothing. Like I said, the room's just sitting there and it makes no difference to me. All I ask is that you don't speak to me unless you absolutely have to."

A mute roommate and free rent? How could I keep getting better deals than the Portland State whorehouse?

"Lonesome," I said, slapping him on the back, "you got yourself a roomie."

Living with Lonesome Louie worked out better than I imagined. The guy was essentially a ghost, a death dog quietly contemplating his own demise. He'd been renting that new apartment for six months and it felt like I was the first occupant: there was still plastic covering the furniture and he'd never had the electricity turned on. ("I like it cold and dark," he told me.) He'd come home from work, walk to his bedroom, shut the door and not reemerge until it was time for work.

How had this happened? One day I'm living in my old wreck of a car and shitting in gas station restrooms, the next I've got a fancy Millbrae apartment all to myself. For *free*, no less! *I must be doing something right,* I thought. On the one hand I felt bad about Lonesome's depression, on the other ... would I even be there if he weren't nuts?

And a little mystery never hurt anyone. Once when Louie was doing a double shift at the airport I snuck into his room. I figured he'd have some snacks around, a few books, maybe even a small TV or radio.

But there was nothing. The bed was made with military precision, the bathroom was spotless, a pair of pants and an extra uniform were hanging in the closet and there was a small windup alarm clock on the bed stand. Other than that the room was completely bare.

What did he do in there all day? What did he eat? What did he drink and think about? I was deeply impressed by the ascetic depth of his despair, the way he seemed to troll the deep end while still functioning in the real world.

But I didn't tell him that: his response to the electricity query was all I needed to know. We soon fell into a regular routine, returning from work in the morning in Louie's sole personal indulgence – a cherry '48 Buick – and disappearing into our rooms. I'd sleep three or four hours before rising to a six-pack and the new portable typewriter I'd bought. I was ostensibly writing short stories as I searched for my narrative voice, but mostly I was just killing time until the booze kicked in. Some days and nights I'd drink alone, other times I'd hook up with friends on the Peninsula, and, occasionally – on my nights off – I'd even talk a girl into the sack.

It was a hard life to judge because I didn't have anything specific in mind. My vague "write a novel" goal was personally soothing and a reasonable excuse for my behavior but, as Canby liked to point out, I'd showed up one afternoon as a regular guy and the next thing you knew I was the wino beneath the porch. I tried to restrict my alcohol intake before work, for instance, and the best I could manage was reasonable success part of the time, so most nights I was pretty juiced when Louie and I left for the airport. There were rarely supervisors around on the graveyard shift and Lonesome was still doing a remarkable job of covering for me. He'd stick me back in that locker when I passed out, drive the cart so I wouldn't steer it into a jet engine, even take my uniform to his dry cleaner occasionally.

Yet we still rarely spoke ... we could go through an entire shift and not say six words. On our breaks I nodded off or read and he disappeared somewhere (to eat, I hoped). An onlooker might have thought we loathed each other but it was really just the opposite. I was fond of Lonesome and would have bullshitted with him the way I did other guys if he weren't such a gloomy bastard. Under the circumstances you could only offer him support or advice and, well ... what did I have to offer? I was drinking beer for breakfast.

Still I did have a small moment of input in mid-October, about six weeks after I'd moved in. As was happening with increasing frequency at the time I woke face down on the living room carpet. It wasn't clear if I'd pitched forward on my face the night before or simply rolled off the couch while sleeping. (Like Louie I hadn't removed the plastic covering, so the cushions were pretty slippery.)

Not that it made much difference to my postmortem assessment. I heard Louie calling my name and slowly raised up onto my elbows. I knew he only came out at night, so figured I must have slept all day, but then I saw the light streaming through the window and the old burlap bag in his hands.

"Jesus," I groaned, my tongue sticking to the roof of my mouth, "is there any beer left?"

"It's nine in the morning, High," said Louie.

"Just check the fridge for me, would ya, pal?"

I heard him pad into the kitchen and scrounge around in the refrigerator (he'd had the electricity turned on so I could keep my beers cold). When I opened my eyes he was handing me a cold 12-ouncer of *Hamm's*. I gulped it down in a series of greedy swallows, stumbled to my feet and went straight to the bathroom for a long, hot leak (careful not to glance at myself in the mirror). Then I returned to the couch and looked expectantly at Louie, who was down on his knees with the sack in front of him.

"Well, Lonesome," I sighed, lighting a cigarette from the pack on the table, "what's the occasion?"

"I have to ask your advice about something, Wilson," he said.

So he was up and around in the morning, plus asking my advice on top of it? This was definitely a new twist; I was curious in spite of myself. "Advice?" I said. "About what?"

"How to kill myself with a minimum of pain and pretension."

I lifted the empty *Hamm's* can and swung it back and forth. "Have you considered ...?"

"No booze! It's messy and it takes too long."

"There is that. What's with the bag you're holding?"

"I keep this in the trunk of the Buick," he said, and abruptly upended the contents onto the carpet. "I call it my 'Suicide Sack.'"

Out rolled razor blades, a can of *Drano*, a revolver, a rope, a plastic envelope with *cyanide* printed on it, a box of rat poison, a prescription bottle of tranquilizers, another of sleeping pills, a long *hari-kari* type knife, a syringe and three sticks of dynamite.

I quickly stubbed out my cigarette. Tried a low whistle but my mouth was dry.

"The dynamite and *Drano*," I said finally. "Those might be a little extreme, don't you think?"

"Maybe. What about you, Wilson? What would you choose? Other than alcohol, I mean."

"Hmmm. Let me take another leak while I think about it." I wobbled to the bathroom, did my business, then went to the kitchen for a second beer. Sipped from it as I walked around and around Lonesome's murderous implements.

"Come on, High," said Louie finally. "You aren't worth a shit at the airport, but this ... this is the kind of thing a guy like you should be good at."

It *was?* "Well," I said, "if the needle, rat poison, sleeping pills or tranqs didn't work you'd *wish* you were dead, and the knife, razor blades, dynamite and gun are as messy as the cyanide and *Drano* are nasty ... so how about if you rent a garage, run a hose from your exhaust pipe into the cab of the Buick and off yourself that way?"

Lonesome looked shocked. "See?" he said, "that's why I did this: I completely overlooked carbon monoxide poisoning. Thanks, High." He shoved the implements back in the sack, walked to his room and shut the door behind him.

It was one of the reasons I quit Delta shortly thereafter and went to work for the Bank of America. I didn't *think* Lonesome would be driving home one morning and steer us into oncoming traffic, or that he'd actually off himself with me in the next room (though I did jump every time a car backfired outside), but there was no sense pushing my luck.

Plus that graveyard shift at the airport was ruining my social life. I answered a newspaper ad for an operations trainee and was hired on at the B of A's South San Francisco branch. The pay was half as good as what I was earning at the airlines but I wouldn't be living like a vampire anymore. When I broke the news to Louie he seemed pretty sanguine about it.

"It doesn't matter," he said. "The countdown's begun, anyway."

We both knew he wasn't talking about Cape Canaveral.

So one November morning I took the train to South City with the other commuters. I had my gut sucked in and was careful not to cross my legs because I was wearing the high school graduation suit my mother had sent me. It *might* have fit before I discovered beer, but for now the coat and pants were unbuttonable and the sleeves were creeping up my forearms. I'd tried to make up for it with a shave and haircut but staying sober the night before would have been better.

The first thing they did at the bank was try to teach me teller procedure. This meant standing beside a teller at her window and watching how she handled the various transactions during the day. I could handle it for an hour or two in the morning, then the hangover would take over and I'd start to doze.

Which is where the trouble began. The bank was hooked up via silent alarm with the South City Police Department and when that alarm went off the cops were supposed to be at the bank within thirty seconds. The button for the alarm was just to the left of the teller window, right where I liked to wedge my ass when I nodded off.

Three times in the first week I pressed the alarm without knowing it. The lobby would be half full, just another dreary day of money changing, when *Bang!* the front doors would fly open and in would run a group of officers with their guns drawn. The first time it happened I didn't know I was the culprit; the second time I prayed I wasn't; by the third I knew I was dead meat. I watched the police sergeant have a long conversation with Jud LeFay, the operations officer. Then he came over, grabbed my arm and took me aside. He was a puffy-faced Irish character with "O'Donoghue" on his name tag.

"Jud wants to talk to you, asshole," he said to me. "And High?"

"I'm sorry about this, Sarge, I really am."

"Shuddup, High. I just want you to know that if I ever spot you on the street? Away from this bank?"

"Yeah?"

"I'm gonna beat the livin' shit out of you."

"Oh great."

My desk was directly across from Jud LeFay's and I walked over and sat down. He was an amiable chain smoker with a long, hound dog face whose sole claim to fame was lighting one match a day.

He fired up a new *Pall Mall* from the butt of the old one, looked me over.

"You're a real fuckup, High," he said finally. "I've had a ton of trainees through here and well, you stand alone, son, you're the absolute worst."

"Hey!" I said. "I've only been here a week."

"You make my point."

"So you're firing me?"

"Eventually I'll have to," he said. "More likely you'll quit. Either way you'll never be an Operations Officer."

"So then you won't mind if I just … hang around for awhile, collecting checks?"

He looked me over and seemed to be trying to decide something. "I know you're only nineteen," he said finally, "and I don't mean to pry … but you're a drunk, aren't you? A young drunk, I grant you, but a drunk nonetheless. Not only can I smell it on you, but you've got this strange, give-a-shit attitude."

"I do like the occasional cocktail."

He thought some more, then stood up, grabbed a thermos from his desk and motioned for me to follow him. "Come on," he said, "it's lunch time."

I walked with him to the back of the bank, lugging my meager peanut butter sandwich. When we reached the vault he pointed to a stack of boxes in the corner.

"See those?" he said.

They were cases of *Royal Gate Vodka*. Maybe twenty of them. "Yeah," I said.

"Watch this." He walked over, pulled a bottle from the case on top. Set it down, unscrewed his thermos and held it up. "This thermos is a third full of orange juice." He grabbed the quart of vodka, unscrewed the cap, poured a good long slug into the thermos, then screwed the cap back on and replaced it.

"Later I'll fill up the bottle with water," he said. "We use this stuff for office parties and the girls out there ... they never know the difference."

I was confused. "I ... eh ... don't understand," I said. "Why are you showing *me* this?"

Jud laughed and puffed on his *Pall Mall* beneath the *No Smoking* sign.

"Shit, son," he said, "I'm telling you to get yourself a thermos!"

Nineteen. All things considered, it was a very good year.

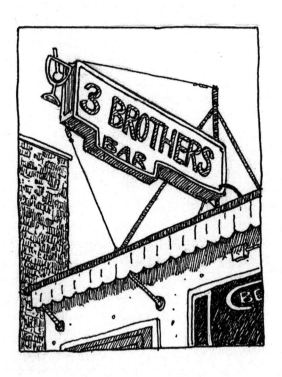

I still think about Jud LeFay. I never saw him after I left the bank, but if it hadn't been for that smoking habit of his I might have tried. As it was I figured he was a goner in five years, maybe ten tops. Even when he was eating he smoked, keeping that *Pall Mall* simmering in an ashtray so he could hit on it between bites. His lunch was tuna fish and screwdrivers; mine peanut butter and jelly and the same. We went through a lot of *Royal Gate Vodka* in the little room where we ate. Jud had been in the business a long time and, as he liked to say, "If I was worth a shit I wouldn't be an operations officer at fifty."

So he gave me manuals to read and simple entry jobs to keep me busy after the noontime cocktails. Then one morning he dropped a manila envelope on my desk. "I talked to Feldman last night," he said.

This was the bank president, a weaselly little character who often gave me disapproving looks. It may have been my suit. Or maybe my *Goodwill* dress shirts with frayed collars. "Yeah?" I said. "What's this?"

"A bank procedures test that the main office sent to all the branches. Feldman told me to have you take it, see if you've learned anything in your five weeks here."

"Take it when?"

"*Now,* Wilson. I hope you read those manuals I gave you."

Oddly enough I had. Plus the only thing I really missed about college were the exams. Especially easy multiple choice problems like the ones on that bank test. There were 50 questions and I finished in fifteen minutes and handed the sheets back to Jud.

"No no," he said, trying to push them back at me, "you're still on probation and you have to *concentrate* on this. The tellers are taking this too and if they score better than you do I might have to can you!"

"It's a silly, silly test, Jud," I said. "If somebody scores better than I do, you *should* can me."

He grudgingly accepted the answer sheets and I returned to filing checks. The next morning was a Friday and when I came in Feldman and Jud were both standing by my desk. The president stuck out his hand as I walked up.

"Wilson," he said, "I wanted to be the first to congratulate you. You scored a perfect 50 out of 50 on that procedures test."

I clasped his hand as Jud, standing behind him, feigned wonderment. "Well thank you, Mr. Feldman," I said, "but it was nothing really."

"Is that right?" he said. "Then how come no teller scored better than 45? Some of them have been with us for years."

I looked beyond Jud and saw the tellers were back there, too, shooting me daggers with their eyes.

"Well, I won't keep you from your work, Wilson," said Feldman. "I just wanted you to know you have a real *future* with this bank."

"Thank you, sir." He returned to his side of the building as I sank down behind my desk and lit a congratulatory smoke, giving a couple of the tellers the A-OK sign with my thumb and forefinger. They, in turn, flipped me the bird.

"Well," said Jud, coming over and sitting on the corner of my desk, "I guess you're pretty goddamned proud of yourself, High."

"You know, Jud," I said, "it's hard to believe, but I think alcohol is making me *smarter!*"

"Is that right? Then you should be perfect for this errand I'm giving you," he said, and handed me a yellow card.

"What's this?"

"A signature card for the Three Brothers Bar down the street. You'll see on Line Three there that Eddie, one of the brothers, forgot to sign it. He works in the morning so I want you to walk over there and get his signature."

"You're sending me to a bar?" I said. "At nine in the morning? Are you sure about this?"

"Oh yeah," he said, "I'm positive. And Wilson?"

"Uh huh."

"Be back in fifteen minutes, okay?"

"Absolutely."

I glanced at my watch. The bank didn't open for another hour so I figured I could stretch that fifteen minutes into thirty easy. I headed west on Grant Street and found the Three Brothers Bar two blocks down. It was a cheesy dump with bamboo décor and plastic palm trees. Sitting on a bar stool was a stocky, middle-aged Italian guy with a drink in one hand and a cigar in the other. Beside him was a younger Mexican woman with a drink of her own.

I walked over and pulled the signature card out of my pocket. "Are you Eddie DeCarlo?" I asked.

"Wow, pal!" he said. "Nice suit!"

"And check out the tie," laughed the whore. I could see that's what she was now, and that she might be even older than Eddie.

Not that it mattered to me. She had eyes like a cat.

"Hey don't fuck with me," I said. "I'm just LeFay's lackey."

"Easy, kid," said the Italian. "I'm Eddie, all right. Jud told me you'd be coming around."

"He didn't tell you to buy me a drink, did he?"

"Listen to him," said the whore. "You lookin' for an early start on your Friday, kid?"

"I was hoping to catch up with you."

"Shit," said Eddie, jumping up and walking around the bar, "we been at it all night ... we're *finishing* here. Now what's your pleasure?"

I thought about it. I knew I should stick with vodka but no one at the bank got close enough to smell my breath except Jud, and he wouldn't know the difference.

"Whiskey," I said, and sat down next to the whore.

"Hi," I said, "I'm Wilson."

"I'm Mitzi. Do you really work in a bank?"

"Oh yeah."

I'm sure she would have given me the blow job she promised if she hadn't passed out. As for the rest of the day ... I remember some kind of drinking contest with one of Eddie's brothers, and dancing with Mitzi to – of all things – "Little Red Riding Hood" by Sam the Sham and The Pharaohs ... but these were details of little consequence as I crawled back to the bank at 7:00 p.m. And I mean literally *crawled*, having fallen so many times that I gave up worrying about my suit pants ripping further. I had my key in my hand and was trying to stab it into the lock when Jud LeFay appeared on the other side of the glass. He stepped out, locked the door behind him, glanced down at me and sighed.

113

"Sorry, Jud," I slurred, shimmying my way up so I could lean against the door. "I shoulda called."

"Called?" he said. "What about coming back to work!?"

"That, too. I mean, well … I guess I'm fired, eh?"

"Fired?" He laughed, took a drag on his *Pall Mall*. "You just made me a hundred bucks, High!"

"What?"

"Oh, Feldman was so excited this morning about your test score and all your *untapped potential* that I bet him a hundred bucks I could send you to a bar at nine in the morning and you wouldn't be back before noon."

"Noon?"

"But *you*, High!? You were gone *ten hours!*"

"…"

"You're a worse drunk than I thought, kid, you should get some help."

"*You set me up you rotten fucker! I want half that money!*"

"No way," said Jud, "keeping your job is payment enough." Then he laughed and walked away, leaving me propped against the door. I sat there simmering for a few minutes, not sure if everything had worked out right or not. Finally I tried to struggle to my feet but the whirlies overtook me and I went to my knees and puked.

Just as a police car drew up in front of the bank. I was bent over, wiping my mouth, when I noticed a pair of shiny black boots.

"Take a good look at those, High," said a voice I recognized as Sergeant O'Donoghue's, "'cuz they're headed up your ass."

O'Donoghue and his partner dragged me behind the bank and gave me a pretty good pounding. Fortunately I was too drunk to defend myself and passed out before they were done. When I woke I found myself in a drunk tank for the first time. It was a full house in there and I was sitting on a bench between a skinny wino and a guy who'd pissed himself. I sat up abruptly, let the two of them collide while I hobbled to the piss hole. I hurt bad. It felt like the cops had left my face alone, but my chest, gut and legs were so bruised it was difficult to straighten up.

When the piss finally came it was pink with blood. I used my one phone call to get hold of Canby. He arrived within the hour, paying my bail and helping me to his car. It was all I could do to fold myself into the passenger seat without crying out.

"So the South City cops beat you up?" he said, pulling away from the curb. "What was that about?"

"I ... kind of deserved it," I groaned.

"Hell, High, you *always* deserve it!"

He drove me to the Millbrae apartment and was likely back home before I made it the one hundred steps from the curb to the door. I remember thinking how lucky I was to have Lonesome for a roommate, how I'd be able to rest in the front room all day without anyone bothering me. I stumbled inside, dragged a six-pack from the refrigerator and made it to the couch. Stretched out slowly and propped the beers on my chest. I had blood and booze and vomit on my shirt, and my suit was hanging in tatters, but there'd be no showering or changing clothes until I had a bit of liquid courage in me. I cracked open a can and gulped it down.

The next thing I remember is waking to the sound of Lonesome's door opening. I was too stiff to move so I waited until he padded into view. It was quite a sight ... he looked like Frankie Avalon in horn rims. He had on a shiny silk shirt, chino pants and, of all things, scuffed white bucks. The last time I'd seen shoes like that was in the Fifties.

"Damn, Lonesome," I croaked, "where'd you get those clothes?"

"A secondhand store," he said. "What do you think?"

"Well, Buddy Holly's dead and Pat Boone's in exile, man. You're like ... out of another time or something."

"Oh yeah? This from a guy who looks like he was run over by a truck? What the hell happened to you, High?"

I raised myself to my elbows and let the sixer slide to my lap. "I don't have time to fuck around this morning, Louie," I grunted, "so I need to know three things quick. One: why are you out of your room? Two: why are you out of uniform? And three: why are you speaking to me?"

He pulled up a chair, sat down and rubbed his hands together. "Wilson," he said, "I've felt *good* the last couple of days, almost *interested* even."

Then he grinned that odd, ice-cracking grin of his, virtually the first time I'd seen it since that morning at the lockers.

"I was even sorry you didn't come home last night," he continued. "I wanted to go out *drinking*."

Oh God, Louie, I thought, *please don't pick this of all days to be my buddy, pleeeaaassse.*

"I thought when I woke this morning the feeling would be gone but it isn't, Wilson! I feel buoyant, like we should go to San Francisco and do the town!"

"Oh Jesus," I groaned, "you gotta be kidding me!"

"C'mon, High! If you felt good once every five years what would you do?"

"But, Lonesome ... the day you picked to feel good is the day I'm home from the drunk tank after being pummeled by cops!"

I tore open the front of that filthy shirt, showed him the black and blue marks on my stomach and hips. "Look at me!" I groaned. "I can't go out partying ... I can barely move."

Louie thought about it for a minute, then jumped up and went outside to the Buick. When he came back he tossed me a pill bottle.

"Here," he said. "That's the codeine some quack prescribed for my shoulder. Take two of those, grab a shower and you'll feel fine, Wilson."

Well, I thought, *pain killers are a start, anyway.* I shook out a handful, gulped them down with another beer. Tried to imagine a day in the city with Lonesome Louie Houston.

"Louie," I said finally, already thinking about a real *dark* bar, "what do you want to do in San Francisco?"

He pulled a newspaper clipping from the pocket of that silk shirt and handed it to me. I unfolded it and saw it was an ad for the Paris Follies Burlesque. Touched-up photos of aging strippers in G-strings. *Beautiful Faces!* read the caption. *Great Bodies! No Clothes!*

I folded it back up. "You want to go to a stripper show?" I said.

"Yeah," said Lonesome, "I'm twenty-five years old and my sister's the only naked woman I've ever seen." He said it like a Texan: *nekkid.*

"Well," I said, "how about we get you a whore instead? I think Canby knows a couple."

"I just wanna *look,* Wilson, not touch! Now are you gonna take that shower and change clothes? Time's-a-wastin' here, I could plunge back in the depths any time!"

I remember the shower better than I do the rest of the morning. It didn't occur to me to decline Louie's proposal; not only had he put a roof over my head and saved my ass time and again at Delta, but I had this fatal fondness for the strange. A chatty Lonesome, in fruity clothes and a good mood, wanting to hit a strip show and drink? What could be more unlikely than that? When the codeine kicked in I thought the day might have a chance after all.

Then I passed out on the ride to San Francisco and was shaken awake by Louie just long enough to follow him into the seedy Paris Burlesque theater, where we plopped down with a discreet seat between us. Over the next hour I floated in and out of consciousness but distinctly remember a stripper named Tempest Storm. She must have been forty but she had this wondrous bush and body and a very sensuous act.

Fortunately I was too sore and groggy to even contemplate jerking off. There was nothing inhibiting the lowlifes around me, though, at least to judge by the way they fumbled beneath their overcoats (you could rent them for a buck in the lobby). I was afraid to see what Lonesome was doing but was pretty sure I heard him gasp a time or two.

Then I passed out again, only to be wakened by a deeply chastened Louie. "Jesus!" he said. "I dry humped myself and it makes me sick. Let's go drink!"

Somewhere between the burlesque house and a small bar off Franklin I began to feel what O'Donoghue and his pal had done to me; it looked like more codeine or drinking if I was gonna be there for my buddy Louie.

I tried both but Louie's enthusiasm had passed with his orgasm. He was knocking back straight shots of tequila and the more he drank the more remote he became. It didn't help that it was five days before Christmas and Bing Crosby was crooning carols from the jukebox. If Louie had family he wasn't admitting it, and even drunk he wouldn't talk about his depression (blaming it on the wrong batch of chemicals in his brain). I made a few vague attempts at cheering him up – suggesting, for instance, that he could at least feel cheated by Fate, that would be a start, wouldn't it? – but from the way he looked at me you could tell the pilot light was flickering.

The next thing I knew I was coming to again. It was three in the afternoon and I was lying on the front seat of the Buick. I sat up slowly, waited for my eyes to focus while I looked around for Lonesome. Was he still in the bar? Had we really ever *been* in a bar? And why was the car parked in an alleyway?

Then I saw the note wedged in the steering wheel:

Wilson:

I signed the Buick registration over to you and it's in
the glove box. Thanks for being the only friend I ever had.

~ Louis Houston

119

Why'd he do that? I wondered. I didn't want his car. Then it hit me. I shimmied over to the door, stepped out and limped around the Buick, thinking Louie would be lying beside it with a bullet in his brain or cyanide foam on his lips.

But no Lonesome. Next I tried the trunk and sure enough the Suicide Sack was right where it always was so I started up the alleyway on foot, wondering how Lonesome might off himself in the city. The possibilities seemed endless. I paused to take a long, hot piss and happened to look up at the tall buildings everywhere. *Oh shit,* I thought, *the fool's going to jump!* The worst possible death, all that time to think and the grisly splat afterwards.

When I reached the street I was so busy scanning rooftops that I almost missed Lonesome. He was at a bus stop on the street corner across from me, the toes of his white bucks hugging the curb as he swayed back and forth.

I was overcome with relief. *He's not going to kill himself,* I thought, *he's had a change of heart and he's taking the bus home.* "Hey Louie!" I yelled, waiting for the light to change so I could cross the street. "Hey Louie wait for me!"

He glanced over just as the Greyhound rumbled up the avenue, cupping his hands around his mouth and yelling something I couldn't make out.

Then he shrugged, waved, and flopped backwards onto the street at the same time the bus arrived.

"OH FUCK NO LOUIE!!!!!!" I screamed.

When the Greyhound ran over him I'd swear you could hear his pelvis pop fifty yards away. The light changed and I forgot my own aches as I limped over there, shoved hysterical bystanders out of the way and bent down beside Lonesome. You could see the tire tracks had flattened his stomach and hips and dark blood was gushing from the corners of his mouth.

"Oh damn Louie, damn …" I moaned. He turned his head, seemed to recognize me and motioned with a jerk of his chin for me to draw closer.

"What is it, Louie?" I said. "What can I do?"

"Wilson ..." he gurgled, spitting up blood, "Wilson ... I even fucked this up. Lots of pain ... takes way too long!"

"No, no Louie," I said, "you did fine, just fine!"

Then someone grabbed me by the shoulders and dragged me out of there.

It was the grisly end of a Death Dog. I followed the ambulance to a city hospital but after a three-hour operation the surgeons assured me it was only a matter of when – not if – Louie would die. I was interviewed by a couple of suspicious cops, then spent the intervening time thinking about every minute I'd spent with Lonesome. Other than work they didn't amount to much, our closest bond being a joint desire for solitude. Still I'd miss him: it felt like I'd lost a benefactor, a dear friend and a total stranger, all at the same time. When I was sure he wasn't going to make it I jumped into the old Buick and headed for the nearest bar.

Or that's my guess, anyway. In one of the rare double blackouts of my drinking career the next thing I remember is waking on a pay toilet. I had no idea where it was but it certainly sounded and smelled like a public rest room. I looked down to see my pants around my ankles and six empty beer cans scattered over the tiles. Not only that, my feet were asleep and the codeine had definitely worn off ... when I tried to pull myself up by the hook fastened to the door I gasped in pain. Had to sit back down and massage the stiff bruises on my legs.

It took a full ten minutes to get my feet and legs functioning, then another couple to pull my pants up and light a cigarette. When I opened the door and stepped out I could see the toilet was across from a wall of urinals. I reached out and stopped a fat guy with a briefcase.

"Eh ... excuse me," I said, "but where am I?"

"Pardon me?" he said.

"Where am I? I woke up here … but I don't know where I am."

He looked me up and down, then spotted the empty beer cans in the stall. "Damn," he laughed, "you party in pay toilets?"

I just stared at him. My tongue was swollen and the jackhammers were starting behind my eyes.

"Okay, okay," he said, "you're at the airport."

What a relief: I must have driven to Delta to tell the people there about Lonesome. "Thanks, pal," I rasped, "at least I'm still in the Bay Area."

The fat guy had turned away but now he stopped and looked back at me. "You're kidding, right?" he said. "This is L.A."

"*What!?*"

"This is Los Angeles. The L.A. International Airport."

"*Los Angeles!*" I said. "*What the fuck am I doing in L.A.!?*"

"You're asking *me?*"

The shock was visceral. I stumbled over to a wash basin, splashed cold water on my face and tried to think of one good reason for being in L.A., or even remember something … *anything* … about what I did after leaving the hospital in San Francisco.

But there was nothing. And what about that empty six-pack? If I flew to L.A., is that what I brought on the plane with me? And where the hell was Louie's Buick? I searched through my pockets and not only were there no plane tickets or receipts, but the keys to the Buick were gone and I had twenty dollars to my name.

It was all too much feeling the way I did. I crab walked out of the men's room, made my way down the terminal corridor until I found an open bar. As luck would have it the fat guy from the bathroom was there, telling the bartender about me. The two of them sniggered as I hobbled up to the counter.

"Hey!" said the bartender. "If I serve you something you gotta drink it here. No takin' it back to the john with ya!"

They had a good laugh over that as I lit my last cigarette, thought, *Welcome to L.A., asshole.*

There are dozens of ways to run an indoor marijuana operation, most of them high-tech and hydroponic. But as an organic, old school, potting soil character I've used the same system for a quarter century now. First I manicure the mature females right in their pots, then cut them down and hang them before dragging out the containers and emptying them into contractor bags for disposal. Next I pull up the room's plastic sheeting so the floor can dry, waiting twenty-four hours before laying down a new sheet and bringing in the 50 plants from the vegetative room. I cull out the 40 best ones, transplant them from two-gallon to five-gallon containers and spread them around the room. Ten days later I snip cuttings from the bottom of each plant, switch the lights from eighteen to twelve hours per day and begin a new cycle.

In the meanwhile the manicured plants have dried (it takes about five days), and I've cut, weighed, bagged and sold them to my twenty-odd customers.

It's a great gig and will be hard to give up until I have to: I once estimated that, in terms of actual labor, I devote about twelve hours a month to the plants.

Finding a lover and/or girlfriend can be difficult at any age … as a sixty-four-year-old dope grower in Portland it's damn near impossible.

Not that being 6'6", skinny and bald helps. I had this absurd notion when I turned forty that, as I aged, my old rogue status would become increasingly attractive to women, that they'd weary of the safe, boring lives they'd lived to that point and want a little of the strange stuff.

Just the opposite is true, of course … like most of us I'm less appealing every day. I was so desperate last fall that I went on the *High Times* website to check out their "Personals" section. I figured any woman who'd post herself there must be *looking* for a guy like me.

So I'm glancing through the photos and descriptions – there are some attractive, interesting women listed in my age group and locale – and at first I'm so sure they *have* to be stoners that I don't look at the "Preferences" section. When I finally do what do I see in response to the "Marijuana Okay?" question but statements like "NEVER!" "NO WAY!" and "ABSOLUTELY NOT!"

What am I missing here? Why would someone list herself in a *High Times* personals ad and not want to get loaded? Or is that simply the code, i.e., if they're there that shows they want to get high regardless of what they say? (And if so, you'd think a simple "NO" would have sufficed.)

But I can't complain: I'm more interested in sex than companionship and hormones will take care of the former soon enough. Plus being monkish by nature is a real boon in Boregon. I have dozens of friends nearby and probably know another hundred people across the state, but I'm the sole single person among them.

They feel bad for me, I feel worse for them.

Mr. Bubbles was a car wash on Colorado Boulevard, about halfway between Glendale and Pasadena. I hired on there three hours and two Bloody Marys after I woke on that airport toilet. My plan was simple. Other than my typewriter I hadn't left anything of value in the Bay Area (unless you counted the phantom Buick and the old Plymouth, which hadn't run in weeks) and when they cleaned out the Millbrae apartment they'd hardly find enough between Louie and me to fill a garbage can. Even Jud LeFay was understanding: when I phoned him at the bank later that week he laughed, told me to keep moving ... with a little luck I'd outrun myself.

And he was right in a way, because what difference did it make where I lived? It was three days before Christmas and I knew my old high school buddy Jim Cable (the same guy who bet me I couldn't win the senior class presidency) was a freshman at Occidental College and would be back after the holidays. It would be good to see him and he might have an apartment or know of a place I could crash. In the meanwhile I had to find some kind of wretched, piecemeal job that would either pay me cash or let me make draws until I was back on my feet.

So I took a bus to the Eagle Rock area of L.A. (where the college was) and started hoofing it up Colorado Boulevard in search of a job. I hadn't gone two blocks when I came to *Mr. Bubbles*, and underneath the sudsy clown on the marquee was a WORKERS WANTED sign.

It was twelve hours a day, seven days a week, $1.25 an hour with no breaks, not even for lunch. They didn't tell you this when you hired on, of course, simply suggesting you'd have a chance to eat or catch a smoke during the "down times." Which as far as I could tell never happened. This was L.A., where even in winter it was so sunny that the cars were in line from sunset to sundown. (We were lucky to get Christmas Day off.) What's more, as the only non-Mexican and the guy with the least seniority among the workers, I was assigned the worst job – scrubbing hubcaps – while tiny illegal aliens half my size struggled to reach the car roofs.

The worst part might have been the blue *Mr. Bubbles* uniform. Like the firehouse outfit it was a couple sizes too small so the first time I bent over to wash one of those hubcaps the ass ripped out. If the boss noticed or cared he never let on and sometimes, dazed and wet

129

from the spray and sweat I'd struggle to my feet, hear muffled laughter behind me and look through the viewing window to see kids my age laughing and pointing. Not a year before I'd looked like one of them; now I hadn't showered or shaved in days, was sleeping in a local park and had thrown away my underwear to live in that silly uniform with the rip up the ass. While I worked like a dog at a job that broke every conceivable labor law.

And it had all been so *easy,* such a seamless transition for me. When each day finally ended I didn't shop for clothes or look into a room at the YMCA, but went straight to the cashier and drew out every dime I'd made. Then I'd walk to a local liquor store and blow it on a six-pack of half quarts, a half pint of whiskey, a couple packs of cigarettes and a soggy, pre-made sandwich. Work my way through them behind some tall bushes at the "Kiddie Park" I called home. I'd made myself a pine needle bed at the base of a tree and the park was usually deserted after sundown. I had a notebook I kept beneath some rocks, ostensibly for writing, but after the whiskey and a few of the half quarts I could rarely make out my scribbles the next day. Mostly I just drank and dreamt the dreams that drunks do, trying to enjoy the haze as much as possible because it was obvious, even then, that I didn't have the kind of alkie stamina I'd hoped for. Every hangover seemed worse than the one that preceded it and the more I drank the more fitful my sleep became.

Or maybe it was just the pine needles. I know I was always at *Mr. Bubbles* at seven in the morning for my shift and finally, just after New Year's, I was able to reach my old buddy Jim at his dorm room. I told him, in a generalized way, that I was working in town and between apartments, and did he think he could put me up for a day or two?

"No problem," he said. He was living in an eight-man studio on campus but I was welcome to stay as long as I liked. He gave me directions and after another long day at *Mr. Bubbles* I showed up at his door with my whiskey and six-pack. Jim hadn't seen me since the draft physical and, even though it had only been six months before, it seemed like another lifetime.

I knocked and it was one of his roommates who answered the door, a grim, taciturn kid in a cashmere sweater. I started to speak but he took one look at me and held up his hand.

"You've got the wrong apartment, wino!" he said, and slammed the door.

I knocked again, heard some commotion inside, and this time it was Jim who answered.

"Cable!" I said, reaching out my hand. "How the hell are ya?"

It was similar to my arrival at Canby's the summer before. Jim's eyes bugged out and he jerked backwards with a start.

"Whooaaa, Wilson," he said, "is that really you? I would have passed you on the street, man, you look and smell *awful!*"

"Yeah, well," I said, "I haven't showered in a couple weeks, but I thought I was getting enough soap on me at the car wash that it didn't matter."

"And what have you gained? Thirty? Forty pounds?"

I looked down to where my gut bulged out of the unzipped uniform. "Yeah," I laughed. "All muscle." When I pulled out one of the beers and offered it to him he noticed I was carrying liquor and quickly dragged me inside.

"Listen," he said, "you can't have alcohol on campus! It's forbidden here!"

I thought he was kidding. Then we were in the living room of the dorm with the seven roommates sitting around on couches. It might have been me, but I could sense a certain hostility in the air. Here were these preppy characters in their cushy college studio and all of a sudden a giant bum shows up looking for a crash pad. Jim introduced me around as his old class president buddy from high school, and other than a certain reluctance to shake my hand – I reassured them, as I had Cable, that it was bathed in soap all day – they seemed like a

131

reasonable bunch of guys.

Then Jim asked me what I'd been doing and how I ended up in L.A.

"I don't know how I got to L.A.," I said. "My Bay Area roommate committed suicide by jumping under a bus last Saturday, and I drank myself into a blackout afterwards and woke up on a toilet at the L.A. airport with twenty bucks to my name and no idea how I got there. I remembered you went to school in the area and would be back after Christmas vacation, so I took a job at the *Mr. Bubbles Car Wash* on Colorado Boulevard."

They all just looked at me and I took advantage of the silence to crack open one of the half quarts. I drank half of it down, then looked around.

"What?" I said.

"Well, eh, where have you been living between the time you landed at the airport and now?" asked Dale, the kid who'd slammed the door on me. He looked like pre-law.

"You know the Kiddie Park over on Taylor?" I replied. "I pass out under a tree there."

"Jesus! With kids around?"

"No, no. They've all gone home by the time I arrive."

"Well," said Darren, another of the roommates, "where'd you spend Christmas then?"

"In a bar."

Silence again. I could tell they were torn. Cable was their pal and classmate, but I was obviously a nineteen-year-old menace to society. Would they be safe at night if I were out in their living room, flopped on those very same couches?

Then Jim started laughing and slowly, tentatively, the rest of the roommates joined in. "I told 'em you were a real kidder, Wilson," he said.

"You did?"

"Yeah," he said. "We know you're actually a *hippie*."

It was January of 1967 and most of what I knew about hippies I'd read in a *Newsweek* magazine article. Jim knew even less but right there on the spot he made up the hippie thing to cover for the fact that his best friend from high school, his old straight A's buddy, had shown up at his door looking and acting like an alcoholic scumbag.

Hippie, I thought. Beard, long hair, ratty clothes, free love, fucked up ... sounds about right.

Well, except for the "free love" part, anyway: even jerking off was difficult when you lived in a kiddie park. I flashed the V sign to those tidy Occidental boys and grinned:

"Hey, brothers," I said. "Peace."

Cable's father died not long ago and I went to the memorial service here in Portland. One of the other mourners was Bob Russert, now a local attorney and once one of those Occidental College roommates. He didn't recognize me, of course, and when Jim told him who I was he did the "ghost" thing:

"Holy shit!" he said, "I can't *believe* you're still alive!"

"Don't worry," I said. "I get that all the time."

"You should. Whenever I hear those stories about some college kid who bottoms upped a bottle of booze and died on the spot? That's when I think of you, High."

"Jesus."

"Do you remember living in the corner of the couch in our living room? And the way you were always dressed in that horrible … what was it?"

134

"Car wash uniform."

"Yeah. And every night you'd sit there and drink 'til you passed out, listening to Barry McGuire's 'Eve of Destruction' over and over and over!"

I cringed ... I'd forgotten the Barry McGuire part.

"Damn!" said Russert, shaking his head. "Wilson High, the alcoholic hippie, actually fuckin' *lived!*"

Like the rest of the roommates he'd wanted me dead the last time he'd seen me. They'd put up with my company for a couple weeks, then one night I came home to find the studio empty. I had a hot shower and was sitting in the front room in my underwear afterwards, working on the boilermakers, when an old guy in a flannel shirt opened the front door and sauntered in. Now he had to be the janitor, right? Who else would have a key to a student dwelling? I dragged out a couple bags of empty bottles and cans I'd been keeping in Jim's closet, asked him to throw them out with the other garbage.

The next night I straggled home at the usual time to discover this had actually been the Dean of Men. It seems he'd been doing his annual "drop-in" dorm check, and the sight of me drunk in the front room, when you weren't supposed to have overnight guests or alcohol on campus, had been enough to place all eight roommates on probation. If I wasn't gone in twenty-four hours they faced summary expulsion.

It was close to midnight when Jim dropped me off on the highway. There was no need to give notice at *Mr. Bubbles* – I'd drawn every cent I'd made at the end of each day there – and for baggage I had the uniform on my back and a pint of whiskey.

"Where you headed, Wilson?" he asked.

"Somewhere north," I said. "Those paper mills around Longview are pretty easy duty, and they pay well."

"Think you'll get a ride out here at night?"

"No."

Cable laughed. "I gotta hand it to you, High," he said. "The way you live would scare the shit out of me."

"That's exactly what I was gonna say to you, Jim." I shook his hand and thanked him for putting up with me. If I could change one thing about those early alkie years it'd be the number of times I sponged shelter from friends. I never forgot them for it, but what greater imposition could there be than a sloppy drunk in your living room? Talk about *Eve of Destruction* ...

In the meanwhile the psychedelic times were exploding all around me and I was eager to jump aboard. I ended up in Kelso, Washington after a series of rides and hired on at a pulp mill, driving a cleanup truck in the chip area. After three months of laying low in a cheap room and even controlling the boozing enough to do my first *real* writing, I bought a red-and-white '56 Ford – the front doors wouldn't close, the back doors wouldn't open and, like the Plymouth, it shook *violently* at speeds in excess of 50 mph – and returned to the Bay Area.

Canby and two other guys had a townhouse on Casa de Campos in Foster City and Tom had written and asked me to be the fourth roommate. It was May of 1967, on the cusp of The Summer of Love, and I was twenty years old with nothing on my personal agenda but accumulating as many good times as possible. I hired on as a data control clerk at Dalmo Victor in Belmont – a defense plant that did missile configurations for the Army – and by night I partied. We lived in that apartment for three months before being evicted and none of us can remember when there wasn't a party going on. Much of the time, in fact, we had no idea who the other partygoers even were. They'd be from around the complex or friends of friends and most of them would bring booze and, more importantly, exotic drugs.

I took LSD for the first time my second weekend back. My old high school friend Carl Sampson had some Owsley acid and claimed he'd be my spiritual guide while I "dumped the lump."

So I swallowed the *Czechoslavakian Purple* tab and we drove to a park near Coyote Point. After an hour sitting under a Eucalyptus tree Carl asked me if I'd come on yet.

"I think so," I said. "That bumblebee's as big as a battleship."

He went over to the car, brought back a pint of cheap bourbon. "Here," he said, tossing it to me. "If things get too weird, drink that."

"Wait," I said. "Where are you going?"

"I'm gonna pick up Dick Hale, maybe do some drinking."

"That's your idea of a *spiritual guide!?* Dropping me at a park, handing me a bottle of booze, then stealing my car!?"

Sampson laughed and sauntered off. "You'll be fine, Wilson," he said. "You were MADE for acid."

Four hours later he and Dick returned to pick me up.

"Well?" asked Carl. I crawled over the front seat, laid down on the empty beer cans in back. Took a sip of the bourbon and a long hit of the joint Hale passed me.

"You got any more of that acid?" I rasped.

"Yeah."

"Hit me with some ... I wanna do it again."

The idea of classifying alcoholism or other addictions as "diseases" wasn't a widely-held notion when I first started drinking, and I find I resist the idea even now.

But I shouldn't ... I had a craving for highs long before I discovered alcohol. I assembled hundreds of car and airplane models as a kid, for instance. Do I remember a single one of them? No. Have I ever even liked cars or airplanes? No. But the odor of the glue? It still rings my bell.

I took numerous oil painting classes between the ages of nine and twelve from several different art teachers. My mother still has one of my efforts hanging in her apartment and when I see it I'm reminded not of the classes or the artistic process, but the intoxicating bouquet of turpentine.

Taste buds are part of the equation, too. Until I was eight years old, and I'd ruined the enamel on my teeth and the acid balance in my stomach, I would sit under lemon trees and wolf down the lemons peels and all. (Sometimes I'd toss the fruit and simply gnaw on the bitter skin.) When I couldn't get lemons or sour oranges I'd suck one of those plastic lemon or lime squeezers, eat unsweetened *Kool-Aid* straight from the package or – best of all – do the Ultimate Sour Combo: three *Bayer* aspirins (chewed) followed by a package of Raspberry *Kool-Aid* and a lemon.

It makes my mouth water just thinking about it. Which isn't to say I neglected the sugar department. This was a staple I hadn't acknowledged until I drove past a couple Bay Area theaters last year. I'd spent plenty of time in them as a kid and as I cruised past The Palm I thought: *Milk Duds*. Then I saw the San Mateo Theatre a little later and thought: *Abba-Zabba*. Pretty soon I was going through a checklist of childhood haunts and realized that my main memory of all of them was the candy bar I liked to eat there, i.e., *3 Musketeers* at the Roller Rink, *Big Hunk* at the Smoke Shop, *Nestlé's Crunch* at the Broadway Theater, *Charleston Chew* at The Manor, etc.

Just so I could grow up to smoke the likes of *Mango, Blackberry Widow, Juicy Fruit, Big Frosty* and *Bubblegum*.

LSD, mescaline, psilocybin, peyote (or combinations of the same) ... these would be my constitutional staples for years to come. It was the shift in consciousness that appealed to me and the younger I was the bigger the shift I needed. It took me decades to run out the string and it was only five years ago that I finally said "no" to mushrooms (when you're young the ride's too quick, when you're old much too long).

But mostly psychedelics made my cigarettes taste better. If I had a long night of boozing ahead and I was dragging from no sleep the night before I'd simply pop a couple mescaline. It was perfect ... weirdness was my beat, anyway. And the higher I got the more inclined I was towards crowds of strangers. This meant grinding a groove from Foster City to San Francisco as I ferried friends back and forth to Winterland and Fillmore concerts. It seemed like an exciting time for everybody but Canby.

He'd always had a hole in his soul. Even when we first met, in seventh grade, he was a sensitive, very pensive guy. Maybe it's the Russian in him, certainly it was his mother's influence. She liked mixing Librium and booze and tried to kill herself fourteen times before succeeding. I was there for a couple of the attempts; and what Tom had to confront as a boy was not pretty.

But he wasn't a talker as a kid, he was a brooder, a guy with a worm beneath the ground. I liked that in a person. He was also loyal and generous and big-hearted and I'd rarely heard him say a bad word about anybody.

Plus he got more pussy than the rest of us combined. He had a square-headed Ricky Nelson look and the same kind of Laconic Stranger routine. When a party started you could pick out the most attractive girl there and know she'd likely be in Canby's bedroom a couple hours later.

So when I'd been at the townhouse for a month and Tom seemed to get more and more depressed each day it was hard to understand. He was drinking a lot, of course, but he'd been doing that since we were teenagers, and unlike me he studiously avoided drugs. ("I'm already nuts," he told me.) I tried to talk to him about his melancholia but not with any particular earnestness. Like the Louie scene it was hard to pose as an upbeat confidante when you drank as much as I did. Mostly he'd just look at me, purse his lips and shrug.

Which was usually the signal for some comely lady I'd been eyeing all night to wander over and introduce herself to him. I was sympathetic, in other words, but not *that* sympathetic.

What I got mostly, in fact, were those same girls coming to me later and wondering what was *wrong* with Tom, why had he stopped calling after a date or two? Or friends asking me to explain his increasingly bizarre behavior, like driving his car into walls twice in three weeks. They assumed (or maybe just hoped) that I knew something they didn't and that, because of the Lonesome Louie saga, I was an expert on suicidal tendencies.

Actually it was growing up with Canby and his mother that had prepared me for Louie. I can sit here at sixty-three, looking back on all the potential and successful suicides I've been privy to, and I'm still ambivalent about them. I doubt I'd do it myself for the simple reason that I've never found nothingness attractive – and if there *is* an afterlife there'll be no bonus points for quitting – but I can empathize with being so depressed or hungover that I'd want to.

I was, in any case, less likely to dissuade a Death Dog at twenty than I am now. Plus there were no anti-depressants in the Sixties, no Prozacs or Wellbutrins or Celexas for the likes of Louie and Tom, so I suppose I wasn't *that* surprised when I woke at three one morning to someone raising my right arm. I was lying on my back on the carpet – I owned no furniture or bedding, of course, not even a blanket – and there seemed to be an increasingly heavy pressure on my sternum. I dragged my eyes open, saw that Canby was bent over me with the butt of a .22 rifle pressed against my chest. He'd wedged the barrel against his own and was dragging my hand towards the trigger.

I sat up with a start and shoved him and the gun away. "Holy shit, Canby," I said, "what the fuck are you doing!?"

"I want you to shoot me, Wilson," he said. "I can't seem to do it myself."

"Why not?"

"I can't reach the trigger and aim, too."

I couldn't remember what I'd taken the night before but I was a *long* way away when Tom woke me. "Damn, Canby," I said, "remember your Hemingway!"

"Hemingway?"

"He used his toe, man, you gotta use the toe when you shoot yourself. *That's* what you hook around the trigger!"

He thought about it, grinned and slapped me on the shoulder. "Thanks, Wilson," he said, "I knew I could count on you!"

"Anytime, pal," I said, and was probably out before my head hit the floor. It's the reason I didn't hear the shot from Canby's room, didn't, in fact, wake until the ambulance was in front of the townhouse and Tom was shaking me awake.

"Wilson," he gasped, "I fucked up, Wilson!"

I raised up on one elbow, saw Canby holding a spot near his left shoulder. There was blood seeping between his fingers.

"I used my toe but the rifle jerked, man. I shot myself in the shoulder!"

"*You shot yourself!?*"

"What'd you think I was gonna do!?"

I hadn't, actually. Just then the door to my room burst open and in came a load of cops and ambulance attendants. After they had Tom patched up and were taking him off in the stretcher I laid back down on the carpet, noticed Jake Milltown, another roommate, in the doorway.

"What?" I said.

"Canby says you helped him shoot himself!"

"Advice ... I gave him advice. I knew he wasn't serious."

"Is that right? So why'd he pull the trigger and nearly kill himself?"

"It's the same as when he ran his car into those walls, Milltown. We're talking about a cry for help here."

He looked down at me as I lay there, fully clothed, my jean jacket rumpled under my head for a pillow and the carpet around me clotted with empty bottles and cans, and shook his head.

"Jesus," he said. "He needs help and he comes to *you?*"

"My point exactly. What kind of serious person would do that?"

I was only half-kidding. His mother had gone through a dozen attempts by then and this looked like more of the same, the death turd tumbling from one generation to the next. Tom did a week in some Club Head in Menlo Park, then was back at the townhouse with a fistful of pill bottles. He seemed lower than before and – as if to prove the point – took up with a stripper named Chili. She was the one who called me a couple weeks later at midnight. There was a huge party at the townhouse and it was hard to believe there was anyone with the wherewithal to answer the phone when it rang, much less find me.

I finally wove my way to the receiver, buoyed by some excellent mescaline, and hunched down so I could hear over the music. "Yeah?" I yelled. "Who's this?"

"This is Chili, Wilson! You remember me?"

How many "Chilis" did I know? "Yeah, yeah ... so?"

"I'm at Tom's grandparents' house!" she sobbed. "He's in the garage, cutting himself with a razor blade!"

"What? A razor blade? Why?"

"Because he wants to die! Every time I get near him he cuts himself again!"

"Oh Jesus ..."

"He says he'll only talk to you. You have to come over here *now* ... he's bleeding a lot!"

I looked across the room at the girl I'd just met, thought about driving all the way to Hillsborough in my condition. "Eh listen, Chili," I said, "maybe you could just have him come to the phone."

"FUCK YOU THIS IS SERIOUS GET YOUR ASS OVER HERE YOU ASSHOLE!"

"All right, all right, I'm coming."

I grabbed a six-pack from the refrigerator, went out and fired up the old Ford and headed north on 101. I didn't think to grab another friend or call somebody for help because what was the point? Canby had been seeing shrinks for years and here I was, drunk and stoned, driving to another of his suicide attempts to convince him to stay around long enough to be drunk and stoned with me.

Or, in his case, graduate to mainlining cocaine for fifteen years. But I didn't know that as I pulled into the driveway of his grandparents' home. I'd no sooner turned off the lights and stepped out of the Ford when the garage door swung open and out raced Chili in an open robe and negligee.

"Oh Wilson you're finally here!" she yelled. "Come quick he's inside!"

I grabbed the six-pack and followed her towards the garage.

"Where's his mother?" I asked. "Is she around?"

"She was earlier but I can't find her now!" said Chili.

"Good. She's probably passed out somewhere." We stepped inside the two-car garage and sure enough, there was Tom at the other end, T-shirt in tatters, blood from his neck to his bellybutton. He held a razor blade in his right hand.

"Oh Tom," I said, "not mutilation ..." I took a step towards him and he slashed across his chest with the blade, opening a long red wound.

"Stay right where you are, High!" he said. "Come closer and I'll slash my wrists!"

I froze, set the six-pack down and lit a cigarette while Chili sobbed and carried on next to me. "Canby," I said, "what the fuck are you doing!?"

"I'm going to kill myself, man ... I can't take it anymore!"

"Can't take what?"

"Life! I feel like an insect!"

"So why'd you get me out here?"

"Are you kidding ... I knew you'd bring booze! Roll me one of those beers!"

"*Roll* it?"

"Yeah, man ... like you were bowling!"

I reached down, pulled one of the cans out of the six-pack, bent over and rolled it across the concrete floor to Canby. He scooped it up while keeping one eye on me, then cracked open the flip top and did a bottoms up, foam and beer running down his chin and neck to mix with the dried blood. He tossed the can aside, managed to belch and wince at the same time.

"Okay," he said, "roll me another one!"

I did, then opened a can for myself.

"How about you, Chili?" I asked. "You thirsty?"

"Are you crazy!?" she screeched. "Tom's gonna kill himself and what? You two are gonna have a couple sociable beers first!?"

"He's not going to kill himself," I said

"Oh yeah?" yelled Tom, finishing off the second beer. "Says who!?"

"Says me. I mean if you're going to slash your wrists what's with all this other crap?"

"I'm working my way up to it, asshole!"

"You mean ... practice?"

"You practice drinking but I can't practice suicide? Roll me another can, man."

This time I took a few steps back, pretended I was at a bowling alley sighting the arrow in the lane and ran up, threw my right leg out and followed through.

The can flew across the garage a half inch above the floor, bounced once and exploded with foam as it reached Tom.

"Fuckin' strike!" I yelled, pumping my fist in the air as Canby struggled to gulp down whatever gushing beer was left. When he was through he sank to his hands and knees, soaked in beer and blood, and looked at me with disgust.

"I give up, High," he sighed. "Take me to the Hillsborough Police Station and they can ship me to the ward again."

"Good choice, old friend." We walked over to him and with Chili under one arm and me the other the three of us straggled out of the garage and into the night. We'd gone about ten steps when someone grabbed my ankle and tripped me, sending the three of us tumbling onto the driveway.

"What the fuck ...?" I sat up and there, lying in the bushes like a beached whale, was Tom's mother. She was wearing a vomit-puckered muumuu and swinging a pint of peach brandy.

"Where ya' goin'?" she slurred. "Where you takin' my boy?"

"Back to the sanitarium, Darlene," I said, helping her up as Tom and Chili straggled to their feet.

"Well bring me, too!" she said, so five minutes later there we were, walking arm-in-arm into the Hillsborough police station: me in the middle, Chili in her negligee and robe, Tom with his T-shirt in tatters and an upper body crosshatched with razor cuts and blood, his mother in her puke muumuu, still clutching the pint of brandy.

The cop at the desk glanced up, barely raised his eyebrows as he turned to the officers in back.

"Check it out, guys," he yelled. "It's a Canby doubleheader!"

Canby was caged for an extra couple weeks this time, and when he finally returned to the apartment we didn't discuss what he'd done or where he'd been. Thirty-seven years have passed, in fact, and we *still* haven't spoken about the rifle and razor blade incidents. For a long time I chalked them up to that psychedelic Summer of Love, a period when many kids did wild and dangerous things. Then Tom began shooting coke and all bets were off.

I was involved in my own self-destruction, I suppose, but it still didn't feel like it. If I had to point to the best four months of my life, in fact, it would be that May through August period of 1967, much of which took place in that lunatic townhouse. I'd just discovered psychedelics and they hadn't been adulterated yet, I could still drink and wake up with nothing worse than headaches and cottonmouth, I made many of the Bay Area friends I have to this day, I had an easy desk job that only required the pretense of consciousness, and everywhere I went people were partying like there was no tomorrow. What more could a twenty-year-old hedonist ask for? How could I have possibly lived in a better place and time? It was a reckless, rhapsodic ride that, all these years later, has a special place in my heart.

It's also when I first met my friend Felice. It wasn't the first time I'd seen her: that was when we were both in junior high and she was a grade behind me. As a cartoonist I was absorbed with faces even then and I'd never seen one like hers. There was something infectious, even slightly goofy about her dark features, crooked grin and feline eyes: she looked like a character from Santa's workshop.

I couldn't walk by her without grinning myself. I was thirteen and busy with girls in my own class, so I was content to leave it at that at the time, attributing my fascination to the cartoonist in me. Then I ran into Felice again in July of '67, caught one glimpse of that mischievous mug and it all came flooding back.

Except now I recognized what *chemistry* was and it seemed the two of us had plenty of it. She was home from USC for the summer and we ended up going out several times. My memories of those dates are the most detailed I have from the period. Probably because I wasn't drunk or *on* anything, which says a lot about how I felt about her. When I was in Felice's company, in fact, we got along so well I damn near forgot to drink.

I was certainly plying her with alcohol, though. We went to a movie the first time and two parties at the townhouse thereafter and they had all the decorum of frat parties. (Even worse, actually ... those were the two blowouts that got us evicted from the townhouse.) What stays with me is that in the midst of all those long-haired chattering stoners – myself included – I'd glance around for Felice and her face was the same beacon it had been when we were kids. I'd swear I could pick her out of a crowd of a thousand.

After the parties we'd make out in the old Ford, then drive to her parents' driveway, park and do it again. Why I'm not sure. I could have dragged her up to my room like I'd done with other girls that summer, or at least found a better place for frantic dry humping than her parents' driveway. Perhaps she was simply too special to me ... it'd been awhile since I had that sort of affection for anyone. (My high school girlfriend, Kathy, always aiming higher, had broken up with me when she found I'd dropped out of college.)

But then came the eviction, and I ended up living in the old Ford. A week after that I got a message that my friend Kit, a dealer in Berkeley, wanted to see me. So I drove up there on a Saturday afternoon. It was always a pleasure to visit the guy, he had the best of everything and plenty of it; he was also a member of the same Cal Berkeley fraternity as Hale and Sampson. He took me over to a closet, swung open the door to reveal a six-foot-high stack of packages.

"Kilos, Wilson," he said. "Two point two pounds of primo Mexican weed. Check the way they squeeze it into bricks."

He took down an open package, let me check out the tight tangle of bud, seed and stems. I was deeply intrigued and couldn't stop fingering it.

"Damn," I said, "how much do you sell these for?"

"Seventy-five apiece," said Kit. "And here's the thing. I just talked to Sampson on the phone. Did you know he's in New York City?"

"No."

"Hale, Mustera, LaRoy and some other guys from the fraternity are living there for the summer. Sampson just arrived and he called me, said you could get ten or twenty times the price of that kilo if you sold it in New York. He's the one who told me to get hold of you. Said you might be interested in bringing some weed back there."

"You're kidding me."

"You'd have to take it on the plane with you, man, or check it in with your luggage. It'd be risky."

"And how much is a one-way flight to New York?"

"A hundred and twenty-five bucks."

So for two hundred dollars – every cent I had in the world – I could fly across the country to peddle dope in a notoriously dangerous city.

"Think it over," said Kit.

150

"I just did," I said, and reached in my pocket for the seventy-five bucks.

That night I was on the red-eye to New York City, the kilo of pot resting in a gym bag beneath my seat. I left a message of resignation at work, the old Ford at the airport and planned to call Felice once I arrived.

But I never did. And when I finally saw her again – thirty-seven years later – the pot was still getting in the way.

What I remember most about New York City is the heat and humidity. Next is Central Park. The Bay Area crew had an apartment near the West 72nd Street entrance, and inasmuch as that meant six big bodies in a single room I often slept in the Park. This was facilitated by the warm weather, my general inebriation and the mounted police: on the nights that were cold they'd invariably find me beneath a bush and, instead of rousting me, would toss me a section of newspaper to wrap inside my jacket.

I guess they didn't realize I was a big time West Coast pot dealer. I should have known something was up when it was Sampson (the only guy I knew who was as careless with details as I was) who suggested I come to New York City. I'd never sold a drug in my life and assumed he'd have buyers lined up for me.

He did. Dozens of them, in fact, shift workers from a Borden's Dairy in Harlem (Carl had a temporary job there building pallets). All I had to do was show up in Harlem at midnight with some nickel and dime bags.

"It'll be the easiest money you ever make," said Sampson.

"Wait a minute," I replied. "Isn't Harlem full of desperately poor black people?"

"Pretty much."

"So you want me to take a subway there in the dead of night, walk through all those black neighborhoods with pot on me, and if I'm still alive when I reach the Dairy ... what? I'll sell the weed to *more* black guys? After which I'll have to walk *back* to the subway with a pocketful of money?"

"Yeah. You want me to hold your hand or something?"

Our friend Dick Hale was listening to us as he burned a giant spliff of my weed.

"Dick," I said, "what do you think?"

"I think if you do what Carl suggests you'll die like a dog."

Two nights later I was walking through Harlem at midnight. I'd tried to sell the weed on my own in Washington Square but *Damn!* I was from the other side of the country: half the Village hippies looked like narcs to me.

And the truth was that, even as I followed Carl's map through the heart of black New York, a hopelessly naïve, middle-class white kid with pot shoved in his crotch ... I was loving it. Being half-drunk and six foot six helped, of course, along with the fact I was dressed like a bum and weighed 230 pounds by then, but mostly it was just feeling young and crazy and immortal. When I got to the Dairy Carl had it all set up at shift change so I sold my five- and ten-dollar wares to a line of black guys in white *Elsie the Cow* uniforms. It was edgy but as easy as Sampson predicted and right away I established my dealer bona fides: (1) I always had good stuff, (2) I was always fair and (3) the more money I made the more I spent. When I got to know the guys at the Dairy I'd even take them across the street to The Paris Bar (where the only drink served was scotch and milk) and get us drunk on the same loot they'd given me.

The rest of the time I partied with my pals. When we left New

York City at the end of August I had a couple hundred bucks and half the kilo was gone. I took it with me through customs to the Bahamas (after a perilous ride down the Eastern Seaboard in a Volkswagen), where I hooked up with Hale and Tony DeBola, another character from the Bay Area who'd spent the summer working construction in Hoboken, New Jersey. I sold bags of weed to rich kids on the beach for a couple days, then we flew to Miami, picked up a Buick Grand Prix from a drive away lot and steered it across the country.

When we reached the Bay Area a week later I sold the rest of the weed in Burlingame, walked to the highway and stuck out my thumb. (It was a cycle I'd repeat often in the years ahead: I loved the ceaseless pace and fast action in California, but inevitably I'd wear myself out and head north to recharge the batteries.)

What I didn't know at the time was that the drunken good times were over and the drunken bad ones just beginning.

Not that it would have made much difference.

I harvested the last *Kryptonite* yesterday. I created it almost 16 years ago and it was my longest surviving and best known hybrid. The father was a *Silver Pearl* and the mother a *Four-Way* (a cross of four different indicas) that was notable for a strange, floating stone and a particularly pungent odor.

I should have called it *Cat Piss*. Instead I went with an obvious, throwaway name like *Kryptonite* because frankly, after smoking it, I thought it would only last a cycle or two. It left a noxious burn at the back of my throat, produced the feeblest of highs and smelled like a litter box.

At least until you lit up, anyway, at which point the odor more closely resembled boiled urine. I was so put off I apologized to customers when I first put it in their bags.

It wasn't the only time I've been wrong about a plant, but it was certainly the most glaring example. I've created and grown hundreds of different hybrids over the years, but every time I tried to shitcan *Kryptonite* I'd hear about it:

"Where's the orange-colored buds?"

"What happened to those weird, stinky nugs?"

"I like that red stuff you can smell across the room."

They even claimed it got them stoned. I couldn't understand it and still can't. "How about *Super Garlic?*" I'd say to them. "That was twice the plant *Kryptonite* is and nobody wonders where it went! Or *Blue Moon* or *Inside Out* ... they had more resin on a bud than *Kryptonite* has on the whole plant!"

"Yeah, but that strange stone ... and that funky smell."

So I compromised and kept just enough *Kryptonite* plants around to stink up the bags. Ten years passed, then fifteen, and I gradually developed a grudging admiration for the old girl. She *was* a unique creation, there was no arguing that, and after all those years she still produced like the original.

But she never got me loaded. So when I came back from a trip to California and all the *Kryptonite* cuttings had died I didn't take more of them or try to regenerate the plant because – as I indicated earlier – I'm here for the highs.

One of the reasons I headed north was to visit my parents in Portland. I suppose it was like many ill-fated homecomings of the time, except in addition to my long hair, beard and ratty clothes I'd also gained fifty pounds since they'd last seen me.

They weren't impressed. My father's health had begun its long, slow decline and with my younger brothers off at college they'd moved into a small apartment on the west side of town. The sudden appearance of their most gifted son, looking and living like a drunken bum, was just about the last thing they needed. After a strained dinner and early evening I spent the night on the living room couch, then woke early and took a bus downtown. I felt terrible about the discomfort I'd caused them but always had this conviction (pure and utter fiction as it turned out) that someday I'd make them proud of me.

In the short term I made my way to the State Employment Office.

I was looking for piece work or agricultural labor, something that would allow me to make a few bucks while getting out of town as fast as possible, but instead I got lucky and stumbled onto a Bureau of Public Roads job. There were four of us hired for a surveying crew and twenty-four hours later I was living in a boarding house in Molalla, Boregon. We did a difficult monthlong stint there – I lost ten pounds of fat right away, traversing up and down hills when I wasn't hacking out forest trails with a machete – then headed north to the Canadian border to survey a road in the Mt. Baker National Forest. For the next two months, until the slow, steady snowfall finally shut us down, I hiked ten miles a day six days a week with a 30-pound bundle of lathe on my back. Through tangled woods, up and down steep, icy slopes, across frozen rivers on felled trees. It was all staggeringly beautiful and physically torturous, so by the time we were laid off in mid-December I was in both the best and worst shape of my life.

Because the drinking had definitely begun its downward spiral. There wasn't *more* of it – that would have been difficult in any case – it was simply a doubling of effects. Not only didn't I handle alcohol as well, but I was having trouble getting it out of my system. So I'd wake drunk and have to sober up on the job, soaked in vodka sweat as I gagged and stumbled on the trails.

And that was the good news. The survey crew lived in a group of cabins twenty miles from the site. My roommate was a Cornell grad named Chuck, an engineering major who was a pretty decent guy. He was also something of a boozer and one night, after we'd spent the early evening in a ratty bar in Concrete, Washington, we were sitting up late drinking gin and watching a *That Girl* rerun on television. I remember it distinctly because I felt like I was *burning up*, as if there were a hot electric blanket beneath my skin. On top of that something was pounding in my ears and I was sure it wasn't Marlo Thomas.

I ignored it and pushed ahead with the drinking, figuring that whatever the problem was, gin would handle it eventually. Then the program ended and Chuck flipped on the light across the room.

He started to get up from his easy chair, took one look at me and fell backwards in shock. "Holy shit, High!" he exclaimed. "What's wrong with you!?"

I could barely hear him over the drumbeat of my heart. "Huh?" I said, my tongue swollen and numb. "Wath that?"

"Your face and neck are fuckin' beet red, man!" Chuck walked over to where I sat on the couch, bent over for a closer inspection. "And look! Your hands are red, too!"

I held my hands up and he was right ... they looked like they'd been dipped in dye.

"Wath the duck!" I staggered to my feet, hurried to the mirror in the front room. Tore off my shirt and stared at myself. My upper body was flushed deep red from my head to the middle of my chest and my lower body from my hands to my elbows. I stepped closer to the mirror and, even as I watched, I could see little red pinpricks appear on my upper arms. They'd slowly spread into quarter-sized blotches, then merge with each other until only my stomach remained white. I couldn't believe it ... I looked like a lighthouse beacon!

Chuck came up behind me, mouth wide in shock.

"Is ith ... on my bath, too?" I asked.

"What?" he said "I can't understand you."

"My bath!" I sputtered, pointing over my shoulder. "My bath!"

"Oh, your back. It's as red as the rest of you, man. And hey!" he said, reaching up and touching my shoulder. "You're fuckin' *hot*, too!"

"Thansth, geniuth!"

"This is really freakin' me out, High. What's going on here? Has this happened to you before?"

"Nevah!"

"Well, how do you feel?"

"*Lithe a motherfussin' foonice!*" I ran to the cabin door, flung it open, stumbled onto the porch. It was ten degrees above zero out there and I was so hot I barely felt it. "FUTH YOU!" I yelled to the uncaring heavens. "YOU DON'T TURN INTO W.C. FIELDS OVERNITHE!"

Sure enough the Flush was gone the next morning (with no apparent after effects, other than a worse than usual hangover), but when it happened again a couple days later I went to a doctor. He was stunned by the extent of my drug and alcohol use, much less my explanation of how I was trying to take advantage of my alcoholism and "get it over with" (never a popular philosophy with the shrinks and physicians in the years ahead). When he was done lecturing me he finally explained my problem. It seemed I was paralyzing my central nervous system with booze, that when your blood alcohol reached .28 or above you were supposed to go unconscious. If you didn't – and continued to drink – the capillaries nearest the skin would open with a flood of blood.

"It's a very bad sign, Wilson," he said, "and I've never heard of it in someone as young as you are. Keep this up and you'll have an old wino's face by the time you're thirty."

And all I could think was, *Whoa! What a relief. I don't have to quit drinking, I just gotta slow down a little.*

The best thing to do with marijuana is to eat it. I have all kinds of pot cookbooks around and have consumed it in everything from cupcakes to pastas, but after two decades of experimenting, the brownie remains my favorite delivery unit. It's ideal both in terms of dosage and convenience and the only brain twister my mind still tolerates. For years I ate one every other day or, if circumstances allowed, even several days in a row, once figuring I'd put away 3,000 of them since my fortieth birthday.

I've tapered off the last couple of years to where now, working on this memoir everyday as I do, I eat pot less often, but it's unlikely the reader would notice even if I were writing on brownies. As long as I've a little *Visine* handy, in fact, it takes a keen observer to know there's more to any of my highs than a joint. This is because my outward demeanor, language and expression remain the same no matter how weird the mental terrain, a little survival trick I learned from both psychedelics and the d.t.'s.

Still like the buds they come from, the important thing with a brownie is the *quality* of the high. There are any number of elements that go into that, beginning with what sort of marijuana you use. Is it going to be leaf or buds and, if the latter, from what part of the plant (THC percentage generally increases as you go up the stem). I use the bottom buds that are too small and fluffy to be included in the ounce bags. Experimentation has taught me that the gram range per batch should be between 12 and 14, depending on the kinds of plants the buds are taken from. This is difficult to assess when you grow as many varieties as I do so I usually make a 13-gram batch first. To do this I melt a cube of butter in a pan, sprinkle in the bud, cover and sautee at low heat for fifteen minutes, then drain the resultant oil into a bowl of *Betty Crocker Brownie Mix*. (The buds, a black griddle cake by then, get thrown out. If, however, you want to get as close to psychedelia as possible on marijuana, you can take those charred remains, squeeze them into a couple tight cubes with a garlic press, and eat them. Just don't blame me for where you wake up.)

Once the brownies are baked I cut them into fifteen separate pieces and try one. It's difficult to describe exactly what I'm looking for in the stone because it's changed over the years and – just as with smoking pot – the range of ingested marijuana highs is very wide. It's certainly not a psychedelic stone and if you try to make it one by increasing the THC you'll get nothing but a weird, rubbery ride and a real expensive shit. To me brownie highs, like their smoked counterparts, should be a subtle, energizing mood elevator as devoid of anxiety as possible. The kind of thing someone eats, for instance, to make a night with the in-laws tolerable.

Plus like their smoked counterparts they help eliminate dreaming. When I haven't ingested THC I'm inclined to have extremely vivid dreams. They aren't particularly disturbing, just very complicated and intense. So when I wake the right side of my brain feels like an empty

162

vault. I can't write, can't draw, can hardly think at all.

Where if I've used marijuana during the day I experience what I call reruns. A boring, inane dream that's repeated again and again – each snippet duller than the one that preceded it – until I wake feeling refreshed.

If the 13-gram batch is too strong or too strange for my purposes, I simply store it in the freezer (they'll keep for years if necessary) and do an 11- or 12-gram bunch (or, alternately, a 14- or 15- if the originals are too weak), extrapolating from the fact that all the batches from a given crop will have a general similarity.

Everything I don't eat I give away to assorted friends across the country. The brownies are incredibly popular, particularly with my male buddies. They often have a wife or girlfriend who won't tolerate smoke in her lungs but enjoys eating pot and, better yet, fucking on it. I get calls all the time from people thanking me for their cooked cannabis experience, or relating tales of how their treat was swiped from the freezer and mistakenly eaten by a friend, house sitter, etc.

Depending upon how many were consumed there's likely to be panic and paramedics involved. But those instances are reasonably rare. In a quarter century of baking brownies there have only been a few occasions where someone had a bad or *freaked out* time on one of my creations.

Because what the hell … it's only pot. Expecting more from it than it can give, as James Ellroy wrote, is "like trying to get to the moon on mayonnaise."

When I was snowed out on that Mt. Baker job I caught a ride to
the Seattle airport and flew back to the Bay Area. I'd been lodged

in government property and given a per diem over the three months of surveying so for the first and only time in my life I had a couple thousand in savings.

It lasted a little over two weeks. I'm not sure of anything but the "Mescal and Mescaline" theme, but everybody who knew me and quite a few who didn't had the wildest Christmas season of their lives. When it was over I was lodged at a wino hotel on Burlingame Avenue with a floor full of empty bottles and ten dollars to my name. It was a sorry example of lowlife profligacy but hardly the worst of my problems. That would be the fact I was starting to hallucinate when I wasn't on drugs. Even that might have been workable if not for *The Dread*, a vicious terror that piggybacked my hangovers and could only be vanquished by more alcohol. In the back of my mind I sensed this rapid descent to wet brain status but how could it be? How could it have happened so fast ... I was only twenty years old for chrissakes! Granted I'd drank excessively in my determination to meet my alkie demons head-on, but I knew a lot of Bay Area characters who consumed nearly as much as I did and still rose every morning pink as a peach, swallowed a couple aspirin with their coffee and went on their way.

It didn't occur to me that my virulent childhood fevers might be involved, that between them and the booze and psychedelics my brain was increasingly allergic to delirium, or that there was a reason why my mother, if she had more than one drink, woke up hungover and shaky the next day. Not only were these the subjects of middle-age reflection but what difference would pondering them have made at the time? The twenty-year-old staring out his window in the Burlingame Hotel just felt cheated.

Plus it was time to get a job again. As usual I took the first thing that came along and it was one of those rare instances where my ragged appearance worked for me. I was hired on as a "shopper," a sort of low-rent store detective. Every weekday morning I piled into a station wagon with my fellow employees and cruised the Bay Area until we reached a specified chain grocery. Then we'd walk inside, fan out in the aisles and pick up a nonperishable item or two before trying to catch a cashier stealing. I don't remember all the techniques now but one of them, for instance, was the *buy back*. You would wait until the clerk had the groceries totaled and his or her cash drawer open, then suddenly pretend you forgot a carton of cigarettes. If they rang up the additional order they were honest; if they simply totaled it in their head and made change out of the open drawer they were probably stealing.

And there were plenty of thieves out there. If five shoppers entered a store it was likely at least one of us would catch a clerk on the take. This was a pretty sad commentary, of course, but we were hardly in a position to judge ... to preserve our anonymity, our bosses only hired losers who looked unemployable.

That's why I was the "group drunk," no small feat when you were as young as I was and everyone you worked with looked like they *ought* to be alkies. There were faded divorcees, damaged hippie chicks, mental ward habituees, leering molester types, shaky grandmas and giant, 300-pound porkers. We'd limp from store to store, six of us jammed together in that station wagon (crippled fringe characters with a serious grudge), and write our "objective" opinions as to the honesty and courtesy of the clerks we'd spied on.

Plus for every clerk you caught stealing you got a one dollar bonus. I turned in just enough of them to keep my job and even those were mostly accidents. The longer I did the job the more convinced I was that it was harder to pick the honest clerks than it was the thieves. The other shoppers would grab their items and race to the lines of the tattooed or black or greaser cashiers, leaving me with the little cherry-faced high school girl who, more often than not, would steal every dime offered her.

Fortunately I had a low opinion of mankind to begin with. I no longer had a car for entertainment so I'd been sticking close to

Burlingame at night. I spent a lot of time at the *Round Table Pizza* parlor directly beneath the hotel. I liked the convenience of it and Bill the counterman was my drug dealer. I was in there one night in late February when he slid me a folded sheet of paper.

"What's this?" I asked.

"A note," he said. "A guy with a Southern accent was in here earlier and left it for you."

I opened it up and read it:

> High -
>
> I'm back.
>
> ~ Lonesome Louie

I set the note down, filled my mug from the pitcher and drained it. Poured another. It had been a long day in the station wagon and I was more irritable than usual. "You know, Bill," I said, "with a sense of humor like yours, it's no wonder you're a beer jockey."

"Oh yeah?" he said. "I guess if I'd played my cards right, I coulda been a big time *shopper* like you."

"Who put you up to this phony note? Was is that jerk Gumbo? Or what about Canby? It better not have been Canby ..."

"The guy that came in and left that said he talked to Canby. That's how he knew you hung out here."

"Yeah? So what'd he look like, this guy?"

"He was maybe five-nine, black hair, big horn-rimmed glasses. Definitely a weird fucker."

Damn, I thought. *Could it be?* I looked at the note again, tried to remember Lonesome's handwriting. It was possible ...

"He had a girl with him," continued Bill. "She was kinda cute ... didn't talk much."

"Jeez," I said, setting down the note, "you had me going for a minute there. The last thing Lonesome Louie would have is a girl around. Not to mention the fact he's *dead*. He's the guy I told you about, remember? The one who jumped under the bus in San Francisco?"

"You could hear his pelvis pop from across the street?"

"Exactly. Even if he somehow survived he'd be a cripple."

The whole thing was somebody's bad idea of a joke. I pushed the note aside, ordered another pitcher and went back to the biography of Faulkner I was reading. (I liked to read in bars, particularly books about drunks.)

A half hour later I felt a tap on my shoulder and spun around to see Lonesome Louie Houston standing there. I gasped and damn near fell off the stool. It wasn't just the ghost effect ... the sonofabitch was wearing regular clothes, grinning from ear to ear, and actually *did* have a girl on his arm.

"Louie," I whispered. "Is it really you?"

"Surprised aren't you, High?" he said. "You thought I was dead!"

I still wasn't sure he wasn't. I stood up, reached out tentatively to touch his shoulder. It felt solid enough, but how could it be?

Lonesome saw the stunned look on my face and cackled that *ack ack* laugh of his. Dragged the girl on his arm forward. "This is Claire, Wilson," he said. "She's my wife."

"Your *wife!?*" I stuck out my hand, numbly, and she took it with equal enthusiasm. She was attractive in a washed-out kind of way, but seemed as puzzled by all this as I was.

"Lonesome," I said, "this is all too much. I mean, you alive ... walking around ... married. The last time I saw you ..."

"Agghh," said Lonesome, "they shoved everything back inside, sewed me right up. It only hurts when I fart!"

"But ..."

"Those quacks told me I wouldn't live, then said my spine was damaged and I wouldn't walk again, and finally that two miracles were enough for any man ... I'd sure as hell never get a boner again!"

He reached over, squeezed Claire and grinned. "But as Claire here will testify," he said, "I can *definitely* get it up!"

His bride looked mortified as I looked around for my beer, downing it in a couple long gulps.

"It sure is good to see you, Wilson," said Lonesome. "You got any idea why I'm in Burlingame? Why Claire and I flew all the way from San Angelo, Texas, on the off chance I'd find you here?"

"Uhhhh ... the Buick?" I guessed.

"The Buick? You still driving it around?"

"No, I lost it the night of your ... incident."

To my surprise Lonesome laughed again. "You *lost* it? What did I tell you, Claire ... he's a real joker!"

Louie stepped forward, took my arm and guided Claire and I to a table. Retrieved my pitcher and mug and set them down in front of me.

"Drink up, Wilson," he said. "This is a special night for all of us."

"Yeah, sure," I said, still dazed. "But Louie ... what's with the upbeat tone? Is this another miracle or are you on something?"

"Well, it's weird, Wilson. When I came to after the operation I wasn't just depressed anymore ... I was *manic*-depressive. So now, if I stay off the Lithium they give me, I have these kind of *jazzy* episodes. Like now."

"I see," I lied.

"Anyway, High ... as to why we're here. You remember my telling you about my grandfather in Houston, the one with all the oil money?"

"You never told me about anyone in your family, Lonesome. As I recall you rarely spoke."

"Oh yeah. Well, anyway, my granddaddy croaked and left me a bundle. I'll never worry about money again."

Claire had been very strange and remote to that point – just what you'd hope for in a madman's bride – but as Louie began talking about the money she flinched. "Hey I'm happy for you, Lonesome," I said, "that's great news!"

"Oh you don't know how great it is, Wilson, because I'm here to share the wealth with you."

"What do you mean?"

"You still writing that novel?"

"No."

"See?" he said to Claire. "*Always* the jokes." He turned back to me and grinned. "Wilson, I'm going to advance you all the money you need to finish your book. *You'll never have to work again!*"

If you're lucky you have a single perfect moment in life, the one against which you measure all others. That night in the pizza parlor, sitting across from Lonesome Louie Houston, was mine. In a flash whole new vistas unfolded in front of me. No more sleazy jobs, unlimited funds for the best alcohol and drugs, nude beauties wrapped around my face.

"Louie," I said, finishing off the pitcher and signaling to Bill for another, "whatever you're proposing ... I'm in."

NED GUMBO

scha·den·freu·de (shäd'n froi'də) *n.* One who takes pleasure in the misfortune of others.

Louie's offer to support me while I wrote my "novel" cleared up any doubts I had concerning his mental health. He'd always seemed as indifferent to money as I was – not charging me rent at the Millbrae apartment, for instance, and even once giving me $100 when I asked to borrow ten – but no one in his right mind would have handed the twenty-year-old me a thousand in cash. He told me to rent a furnished apartment, buy myself some groceries, then have a telephone installed so I could call him in Texas when I needed more loot. There was also some perfunctory bit in there about how he wanted to "invest" in me, and that the funds were really "an advance against royalties" and so forth, but this, I figured, was simply said for Claire's benefit. What I was hearing was, *I can't take it with me, fucker, so use granddaddy's bucks on the biggest binge ever!*

So the day after Louie reappeared in my life I saw he and Claire off at the airport. Had a couple pops in the nearest bar to get my equilibrium back, then grabbed a cab to 1506 Burlingame Avenue. It was a gardener's cottage behind a larger house and the home of Ned Gumbo, a local *schadenfreude* with whom I'd developed an intense and complicated relationship. We clashed so strongly that it was war all the time, a mutual antagonism born of stubbornness and cross purposes (even as we both conceded a grudging respect for the other guy's audacity).

And Ned Gumbo was as audacious as his cartoon name. He lived solely on his wits, a kind of low-level hustler who was constantly moving a car or a drug or a confidence from one person to another. Like most people I thought my possession of personal scruples made me better than him but that was, again, only half the story, because how could I not admire the way he never worked?

Plus he was cagey as a weasel and as comfortable with extreme behavior as I was. I'd met him, in fact, at a Christmas party he'd given after I returned from Mt. Baker. I'd ignored my winter sinus infection and eaten a tab of "Green Machine" acid with *way* too much strychnine in it. Halfway through the party I developed a serious earache in my right ear. Despite my cries of agony my stoner pals were reluctant to take me to a hospital, suggesting I go see a movie instead.

Finally Big Mac, a medic who was home on leave from the Navy Reserves, drove to his parents' house and came back with a bottle of Novocaine. He and Gumbo bent me over the couch so I was upside down with the left side of my face resting against a cushion. I lay there, drool slopping out my mouth, a hot lance drilling through my skull, as they and some others debated how much Novocaine to give me.

172

"I think two drops should do it," said Mac.

"I don't know," said one of the girls. "He might be oversensitive on acid."

"No, no," scoffed Gumbo. I heard some fumbling and scuffling as he wrestled the bottle from Big Mac, then leaned an elbow on my back. "On acid he'll need MORE Novocaine to cut through the pain. I'm pouring the whole bottle in!"

Lost as I was with the ache in my head I barely noticed Ned filling my ear canal with the thick, cold syrup.

"There!" he exclaimed. "That'll do 'er!" I heard him out of my left ear, because I wouldn't be hearing anything out of the right one for awhile. Then I tried to stand up but he and Big Mac pinioned my arms behind me and shoved my head down. "Let that Novocaine sink in good!" laughed Gumbo. "You don't want it leaking out!"

When I was finally upright I thought he might have known what he was doing after all. Slowly the pain in the inner ear receded, then disappeared altogether. It would have been fine if it stopped there but slowly, millimeter by millimeter, the whole side of my face went numb. I stumbled over to the only mirror in the cottage and gasped in horror. The right side of my head was stiff as concrete and I watched as the lid drooped shut over the eye and froze there. I whirled around, seized Gumbo by the throat and started choking him.

"ARRAAAH GONDA KAKKARAY ...!" Jesus, I couldn't even talk, my tongue was swollen, too. At this point, as Ned slid from my grasp, our memories of the incident diverge. I remember chasing him down Burlingame Avenue with homicide in mind. He remembers me running down the avenue all right, but insists I was completely alone, waving my arms and raving like a madman.

The truth is probably somewhere in-between. All I'm sure of is that for most of the next two days the right side of my face was numb. I had to drink my beer through a straw and every spastic suck reminded me of Gumbo's treachery (even as, once again, part of me admired the simple *outrageousness* of what he'd done).

So what Ned and I have had for most of our adult lives – and we still speak on the phone every month and see each other several times a year – is a hard-won truce. Back then, as I got out of the cab and walked up to his cottage, all I was looking for was a drinking buddy.

I strolled straight through the front door to find him vacuuming the floor. He knew I hated the sound of vacuums so immediately pushed the machine as close to me as possible, slowly running it back and forth at my feet.

"Turn that goddamn thing off!" I yelled.

"What's that?" said Gumbo, smirking. "I can't hear you, High, I'm VACUUMING!"

I reached in my pocket, pulled out the $1,000 in twenties that Lonesome had left me. Waved them in front of his face.

That got his attention. He shut off the machine and stared greedily at the bills. "What's all that?" he asked. "I thought you ran out of surveying money."

"I did," I said. "This is compliments of my old buddy Lonesome Louie. I told you about him, the Millbrae roommate who jumped under the bus?"

"You said he was dead."

"Turns out Texas Death Dogs are hard to kill. He's married now and his granddaddy left him a fortune that he wants to share with *me!* An 'advance against royalties' he calls it. All I gotta do in return is work on my novel."

"What novel?"

"The one I'm going to write someday."

Gumbo stepped over, got a closer look at the money. "You suckin' this guy's dick or something?" he said. "It all sounds pretty fishy to me."

"He's not queer, Ned ... just crazy. This is a guy who jumped under a bus for chrissakes, and carried around that suicide sack and

174

never spoke. Now, of all things, he's giving a bum like me money. These are not rational acts."

"But who better than you to spend it, right?"

"Only you, Ned. What do you say we retire to the nearest bar for a week or two? The drink and drugs are on me."

"What about your job?"

"What job?"

That is honestly the last thing I remember of the next two weeks and Ned (as usual) only *pretends* to be clearer on the details than I am. I know there was a trip to Nevada involved, plus gambling and whores and a bag of mescaline capsules, and that I managed to blow that first thousand without ever moving from the hotel. I called Louie, had him wire me another grand, and when that disappeared as fast as the first advance he airmailed me a plane ticket, told me to be on the next flight to San Angelo or else. He was going to oversee my writing efforts "for my own good."

That was all right with me; it didn't much matter where I was living and, at least to hear Ned tell it, I'd alienated all my Bay Area friends, anyway. When I came out of my haze I was slouched in a seat at the airport, watching him beg a group of ticket agents to let me on the plane. Apparently I not only looked and smelled drunk but had difficulty speaking coherently. Whatever he said to convince them, they finally came to an agreement and he shook hands all around, walked back over to me and stuffed a ticket in the pocket of my jean jacket.

"I've been begging those people to let you on the plane for the last half hour, High," he spat, "so I want you to walk down that runway without a word to anybody!"

"Fug off, Ned," I slurred. "You're a weasly little bastard."

"GET ON THAT GODDAMN PLANE AND NEVER EVER COME BACK YOU FUCKIN' ASSHOLE!"

I was mortified ... the fool was barely sane. It took numerous

175

cocktails on the flights to Dallas and San Angelo before I felt like myself again, at which point I was so delirious the transfer airline had me met at the airport.

Decades later I saw Claire at a San Angelo Emu convention, and she clearly recalled my arrival in that small Texas town:

"Louis and I had been waiting at the airport and just before the plane arrived three police cars pulled onto the tarmac. I remember because Louis turned to me and said, 'Well, at least we know Wilson made the flight.' I thought he was kidding but as they brought the exit ramp over six cops ran up, disappeared inside the plane and reappeared a minute later with you in tow. You were kicking and screaming and carrying on, and they were beating you with their clubs, until finally they pushed you onto your knees, then your belly, and dragged you face first down the steps. It was scary!"

"Jesus!" I said. "And what was Louie's reaction to all that?"

"He was cheering on the cops. Yelling to 'em that you deserved every lick. That was a real wacky friendship you guys had."

"You can say that again."

Other than using organic marijuana (which is often difficult to obtain), here is the best, most heartfelt advice I can give to anyone who smokes pot:

Roll it in joints ... don't smoke it in pipes or bongs!

Not only is this substantiated by every test study I've seen (joints rolled in good ol' *Zig-Zag* papers are less harmful to your lungs than any device this side of a vaporizer), but the empirical evidence is overwhelming. If you're in Amsterdam in a crowded coffee shop, for instance, do you know how you can be certain who the Americans are? Their coughs. Big, skull-rattling, chest-heaving hacks. Since they took their first toke these characters have been caving in the backs of their heads with bong hits. So at twenty-five, thirty years of age their lungs are already the texture of hash browns.

Regular pipes – be they wooden, glass, water or whatever – are nearly as bad. Primarily because it's too much trouble to clean them and people leave the screens in too long. What's always mystified me is why anyone would want to use a pipe in the first place. They're a pain in the ass and the only good hit is the first one; after that it's just progressively harsher ashes. I grant you that huge lungfuls on pipes or bongs are more likely to get you higher than hitting on a joint, but all that means is you need better pot.

I don't say this for my sake … I've always rolled joints. And when I need empirical evidence I simply observe the other forty-year smokers I know, all of whom are pipe users and get up every morning to hack phlegm in the toilet.

I rarely even cough.

Roll it in paper.

Judging by Gumbo's performance at the airport, and the reaction of those cops to my antics on the plane, it seemed I could safely add belligerence to my list of alcoholic afflictions. I know I woke up the next morning angry, beaten and bruised in San Angelo's drunk tank. Fortunately I was still inebriated, too, so when Lonesome bailed me out and helped me to his Plymouth Barracuda I was just starting to shake and hallucinate. I eased into the passenger seat with a low groan, got my first look at the West Texas landscape.

"Here, Wilson," said Louie, handing me a fifth of tequila. "Welcome to San Angelo."

"You're a lifesaver," I gasped. I twisted off the top, took a long, noisy gulp as Lonesome pulled away from the curb. Shuddered and cradled the bottle between my knees. "You know, Louie," I said, "I get the feeling that San Angelo is no place for an alcoholic hippie."

"What the hell'd you *do* on that plane, High? The cops booked you for public drunkenness and resisting arrest, but the airline is threatening assault charges."

"I don't know, man. I've been thinking about it since I woke up and I can't remember anything after the first plane landed in Dallas. Did you see the police report?"

"My lawyer did. Something about you shoving the liquor cart up the aisle and smashing it into the bulkhead because they wouldn't serve you more cocktails. Then you got down on your hands and knees …"

"That's enough!" I blurted, holding up my hand and taking another pull on the tequila. "It's hard enough being responsible for the things I remember."

"Don't worry," said Louie. "This is a good attorney and my father's a big wheel here. We'll get you out of it with a fine or something but Wilson … this *is* Texas. You have to be more careful here."

"Thanks, Lonesome, I'll try. And while we're on the subject … what exactly *am* I doing here, anyway."

"This is a place where you can write, High. There won't be any Bay Area-type temptations around here."

There wouldn't be anything at all. We were driving down the main street of San Angelo by then and looking at it made you wonder who lived there and why. Everything was beige. The buildings, the people, even the sky had a creamy tint to it.

"Lonesome," I said, "what's this sudden interest in my writing? Have you ever actually read anything I've written?"

"Nah, I hate fiction. But when I gave you that $2,000 and you spent it so fast just screwing around … it made Claire pretty nervous. Especially when my family's encouraging her to have me committed again."

"Why?"

"Oh, the usual stuff, plus subsidizing you."

"But if you get committed ..."

"Your meal ticket disappears. So you'd better start writing, High."

It looked like I was going to be in San Angelo for awhile. I told Lonesome to drop me at the nearest wino hotel but he said he had a better idea and five minutes later we stopped in front of a dingy garage.

"What's this place?" I asked.

"A property my grandfather left me. Gail and I live in the flat upstairs."

It was hardly the digs I'd imagined for a Texas oil heir. I stepped gingerly from the Barracuda, retrieved my new portable typer (the only luggage I'd brought), and followed Louie up the rickety stairs to the studio above the garage. It was a single large room with a double bed in the center, a couch against the far right wall, a stove and refrigerator in one corner and a bathroom in the other.

Claire was sitting on the bed. She was kind of zombie pretty, as if the blood had been drained right out of her. Marriage to Louie would do that to you, I supposed.

"Hello, Claire," I said.

"Hello, Wilson," she replied. "So glad you could make it."

There wasn't a trace of sincerity in her voice and I soon discovered why as Louie plopped down on the couch. "Well, buddy," he said, patting the shabby cushions, "this'll be your bed for awhile."

"What do you mean?" I said. "How long is *awhile?*"

"Oh, just a month or so."

I sat down next to him, grinned. "Make that twenty-four hours, Lonesome," I said. "I'm not going to sleep in the same room with you and your wife for chrissakes."

"Sure, man," said Louie. "We'll take care of it tomorrow."

Three weeks later I was still sleeping on that couch. Everyday Lonesome and I were going to rent me a room of my own but when I'd wake in the morning the first thing I'd see was a case of cold *Pearl Beer*. twenty-four longneck bottles resting in a tub of ice. Louie rose early and set them there while I slept, and it was only out of deference to Claire, across the room in their bed, that I'd get up and take a leak before indulging. Or I'd carry the first *Pearl* along with me, work it down while I enjoyed a good beer shit in the tiny bathroom.

I usually had three beers down by the time Claire fixed breakfast for the two of us. Then I would retire to my typer and a desk Louie had set up so I could work on *Blue Yonder*, my Great American Novel. As I recall it was (at least in that version) the story of an old man and his two sons, all of them living in different towns, and the things they did to end up in the same mental ward together.

I rarely saw Lonesome. He'd set out the *Pearls* and slip my twenty-dollar daily allowance under the carriage of the typewriter before disappearing for the day. After a couple hours of rarely successful writing I'd do the same. Twenty bucks went a long way in 1968, particularly in the dive bars I frequented.

Six months before I'd been the only white guy in Harlem's Paris Bar and been way more comfortable than I was in those grim West Texas ratholes. The biggest problem (other than my long hair and beard) was my size: in most places, being 6'6" and 230 pounds protected me.

In Texas it just made me a trophy. I got in more fights my first two weeks there than I did the rest of my life combined. Fortunately many of my foes were drunks themselves so I more than held my own, particularly for a *goddamned hippie*. I'd make it a point not to return to the studio apartment until well past midnight, when Louie and Claire were asleep. Otherwise Lonesome would have sex with her while I lay ten feet away on the couch.

Everything he and I did, in other words, seemed calculated to get him recommitted to a nut house as quickly as possible. On those rare occasions when we actually spoke he professed to want the opposite, of course, but the manic episodes were tapering off even as the Death Dog reappeared.

As for me ... I had all kinds of conflicting emotions. On the one hand I enjoyed the strangeness of every day I spent in Texas, had zero qualms about spending grandpa's bundle and honestly felt "the writing" was a ruse Lonesome and I could perpetrate with a minimum of angst between us. (I hadn't actually discussed the matter with him, but surely he didn't believe I'd get his money back with words.) On the other hand I was vaguely troubled by my lack of ambition, how there I was at twenty years old, with a golden opportunity to realize my literary "dream" ... and it was just another prop for the booze cruise.

Mostly, however, I felt bad for involving Claire in the whole mess. So guilty, in fact, that every time I left the house I was determined to find a cheap room downtown. Twenty dollars would buy a week at a wino hotel then, but after a stop at The Pack Train Club I'd be down to three nights, and by the time I finished up at The Shenandoah or Billy Bob's I'd be stumbling back to the studio with my pockets turned out.

Who knows how long it would have gone on if Lonesome's parents hadn't shown up. He bought me a new pair of jeans and a shirt, and most of the bruises on my face had healed by then, but his family was a real deal breaker. One look at me in the flesh, and maybe a half hour of conversation (during which I made it clear to Gail, Louie's sister, that I found her *very* attractive), and the three of them were ready to commit Louie immediately.

Instead Lonesome dragged me out to his Barracuda and the two of us went for a drive. I hadn't been in his car since we left the jail that morning and it was one of the reasons we hadn't communicated much ... if you wanted a decent conversation with Louie it had to be in his vehicle (for someone with an IQ of 160 the guy had a lot of low rider in him). We tooled around town for awhile as he finally admitted he'd faked much of the "manic" stuff just to get out of the mental ward. He was, in fact, more depressed than ever. To prove it he motioned with his thumb towards the trunk.

"The sack is back," he said.

So the issue was no longer keeping Claire happy, but Louie alive: if she tried to commit him, he'd off himself for sure.

It was time for Lonesome's only friend to stand up and be counted. "Louie," I said, "let's withdraw a bunch of money and head for Mexico! We can live for years down there, give things a chance to settle down here."

For a moment his eyes glazed over and I thought he might be going for it. Then he surprised me by saying that the pages piling up next to my typewriter were vaguely inspirational to him and he wanted me to keep writing.

"Hell, Wilson," he said, "maybe one of us'll make it."

Great ... my work was more important to a Death Dog than it was to me. I told him that everything I'd written thus far was garbage, that until I was killed or cured booze would always come first, but he just wasn't hearing it.

At least until we returned to the studio and his sister besieged us: once inside the door she *flew* at us with a sheath of papers. She tossed them at my chest and laughed triumphantly.

"I've been reading your manuscript, *Wilson*," she declared, "and it's *all the same page!* You type the *same page* over and over! You're nothing but a drunken fraud!"

Lonesome seemed surprised. "Wilson," he said, "is that true?"

"Well, not *strictly* speaking," I said. "I change a sentence here and there and I switched a couple paragraphs around but hey! I'm just getting started, these things take time."

"Oh sure," sniggered Claire. "You can't pressure *genius!*"

So much for getting in Gail's pants. I looked around and Louie had already slunk out the door and disappeared. This left me to deal with Claire and that loony family and the way they carried on you'd think I was getting *$50 a day!*

I took it for as long as I could, then headed out for a last round of cocktails. It was 3:00 a.m. before I straggled back to the studio, tiptoeing up the stairs and gently coaxing open the door. I was dismayed to find the room fully lit, which meant Louie and Claire would still be up, but I'd already stepped inside so it was too late to turn around.

Then I saw Claire. She was naked and spread-eagled on the bed in front of me; as best I could discern (without openly staring at her), she'd been cinched down to the mattress with barbed wire, then covered with ice cubes.

Most of which had melted as she shook uncontrollably. I glanced around for Louie and couldn't see him. Thought, *Well, what's protocol here? Is this torture, some kind of weird sexual practice, or both?*

In the end I opted to mind my own business. Began edging around the bed toward the couch.

"GODDAMN IT HIGH WHAT THE HELL ARE YOU D-D-D-D-DOING?" chattered Claire.

"I'm ... eh ... trying to be discreet here. It's a little awkward, you know?"

"D-D-D-D-DISCREET! Y-Y-Y-YOU'VE SEEN SOMETHING LIKE THIS B-B-B-BEFORE!?"

"Noooo ..."

"THEN UN-UN-UN-TIE ME YOU FUCKING M-M-MORON! I'M BEING TORTURED HERE!"

"Oh riiiight!" I hustled over to the bed, found some wire cutters on the nightstand and gradually snipped her loose. Helped her to her feet, then into the bathroom where I started a hot shower for her. I left her there and meant to wait until she came out, make sure she was okay, but passed out on the couch instead. Was wakened a couple hours later by Claire shaking my arm.

"Get up, Wilson," she said. "I've got something I want to show you."

I groaned, tried to roll over. "No thanks," I said. "I've seen enough."

She responded with a stinging slap to my cheek; this sat me up immediately.

"Here," she said, her voice dripping with sarcasm as she handed me a six-pack of *Pearl*. "I packed you a breakfast."

I took the beers from her, still rubbing my cheek, and after a leak followed her downstairs to her Chevy Nova. We drove silently through town as I worked on the first of the *Pearls*.

"Now Claire," I said when I'd finished it, "about last night …"

"He's crazy, Wilson," she said. "I love Louis, but he's crazy … even *mean* crazy now. Not just wanting to kill himself, but hurting me like that, too."

"So the barbed wire thing … that was new?"

"Well, not exactly. But the ice cubes were."

"And Louie was counting on me coming home to find you?"

"Nobody counts on you *but* him, Wilson. And if that doesn't prove how nuts he is, what I'm about to show you will!"

"Proof isn't necessary, Claire. I was there for the bus scene, remember? I'm a believer."

"Good," she said, pulling into the park in the center of town. "Then you'll understand when I have him committed later today."

So … the gravy train *was* leaving town. *I better get bus or plane fare from Louie first,* I thought. I was wondering if Gumbo would let me stay at his place – surely he was over whatever difficulties we'd had between us – when Claire stopped the car beside the park's artificial lake. I looked up as the bright Texas sun peeked over the trees.

"Ever wonder what Louis does from 4:00 to 8:00 a.m. every morning?" asked Claire. "After he leaves you your money and beer?"

"Occasionally I do, yeah."

"Well, here's your answer. Look out on the lake."

I followed her finger and sure enough, there was a naked Lonesome Louie, floating twenty feet offshore in a white inflatable duck. He even had a flash light that he was using to read a paperback book.

It was as odd and incongruous a thing as I'd ever seen.

"How does he ... get away with that?" I asked. "Whatever it is he's doing."

"Oh, his father knows every cop in town. But look, High ... there's a new twist this time. Louie's wearing a *sombrero!*"

I glanced back out there. She was right. He'd had the hat slung over his shoulders and was pulling it atop his head as the sun rose.

I was pretty sure I knew what *that* meant!

I jumped out of the car, strolled over to the shoreline as Louie looked up.

"Hola, High!" he yelled. "Que tal?"

"'Que tal' is right, buddy," I laughed, and took another pull on the *Pearl*. It seemed the gravy train hadn't left yet after all, that it was still rounding the far turn, headed for a smash-up south of the border.

I wanted to be part of that. Louie held up the paperback and pointed to it. It was an English/Spanish dictionary.

"We leave in an hour, partner," he called.

"Si, si, amigo."

MY FIRST LABEL

I started drawing labels for my pot bags sometime in the late 90s. I'd thought about it for years, ever since I was working in a casino in Stateline, Nevada in 1973 and my roommate brought home an ounce of *Skunk No. 1* from the *Sacred Seed Company*. It was the first labeled marijuana I'd ever seen and the little cartoon seed on the front left an indelible impression on me.

But I didn't dare design labels of my own, not when anonymity was everything in those early years of cannabis cultivation. It took the gradual onset of medical marijuana and an article in *The Stranger*, one of Seattle's alternative weeklies, to convince me. It concerned a local dealer with pounds of slow-moving, mediocre weed who, in desperation, finally designed a bunch of "Pol Pot" (the lethal Cambodian dictator) labels and stuck them on his bags.

Not only did they sell out immediately but he was inundated with calls for more. So I thought fuck it and started my *Scud Bud* line. At first I'd use the same label for three or four cycles, then eventually I created a new design for every crop. There's forty of them now and I can safely say that, as an artist, they represent the most fulfilling and successful work I've ever done.

Even if it takes all the imagination I have to come up with fresh approaches. This is weed, after all, and the difficulty in representing it in novel and interesting ways is obvious when I attend pot exhibitions and see hundreds of marijuana T-shirt designs and zero new ideas.

Fortunately I've plenty of time on my hands and I'm genuinely intrigued by the challenge. Plus when I gather all the labels together I not only see my progress as a pen and ink artist but a record of the hundreds of varieties I've grown. (Is there anywhere on the planet – outside of a medical dispensary – where a stoner has access to so many different varieties? I think not.)

And except for the plants I'm currently raising they're all dead and gone now. All those gorgeous ladies, all those fantastical hybrids, lost to time and smoke and memory.

Replaced by beauties that might ... just might ... get me a litttttttle bit higher.

I sleep on an old futon in my living room. It's something I hadn't given much thought to until a friend's wife returned some books the other day. She saw the futon was still turned down and asked me if I'd had an overnight guest.

"Oh no," I said. "That's where I sleep."

"All the time?"

"Yeah."

"You live alone in a three-bedroom house, and you sleep on the couch in your living room?"

"Well, yeah."

"Why?"

I had to think about it. One bedroom I save for guests, another is the one I'm sitting in now (my ostensible studio), and the third is the room upstairs where I store stuff. All my relationships with girlfriends have transpired at their homes, and when I take in destitute friends it's hard to convince them I'm not giving up a bedroom for their sake.

I guess it's just that I do all my drawing, reading and thinking in the living room, so it's simply *easier* to sleep there. I'm a monkish type

... if the ceiling is tall enough I have no problem with small spaces. Hell, I prefer them.

Mostly, though, it's a simple matter of arithmetic: I sleep so few hours a day, and at such odd hours, that it isn't worth messing up a bed. When I'm tired I turn down the futon, wrap a blanket around me, roll over and hope for the best.

Or as I said to my friend's wife that day: "I guess I'm still a bindle stiff."

In 1968 my alcohol psychosis remained quiescent enough that when I felt The Dread, when I woke in the morning to that icy terror clawing at the edge of my consciousness, hair of the dog still flushed the demons.

But it was taking longer and longer and leaving me stranger and stranger afterwards. So as Louie and I pulled into Juarez, Mexico I was thinking, *This is it. All the money I can spend, all the booze I can drink, all the whores I can fuck ... if I can just beat madness to the finish line.*

Which, oddly enough, is more or less how it worked out. It seemed pretty selfish of me, of course, worrying about personal pursuits when my friend and benefactor was tottering on a mental health precipice of his own, but noose or nut house ... Lonesome's chips were already cashed. You could see it in his expression (or lack of one), the way he had that Death Dog vacancy in the eyes again. The only thing that seemed to give him pleasure was learning Spanish. So as we drove south in the Barracuda (with Mexico City our ostensible destination), not sightseeing or shopping or trying out quaint little restaurants but simply gliding from one roadside bar to another, Louie would chat with the locals while I drank mescal and got blow jobs from whores in the back booths. It was the most intense drinking bout of my life and I confess to no serious memory of anything but the green neon glow behind the bars. Anyone watching us, in fact, would have concluded that I was the suicidal one.

Louie's burgeoning mastery of Spanish, however, did make my sole responsibility easier, i.e., reminding him to send a postcard to Claire everyday. Now he could write her notes in Spanish, make her think he was up to something worthwhile.

Inevitably, though, (especially after he caught me butt fucking a nasty Indian whore in the front seat of his Barracuda), it became a question of whether hanging out with me was any worse than a stateside mental ward. Louie grew more and more distracted until one night we rented rooms in a nice hotel for the first time.

When I woke in the morning I actually knew where I was. I showered, shaved, put on a garish nylon shirt with parrots that I'd bought in a blackout, then met Louie in the restaurant downstairs for breakfast. I was feeling so good I had a single *Cerveza* and was halfway through my eggs when Lonesome sprung his news.

"Wilson," he said, "today *I'm* gonna drink."

My spirits tanked. "Now, Lonesome," I said, "remember what happened the last time."

"That's the point, High," he replied. "Practice makes perfect."

So the train wreck was here. I felt bad for both of us, but it had been a damn good run and I still had my own hide to protect. "Eh … you don't plan on taking me out *with* you, do you, Louie? If you get drunk and do something crazy I mean."

"Forewarned is forearmed, High."

Platitudes. This was the worst sign yet, particularly from Lonesome. The big question now was: did I drink to prepare for what lay ahead, or try to stay sober for the same reason?

I compromised on sipping *Cervezas* as we drove to the outskirts of Chihuahua. Louie wanted to start there because it was where Pancho Villa died and had a reputation as a very volatile place. He was moderately buzzed on beers by then and idled the Barracuda through a series of grim neighborhoods. When he located a particularly ugly bar he stopped and turned to me.

"What do you think, Wilson?" he asked.

"Looks pretty scary to me."

"Exactly. Let's try it out."

I slipped from the passenger side as Louie pulled his polo shirt from his pants, stepped onto the gravel and walked to the trunk. Opened it and withdrew the ridiculous sombrero he'd been wearing in San Angelo.

"Oh fuck, Lonesome," I begged, "not that stupid hat!"

"It's my Pancho hat, High. It's riding into the sunset with me!"

This is getting worse by the second, I thought, then we walked inside that bar and the tension ratcheted even higher. It looked like the Mexican Most Wanted List in there: scarred, skinny, thin-lipped men and hawk-faced women, all of them watching us intently.

Lonesome sauntered to the bar like he owned the place. Slammed his fist down and motioned to the fat, oily bartender.

"Hey Jose," he said, "two fifths of your best tequila here!"

The bartender came down and looked us over. "That will be four hundred pesos, señor," he said.

Louie laughed, pulled out a wad of bills so thick I don't know how it fit in his pocket. He flung it down on the bar. "Fuck that," he said. "I've got money comin' out my ass!"

I turned to my left and every killer in the place was looking back at me. Then I felt something wet on my right elbow and glanced down. The little asshole next to me had spit on it.

The bartender set the two fifths in front of us and Lonesome shoved him a chunk of money. He was still acting like we were alone in there.

"A toast, Wilson," he said, lifting the bottle.

I lifted mine. "To Mexico!" he said, and took a long pull on his fifth as I ventured a quick sip of mine and set it back down.

When Louie finished he gagged, slammed the bottle back on the

194

bar and belched hideously. "The stinkin' beaner shithole!" he yelled, looking around with a laugh. Then he took another slug of the tequila and still one more.

"Louie," I said, leaning close to him, "we're gonna have to fight our way out of here if you don't shut up. And we're outnumbered big time."

"I'm counting on it you drunken asshole!"

"But you've never been in a fight in your life!"

"High time I started then, eh? Get it ... that's a pun, High." He took another long drag on the tequila bottle as I stepped back from the bar, started checking out escape routes. There was only the door we'd entered through and between me and there were a dozen guys at least. What's more they were all short and wiry and it was easier fighting King Kong than little fuckers. I leaned on the bar, watched Louie take one more pull from the bottle.

"You know, Wilson," he said, his voice rising in indignation, "this tequila is *rotgut!*"

"All tequila is," I said. "That's the point."

"Nah, this is *major* rotgut! Hey Jose!" he yelled, motioning to the bartender again. "Hey Jose your tequila sucks!"

"Ees the very best, señor," he sighed. "Top quality stuff."

"You drink it yourself, do you?"

"Si, señor."

"Well have some on me then!" spat Lonesome, and he drew back his arm and flung the fifth at the mirror behind the bar.

In the instant before the glass shattered I remember thinking, *This is it!? I'm gonna die in some piece of shit bar in Chihuahua, Mexico!?*

Then the shards went flying and there was no time to think at all. I wrestled the guy next to me to the ground and started flailing at him as his buddy dove on my back and got me around the neck in a chokehold. I was trying to knee the bastard beneath me while pulling his pal over my head when I heard the gunshots. Four or five

of them in rapid succession, just off to my left. *Blam blam! blam blam!*
I staggered to my feet as the two Mexicans scrambled away and a guy
in front of me turned over a table and hid behind it as still more shots
rang out. I fell to my knees, crawled over there and body-slammed
him out of the way so I could have his shelter. Huddled down and
watched as the shots rang out behind me and light bulbs and pieces of
ceiling exploded overhead. The customers were knocking each other
over in their haste to escape and when there was a momentary lull in
the shooting I remembered Louie and peeked around the table.

There he was, braced against the bar with the pearl-handled Colt
.45s he kept beneath his seat in the car. He must have slid them under
his shirt in the parking lot.

"Jesus Christ, Lonesome," I yelled. "It's me!"

"Who?" he said, his glazed eyes tracking me. "You mean Wilson
High, the *writer?*"

"Yeah, yeah, Louie, that's me!"

He swung the guns toward me and I was barely behind the table
when he buried three shots in the wood, missing my head by inches.
When I peeked out again, saw he was reloading, I charged him and
knocked both guns to the floor. Lifted him off the floor in a bear hug,
rolled him onto the bar and started strangling him.

"YOU FUCKIN' SUICIDAL ASSHOLE!" I screamed. "YOU
COULD HAVE KILLED ME YOU MOTHERFUCKER!"

I squeezed his throat even tighter, realized he wasn't resisting me,
that his eyes, in fact, seemed to be pleading with me to squeeze even
harder ... so I cursed and shoved him aside. Looked around the now
empty bar and tried to think. "Okay, Lonesome," I said finally, "it's
time to see if you really *can* drive that hot rod." I shoved the guns in
the front of my jeans and ran behind the bar, started grabbing bottles
of booze. Stacked four or five in Louie's arms and another half-dozen
in my own. Left most of Lonesome's money on the bar and ran for the
door.

I was afraid the lowlifes we'd ousted would be outside with guns of their own. Instead they were hiding behind the other cars in the lot and one of them, apparently, had contacted the police, because as Louie and I ran into the sunlight I spotted a half-dozen Mexican Federales headed our way. They were a hundred yards up the street with rifles in their hands and ammo belts bouncing on their chests; as they spotted us they lowered their guns and started shouting.

"HOLY SHIT LOUIE!" I yelled, reaching the Barracuda first, swinging open the door and following the bottles into the front seat. "IT'S THE FEDERALES ... HAUL ASS!"

He jumped in, fired up the engine as the first shot shattered the window behind my head. The next fusillade took out part of the back windshield as Louie squealed out of the gravel lot in a roar of dust and rocks. We were a mile north on the highway before either of us spoke.

"Give me a direction, Wilson," snapped Lonesome, sobered by the sudden flurry of action. "Something off the main drag!"

I ripped open the glove box, spread out the map. "Okay," I said, "there's something ahead called Road 16. It heads west for awhile, then curves back toward the border."

"Sounds good. Tell me when to turn." Lonesome was in his element now, the gritty racecar driver humping his fire-eater. The turnoff for Road 16 loomed up, we hung a left and burned down a strip of recently-tarred road. Chihuahua was a half hour behind us before I felt safe giving the guns back to Louie. He slid them beneath the seat, shook his head in amazement.

"Godalmightydamn!" he said. "That was fuckin' somethin', wasn't it? I've never been shot at before!"

"It was a real shitty idea, Lonesome," I said, yawning as I opened a bottle of mescal and took a slug. "Can't you kill yourself like a normal person?"

"All my ideas are shitty, Wilson," he snorted. "Jumping under a bus, marrying Gail, going into partnership with you ... they all suck!"

He had me there. "So what now?" I asked. "We'll have to get back to Texas after this, but if we can escape cleanly … will that be enough for you? You aren't going to crash us into a wall or anything if I take a nap?"

"Relax, High," he said, blowing down that empty, faceless road. "I'm *engaged* now. I've got *purpose!* You can sleep like a baby."

What the hell, I thought, adjusting the seat backwards and closing my eyes, *how much worse can it get?*

When I came to in the cab of the Barracuda I'd been asleep for a couple hours and was still groggy. I rubbed my face, felt a breeze on my neck from the blown-out windows in back. Then I heard the bottles clinking around at my feet and realized the car was going up and down in a gentle rocking motion. I looked out the window, saw nothing but cactus, sand and rock in all directions.

Not to mention a rut where the road used to be. "Jesus, Lonesome," I said, "what've you done now? What happened to the goddamn road!? How'd we end up in the middle of a desert!?"

He looked over at me and grinned. "Only in Mexico," he said. "Your Road 16 ... the paved part, anyway ... just fucking *ended!* One minute you're on tarred highway, the next it's a goat trail. That's what I'm following now, because there's supposed to be a town ahead."

"What if there isn't? We could run out of gas and die here!"

"You want to turn around?"

I thought about it. We might make it back to the main highway all right, but we'd have to head north and the authorities were sure to be looking for us at the border.

Or were they? Maybe shootouts were simply par for the course in Chihuahua. I looked behind me at the shattered windows, decided maybe not. What's more I'd expected our Mexican sojourn to end badly and now it had. I reached down, found a bottle of tequila, winced as I took a pull.

"I'm going to be twenty-one next week, Lonesome," I said, waving the bottle in the air. "Consider the irony of me dying a drunk before I even reach legal age."

"Oh we'll be fine, High," he scoffed. "The fun's just beginning."

I'd swear we were running on fumes when that Mexican village appeared. It was a shabby circle of huts with a small plaza in the center and, miracle of miracles to my eyes, a single gas pump. Louie fueled up the Barracuda while I bought canned goods and jugs of water. When we were fully provisioned and ready to roll we sat in the shade of a tree eating tamales.

I looked around the quiet little town. "Hell, Lonesome," I sighed, "maybe we could just hole up here for awhile, get a taste of village life. Then go back the way we came when the heat dies down."

"When will that be? And what if we're followed here? It's not like we're inconspicuous."

"Well, what did the villagers say about Road 16? Does it reappear farther north?"

"It's some kind of local joke, I think. I mean there's sort of a road there, apparently, and the government says it'll finish paving it someday, but in the meanwhile we've already seen the best of it. The locals say no one *drives* further north, anyway ... they use burros and horses."

"But *we're* going to drive, of course."

"Sure. I thought you liked adventure, High."

"And it's how far to the border?"

"About one hundred miles. Twenty miles before that, though, is a little village where the trail ends. We'll get more directions when we reach there."

"*If* we reach there."

"Right."

"So we'll bunk here and leave early in the morning?"

"Hell no! We're heading out right *now*, High."

"But the sun's going down!"

"That's the point. The desert's much cooler at night."

So we took off in the dark to find a village smaller than the one we were leaving on a trail that barely existed. For the next day-and-a-half we inched through a Mexican No Man's Land, Louie steering while I stumbled around doing the yeoman's chores. Clearing away rocks, shouldering the Barracuda up sandy inclines, digging us out of soft ruts with a tire iron. When I wasn't working I was slumped in the front seat, head lolling out the window as the spring sun baked us and the temperature at night dropped below freezing. The enormity of what we were doing, trying to cross a hundred-mile desert in a goddamn Plymouth, was as terrifying to me as it was exhilarating to Louie. The farther we went the more excited he became and I couldn't figure out if that was because he thought we *were* going to make it ... or we weren't.

It was up to him, in any case: I sure as hell wasn't going to save our asses. When we finally climbed a hill and saw the village in the valley below I thought it was a mirage. Lonesome whooped in triumph, steered us down the slope and into the center of a small plaza. Mexicans and their dogs ran away from us at first, then gradually trickled back as we stepped from the car. Kids, old people, groups of young men and women, they all pawed the Barracuda and pointed excitedly at me.

"What's going on, Lonesome?" I asked. "What are they saying?"

"*Muy Gigante!* You're a giant, the biggest person they've ever seen."

I looked around. The tallest of the villagers was five-six and most of them were no bigger than children. "What about ice?" I said. "Is there any ice for my drinks?"

"There's no electricity here, High," said Lonesome. "Hell, from the sound of it, most of these people have never even see a car before!"

Louie elbowed his way through the crowd, opened the hood of the Barracuda. At the sight of the engine the villagers gasped and pushed forward, chattering as they ran their hands above the hot parts. *This is it for them*, I thought, *the miracle of modern technology, brought across the desert by a madman and a drunk*. Lonesome and I had done something no one had even attempted before ... we were pioneers, heroes!

And all I wanted was some ice. I wandered over to a nearby stable, found some hay that the donkey hadn't shit on and curled up for a nap. Woke a couple hours later to Louie shaking me. He handed me a plate of chicken and refried beans, introduced me to a teenage boy.

"This is Paco," he said, "the mayor's son. He's going to guide us the rest of the way."

"They've got a *mayor* in this town?"

"Well, leader, you know. The point is we need a guide."

"Why?"

"The trail ends completely here, remember? And it's another twenty miles to the border. Without Paco showing us the way we'd never make it."

I worked down some beans and chicken and thought about it. "And say we do make it to the border? How does Paco get back?"

"He'll walk."

"Twenty miles across the desert?"

"He says he's done it before."

"Jesus. How much are you paying him?"

"A hundred pesos."

"That's twelve bucks, Louie!" I reached in my pocket, drew out

202

the pesos I had and stuffed them in Paco's shirt pocket. The little lizard barely blinked.

"You know, Lonesome," I said, the three of us walking to the Barracuda as the villagers milled around, "if we do this, if we actually make it to the border, no one'll ever believe this yarn."

"And you know why?" he asked.

"Because it's sounds so improbable?"

"No, because you'll be the only one left to tell it."

He was right about that. And even though I spent most of the night shoving rocks out of the way and pushing us up sandstone inclines we still made excellent time and were staring at a Rio Grande sunrise eight hours later. Paco accepted another hundred pesos from Louie and started back across the desert with only a thermos of water and a small bag of provisions. At a mesa far away he turned and waved.

"So long, Paco!"

"Adios, amigo!"

Lonesome and I slapped each other's backs in amazement. "Goddamn, Louie," I said, "years from now that kid'll be a legend in his town, the boy who guided the gringo's chariot across the desert."

"Sure he will!" crowed Louie.

We had a good laugh, then I looked out at the churning white water of the Rio Grande, foam splashing the rocks as the river roared in our ears. "So?" I said. "How far is the bridge?"

"Bridge?" said Lonesome. "There's no bridge around here."

"What do you mean?"

"There's no bridge. We've gotta cross the Rio Grande in the Barracuda."

"What the fuck are you talkin' about, Houston? Those are *rapids* out there!"

"And that was desert behind us, man. We'll be cool."

Suddenly I wanted to strangle him again. I was contemplating it when, just like that, up rides the Mexican Marlboro Man. Some sunburned gaucho character on horseback, trotting along and waving his hat like he saw gringos parked next to the river everyday. I watched, stupefied, as Lonesome hailed him over and chatted with him.

"Hey, High," he said finally, "Diego here knows a guy who'll guide us to a shallow part of the river."

"Really?"

"All he wants in exchange is some cigarettes."

I walked over to the Barracuda, reached in, grabbed one of my cartons of Chesterfields and handed it to Diego. Piled into the car with Louie as we followed him for a mile along the river bank. We finally reached a corrugated shack with a fat Mexican in front of it. He, Diego and Louie held a hurried conference, then Lonesome waved me over.

"Don't tell me," I said. "This guy wants booze."

"How'd you know that?" said Louie.

I grabbed one of the whiskey bottles from the Chihuahua bar and gave it to Louie, who in turn handed it to Felipe, our new guide. Everybody shook hands all around, then Diego rode off and Louie and I followed Felipe in the car. We went another five hundred yards or so, then he held up his hand and motioned towards the water.

"This is the place," said Lonesome. "He claims we can cross here."

I stepped from the car, stared out at the Rio Grande. The section Jose was pointing to was about twenty yards wide and looked as dangerous as the rest. The current seemed slower, all right, but there was still plenty of white water and rocks and you couldn't see the bottom. I balled my fist and shook it at Felipe.

"Who you kidding?" I yelled. "A fish couldn't cross that!"

He shrugged, stepped into the river. Grinned as the cold water lapped around his knees, then began a slow waddle across.

"See?" said Lonesome, standing beside the idling Barracuda. "It's a piece of cake, High."

The water was around Felipe's waist by then and he seemed to be struggling. I was sure the current would sweep him away, but he kept plowing ahead and gradually the water receded from his stomach and he stumbled onto the far shore. He turned and waved us ahead.

"Well?" said Louie. "What are we waiting for?"

"It won't work, Lonesome," I said. "I mean this is just insane … there's gotta be a better way."

"Here's how we'll do it," said Louie. "You spread-eagle yourself on the hood of the car for weight, hold really tight, then I'll back up as far as I can on the riverbank … and gun it! Hell … we'll be halfway across the river before we even set down!"

"That's suicide you Death Dog fuck! I'm not doing that!"

"Then walk across like Felipe did. I'm going for it with or without you, Wilson!"

He knew I'd give in, that at this point we'd get out of Mexico together or not at all. I cursed his suicidal soul as I laid down on the warm hood of the Barracuda, grabbing either side of the windshield as Louie positioned us across from Felipe, then backed up as far as the bank would allow. He revved the engine, gave that little *ack ack* laugh before *Bam!* he popped the clutch and we flew forward, twisting across the dirt and rocks.

I was flat out terrified. "AAAAAAHHHHHHHHHHHHH!"

We hit that rise at 30 mph and shot a good five yards over the river before splashing down with a *Whomp!* that soaked my legs and crotch with freezing water. The car found the bottom, started to drift, jerked back in line and drifted again as we wove forward. I tried to concentrate on Felipe, riveting my eyes on his dripping beer gut as we bobbed up and down in the icy current. Just when I was sure we were doomed, and was telling myself to roll *behind* the Barracuda when it started down river, the tires found the far embankment, climbed it with one last gasp of power and we were home free, steaming onto shore with loud whoops from Felipe.

For a long time afterwards I didn't dare move, staring up at a cloudless sky that somehow looked better on the Texas side. Then I slid off the hood, stepped around and fell into the seat beside Lonesome.

"Louie," I said, "you know how I'm going to remember you, my friend?"

He looked at me, already deflated at the prospect of San Angelo.

"How's that, High?" he said.

"As a good man for trouble."

And I do.

It's hard to say what went on with Louie and Claire once we returned to San Angelo because I insisted he drop me at a dive hotel on the outskirts of town. I was feeling all kinds of bad from my extended binge and spent a couple days in bed, drinking more *Maalox* than booze and running back and forth to the community toilet down the hall.

Then on the second of April, just two days before my twenty-first birthday, Louie showed up at my door and handed me a wad of cash. He appeared to be his old moribund self again.

"Lonesome," I said, "what's happening on the mental ward front? Is Claire still threatening to commit you?"

"No, it's *divorce* now."

"Uh huh. And is that good or bad?"

Louie shook his head. "Just forget about me," he said, turning to leave. "What you need to think about is being careful. My family loathes you and they're big wheels in this town."

That gave me pause because it *was* Texas and they played by their own rules down there. So that night I went to a local pizza parlor instead of a sleazy bar, figuring that I'd be less likely to get in trouble in a family environment.

The paucity of that decision became clear as I settled down in back with my pitcher of beer. I was wearing the same Levi jacket, jeans, shirt and boots that I'd left Burlingame with six weeks before and hadn't shaved or cut my hair since September.

If there was another long-haired hippie in 1968 San Angelo I hadn't seen him; neither, seemingly, had the other people in that parlor. Whole families were staring at me with thinly-veiled menace; I kept my eyes down until the pizza arrived and was on my third piece when the parlor turned quiet.

I glanced up and looming over me was a classic Texas Ranger character: lantern jaw, wide-brimmed hat, starched uniform and rigid posture. Behind him was a shorter, stockier guy with a flat top and shiny suit.

Be cool, High, I thought, and went back to my drinking.

"Sir," said the officer, "is your name Wilson High?"

He knew my name? This was not a good sign. "Yeah," I sighed, "that's me."

Just like that the silly cowboy whipped his pistol out of its holster and aimed it at me. "Stand up slowly, Mr. High," he said, "and raise your hands over your head."

I stared down that long metal barrel into the darkness beyond. "Are you shittin' me, Hopalong?" I said. "Don't you think you're overdoing the underage drinking bit? I'll be twenty-one in a couple days."

"On your feet, sir! And raise those hands high!"

"I'll just finish my beer if …"

"Now!"

I pushed away from the tiny picnic table and put my hands above my head. Then the Ranger and his sidekick lined up behind me and we marched through the parlor with everybody staring at us.

"Must be a draft dodger!" yelled someone in back.

"Or a Red!"

"Looks like a welfare hippie to me!"

A little fat kid with sausage and tomato sauce on his cheeks slapped me on the thigh. I stopped and looked at his mother.

"Those pants?" I said. "They haven't been washed in a year."

She screamed, grabbed for the boy as the Ranger jabbed me in the back with his gun. I was marched outside and told to empty my pockets, then strip off everything but my underwear and jeans and spread-eagle myself against the parlor. It was one of those prefab cedar jobs, encircled with seven-foot high windows, so everyone inside the parlor could see me looking back at them even as the flat-topped guy gave my crotch and legs a thorough frisking.

"Who's the Junior G-Man?" I asked. "I'd like to see some identification here."

Flattop grunted and reached inside his suit coat. Pulled out a small leather packet and flipped it open. "Agent Joe Harrison," he said. "FBI."

I laughed. "I should have known," I said.

"Been expecting the FBI, eh, High?" said the Ranger.

"No," I laughed. "That his name'd be *Joe!*"

Uhhhhhh! The Ranger whipped out his long club and slammed it against my back, squashing my face and beer gut against the glass as the crowd inside roared its appreciation. *Fuckin' Texans*, I thought. I started giving them the weird facial expressions I used to use on the basketball court, but in the back of my head I was thinking, *FBI, FBI … what have I done that the FBI would give a shit about?*

And whatever they were looking for they didn't find it in my old rags. At that point in time (maybe still) you could do a life term in Texas for a single joint. That's why I'd used some cross tops and reefer in Mexico but next to nothing in the Lone Star State.

"He's clean," said Joe finally, tossing the clothes at my feet.

"You're sure?" said the Ranger. "So was his room."

"I know my job, Sergeant. Someone gave you a bum steer."

"Sorry, Harrison."

"No problem." Joe wiped his hands with a handkerchief, stepped up next to me and grinned. "You're on file now, High," he said. "You've got your own little folder and we'll be watching you."

"Yeah yeah." I bent over, put my shirt and jeans and boots back on and figured that was the end of it. Instead the Ranger spun me around, jerked my hands behind my back and slapped on the cuffs. Again there was a muffled cheer from the crowd inside.

"Hey!" I said. "What the hell are you doing!?"

"You're coming downtown, big guy," he said. "And if you make one more crack I'll bust you open."

He dragged me over to his squad car, opened the back door and shoved me inside. Took me to the police station and booked me for public drunkenness and underage drinking. It was maybe my fourth stay at that jail and it wasn't getting easier. Fortunately Louie bailed me out before I could even call him in the morning.

"What's up?" I asked him when we were back on the street. "How'd you know I was in the drunk tank again?"

"Look," he said, handing me a pint of cheap vodka. "That stuff with the FBI last night ... what'd you think it was?"

"A drug bust."

"You're right. Or at least it was *supposed* to be. Claire won't continue our marriage unless I sever my partnership with you and when I told her I couldn't do that ... well, she and my father handled it their way. They were sure you'd come back from Mexico with drugs, that that's why we crossed the Rio Grande River in my Barracuda, and they told the authorities you had narcotics on you."

I laughed nervously. "Christ," I said. "I'm surprised they didn't *plant* something!"

"My father and the mayor are old fraternity brothers, Wilson, and that's *exactly* what they plan to do next. I was told that if you aren't out of town in twenty-four hours, marijuana will be 'found' in your hotel room."

I shook out a cigarette from the pack in my pocket, noticed it was bobbing around as I tried to light it. "Drive me to the bus station," I said. "Quick."

"What about flying?"

"You know the only flight out of here is at night. I can't wait that long."

"Don't you want to go back to your room, get your typewriter and writing first?"

"You get 'em if you want 'em. *I'm out of here, Lonesome!*"

There was nothing, absolutely nothing short of death, that was more terrifying to me than the prospect of spending the rest of my days in Texas, much less a Texas jail. We drove straight to the bus station and I booked a Greyhound to the Bay Area. Lonesome handed me five hundred bucks and I hugged him good-bye in the terminal.

"If there's any justice, Louie," I said, "your granddaddy's looking down from heaven, pleased as punch with how we've pissed his money away."

"Oh right," he said. "Now you rent yourself a decent place, Wilson, and be careful with the money this time. I have a feeling I'll be out to see you presently."

I doubted that but I gave him another hug and thanked him for all he'd done for me. Then I jumped on the bus and settled in the last seat with my pint of vodka.

We were crossing into Utah before I breathed easy again.

I buy only the best organic soil and wish I could use it more than once. But that would require a lot of rinsing and lime treatments, so it's easier to start anew each time while giving friends the benefits of the nutrient-soaked root balls. You throw them in your garden with a bit of hydrated lime and bone meal – or simply let the rain leech them out – and *Bingo!* a month later you have a rich mound of loam.

Well, except for the white chunks of perlite, that is. They're necessary for air and moisture retention in pots, but if you spread that same soil around your yard (particularly in Boregon's rainy climate) you end up with *snow gardens*. Thick white swatches that work their way up through the heavier soil inch by inch, year by year, until your vegetable patch crunches like pie crust when you walk on it.

Fortunately there's no one to see mine but the Alzheimer's patients in the four-story clinic behind my house. And to them it might as well *be* a snow garden ...

When I returned to the Bay Area I got my old room back at the Burlingame Hotel. I also picked up another typer at a pawn shop but didn't do much writing. Mostly I sat at the window facing the street and sipped $1.50 quarts of *Ernie's Black Label* whiskey. The irony of finally reaching the legal drinking age at the same time I was finished as a drinker was hardly lost on me. I was going to keep sucking up whiskey and anything else I could get my hands on, of course – and I'd be doing so as long as I could, I was pretty sure of that – but the tolerance was gone and in its place was that dark Dread I only kept at bay with more booze.

It pissed me off, of course, as I was caught in the great conundrum of my young life. On the one hand … where was the long run, the golden years sipping mescal in a trailer park? Hell, my *good* drinking days had stretched a year-and-a-half maximum and now they were over! All that lay ahead was payback.

On the other hand … wasn't that the rationalization I'd set out with in the first place? I was an alkie and I needed to run the need for booze, the craving for what it did, the release it gave me, right out of my system? Beat it before it beat me? So was I surprised I was right

213

or, worse, *afraid* I was?

Oh well, I'd find out one way or another, and it didn't do any good wishing I had another five or ten years to enjoy the process, or a few more laughs before the Reckoning; there was trouble ahead and these would not be the dating years. The best reminder of that was catching a glimpse of my friend Felice one morning. She was the dancer/musician I'd dated the summer before and I hadn't seen her since I left for New York City so abruptly. I was shambling up Burlingame Avenue – after waking in some bushes east of there – and spotted her driving by in the opposite direction. I felt the same jolt I always did when I saw her elfish mug and raised my arm reflexively … only to lower it with a sigh, remembering as I did why I hadn't phoned her. It was only nine months since we'd gone out and I'd become a filthy, bloated wino (living on a lunatic's charity) in the interim.

Sometimes at moments like that there'd be a *tinge* of regret for who I might have been if I weren't me. Fortunately it would pass as quickly as the next drink because an alkie, after all, is exactly what I was. So as I watched Felice disappear up the Avenue I wasn't sure if my heartache was for me, her, or the fact I might be dead or crazy soon.

Perhaps all four. A month after my return from Texas I came back one afternoon to find Lonesome Louie sitting on the bed. He'd picked up the empty *Black Label* bottles and arranged them in rows on the floor.

"Wilson," he said, "there are thirty empty quarts here and you've only been back four weeks!"

"Well hello to you too, Louie," I said, setting some fresh bottles down in the sink. "And how do you know I haven't been partying, that it wasn't a *bunch* of people who drank that?"

"This stuff is rotgut, Wilson. Who else would drink it?"

"Point taken." I sat down next to him on the bed. "What the hell are you doing here, Lonesome?"

"I'm moving back to the Bay Area. I rented a house in San Mateo and Claire will join me this summer." He stood up and walked to the little desk where the typewriter was. Looked in vain for some paper. "You haven't been writing anything, have you?"

"No," I said, "but I've thought about it."

He sighed, shook his head and walked out of the room without another word. I had no idea when I'd see him again and was surprised when he returned three hours later.

"Wilson," he said, striding into the room without knocking, "I've just had a long conversation with your friend Ned Gumbo."

"I wouldn't call him a *friend*, Lonesome," I said, already vaguely drunk. "*Scheming little shit* is more like it. And whatever he told you? It's all lies."

"To the contrary." Lonesome started to sit down, got a good look at the musty chair and leaned against the wall instead. "I think he's a bright fellow who has your best interests at heart, High, and is really, really concerned … like I am … about you drinking yourself to death."

I didn't like where this was going. A Death Dog worrying about me killing myself? Gumbo acting like he wished me long life?

"So here's the deal Ned suggested," continued Louie, "and I think it has real merit. I know you won't stay completely sober, so I'll continue to pay your way as long as you drink only a pint a day."

"Make it a quart," I said.

"No, no, Ned said you'd say that and it's just too much, High. No one can drink a quart of whiskey a day and still write! This is for your own good, you know."

"How about a fifth then?" I asked.

"No."

"This *pint* figure. Ned's the one that came up with that?"

"Yeah. He said that's all you can handle, anyway."

I'll get Gumbo for this, I thought. *I don't know how, or when, but it'll happen.*

"Anyway," said Louie, pushing off the wall, "I'll give you some time to think about it."

"I don't need any time, Lonesome," I sighed. "The answer is no."

"Come on, Wilson. This is a deal breaker. If you stay drunk and don't write it just causes too much trouble with Claire and my family … they'll try to lock me up again."

"And if you subsidize me any further they should." I stood up, walked over to Louie and slapped him on the back. "I can't live on a pint a day, man. I could try, but it just won't happen. And I've blown enough of your granddaddy's money, anyway … let's just go our separate ways, Death Dog."

"But what'll you *do*, Wilson?" he said. "You'll have to get a shitty job again."

"Yeah," I said, "but when you think about it … that's better for me than a pint a day."

Lonesome shook my hand, gave me a stiff hug. "Goddamn," he said, "that Mexico trip was a ride, wasn't it?"

"Yeah, it was, man. And I'll be seeing you around, Louie … you can always find me here."

He nodded, hung his head and started for the door.

"Eh, Lonesome," I said, "aren't you forgetting something?"

"Oh?" he said, turning around. "What's that?"

"What about my severance pay?"

CARL SAMPSON

Carl Sampson called me six weeks ago. I hadn't heard from him since mid-October, when he was selling subscriptions to the *L.A. Times* in Desert Hot Springs, California. I'm sure about the date because I still have the postcard he sent me on my refrigerator. It's a photo of a murky motel pool encircled by rundown rooms and beach umbrellas, with a patch of ugly gray mountains in the background. On the flip side he wrote: "This is the Stardust Motel. It's the best place I've ever lived."

No wonder we're still friends. Then I get that phone call. Now Carl's living in the *Pair-A-Dice Motel* in Las Vegas and selling gold coins over the phone. The problem is that he blew his thirties, forties and fifties drinking the way I did in my twenties, studiously ignoring his teeth in the interim. So now they're falling out here and there and he's in so much pain he can't talk, which puts a real damper on the phone sales. He can get a temporary fix at the dentist, he tells me, but that'll leave him broke, so he wondered if he could come stay at my place for awhile afterwards.

I told him he was always welcome. He could have my last dime if he wanted it, so giving him the room down the hall was nothing. He was here for a couple weeks, then Tony DeBola (who lives in Central Boregon) gave him a tile setting job and a free place to live. It's a hundred year-old hunter's cabin that sits alone – miles from nowhere – in the middle of a national forest. He's got some chickens in a pen and chipmunks and kangaroo rats coming through the walls, but assures me the place is right up there with the Stardust.

Or at least The Burlingame Hotel. That's where Sampson found me the first week of May in 1968. Lonesome had given me a couple hundred bucks in "severance pay" and I'd just about gone through it by then. In the meanwhile I hadn't actually spoken to Louie but still managed to see him everyday. Around noon he'd show up on the sidewalk beneath my hotel window, carrying a stopwatch and wearing nothing but a pair of shorts (even though it was still chilly outside). Then he'd casually stop people and offer them a five dollar bill if they could tell him – without looking at their watches – when sixty seconds had elapsed.

Sounds silly enough on the face of it, right? Except the kicker was the jewelry store across the street. It had a HUGE clock in its front window that must have had a yard-long second hand. Louie would say "Go!" and put the stopwatch behind his back while participants pretended to count to themselves. I say "pretended" because their hundred percent success rate indicated that most (if not all of them) couldn't help but peek at that clock. And every time one of them "guessed" right Lonesome would widen his eyes or slap his forehead in a pantomime of amazement, then hand them their five-buck prize.

"Amazing," he'd exclaim. "Simply amazing. What a time sense the people of Burlingame have!"

Soon there would be a line 5- to 15-people long (most of them broke hippies or bums like Gumbo, who came by everyday for lunch money) waiting to participate in the charade. What was Louie's point, I wondered? I'm sure he was aware of the clock across the street, so did he fancy himself a latter-day Diogenes, seeking out one honest person? If so, why do it directly under *my* window? And weirder yet … what was this glib new bent in his character that had him interacting with strangers?

He might have had some mania going but I preferred speculating to asking him: after our time in Texas and Mexico a little separation suited both of us.

Then Sampson showed up. I hadn't seen him since New York City and though he was no longer enrolled at Cal he was still living in Berkeley. He paced around the room for a minute, winding in and out of the empty bottles, then threw up his arms and turned to me.

"Goddamn!" he exclaimed, "no buddy of mine is going to live in a dump like this! I want you to pack up your stuff, High! You're coming to stay with me in Berkeley!"

"Really?" I croaked. "Are you sure that's a good idea?"

"Absolutely," he said. "This place is a disgrace!" He found an old paper bag on the floor, scribbled a map on it. "Meet me on the corner of Shattuck and Grant at noon tomorrow. You can take a bus from here."

I was so heartened by his generous gesture that I stayed sober the next morning. I didn't have much to pack, just some dirty socks and underwear that I wrapped around my last fifth of whiskey and shoved inside the typer case. Then I walked over to California Avenue and grabbed the Greyhound to Berkeley. Sampson was waiting for me when I stepped off the bus and after lunch at a deli we took a long stroll up Shattuck.

"Well, Carl," I said finally, "I'm getting tired of lugging this typer around. Where's your place?"

"Relax," he said. "We've gotta wait 'til dark. We'll go to the park up here for now, smoke some dope and check out the pussy."

"What do you mean *dark?*" I asked. "Why do we have to wait 'til dark?"

"Hey, pal," said Carl, "you don't want to be sneaking into people's garages in broad daylight."

"Garages?"

"Yeah. All these years I'm paying rent for apartments, High, and suddenly it occurs to me ... people don't use their garages at night, so why don't *I* sleep in them? Hell, I'm an early riser. You are, too. So we'll sneak in the side door of garages at night, get some rest, be gone before anyone even knows we were there. I've been doing it for weeks now ... it's a snap."

"Fuckin' *garages!* You think that's better than the Burlingame Hotel?"

"Come on ... anything's better than that loser hellhole, High."

I stopped in the middle of the sidewalk, extracted the fifth of whiskey and took a long pull. Belched quietly as a woman passerby sneered at me.

"Let's follow her, Carl," I said. "I wanna sleep in her garage."

220

The odd thing about sleeping in garages with Sampson is that he was right ... it *was* better than living at The Burlingame Hotel. For openers it meant I was outside more because I had no place to return to during the day. This in turn translated to less morning drinking and more quality time with my peers. '68 Berkeley was a fringe character's vortex, a place where the loose ends met up, and now that I was officially a street person I was free to explore its psychedelic underbelly. Carl knew a lot of people from his time at Cal so we spent most of our afternoons in students' homes and apartments, backing hits of mescaline and acid with whatever smoke was available. Sampson slept with all kinds of women in the process while I was relegated to mercy fucks from girls in blackouts.

Assuming they didn't throw up first, of course, my rotgut whiskey being generally underappreciated. Mostly I was just grateful for whatever pussy came my way, particularly when it was with a horny, unshaven lass I'd never see again. I've always liked hair on a woman; it makes them more real and – though you'd think a guy sleeping in garages would have had too much of it – I needed all the reality I could get.

If we outlasted everyone else Carl and I slept on a carpet or couch right where we'd been partying. When forced to seek a garage for the night, however, inebriation proved a boon. Those concrete floors were cold and hard and it wasn't like we carried sleeping bags around. We'd stumble out of a house or apartment building and immediately start checking the neighborhood for likely places to crash. All we needed was an unattached garage with a side door entry; when we found one we'd do a quick survey of the lawn out front, searching for piles of dog shit. (A bowser on the property was generally a negative; if they weren't overnighting in the garage itself, they might raise a ruckus from inside the home.)

Individual details are a little hard to distinguish when you're blind drunk at two in the morning, though, so mostly we just took our chances. Once inside the garage we'd try to pass out on the side of the car furthest from the door we'd come through (or at least between the cars in a two-car garage). This way if the owner entered while we were asleep we'd have something between him and us. This happened only a couple times because I rarely slept past dawn no matter how fucked up I was, and on the two occasions when we were caught by a homeowner (both of them male), they backed off quickly when Carl and I rose to our feet. Sampson was the toughest guy I knew, a grizzled ex-rugby player who looked like a force of nature, and at 6'6" and 250 pounds, with long, matted hair and booze-drenched rags for clothes, nobody wanted a piece of me first thing in the morning.

Myself least of all. Then Carl found a garage we could rent for $20 a month. That was all the money we had between us, so we spent a week going back and forth to Union City to pick beans. We'd catch a 4:00 a.m. city bus on San Pablo Avenue, then get off at the end of the line and board a ratty black bus in an alley. I thought we were the only pickers the first time we went, then right at five in the morning a paddy wagon backed up and unloaded another fifteen bums. They were shaky alkies and addicts working off jail time and still managed to pick more beans than I did. It felt like it was a hundred in those sun-baked fields and sometime during the afternoon I'd gravitate to Amos, an old black guy who bussed there everyday from Richmond and drank something he called "rocket fuel." A horrid, brain-numbing grain alcohol that would lay me out quickly. More than once he and Carl had to help me back on the bus at the end of the day (Amos mumbling biblical homilies as Sampson cursed and shoved me) and eventually I did what I should have done months before, which was apply for unemployment benefits. Except after one look at me the State sent me to a doctor who okayed me for disability benefits instead. Essentially the State of California was going to pay me $70 a week – way more than I made as a bean picker – to be a worthless drunk.

I had some scruples about it at first but they passed quickly in the luxury of our new garage. Sampson had scrounged up a mattress for himself and I'd found an old blanket to sleep on. When my check came there was some retroactive money in there so I got my typer out of hock and even bought us a little space heater. The first time we used it I was so relieved to be warm at night that I cozied up right next to it. Woke to Sampson yelling and the back of my long hair on fire. We put it out but I still ended up with a reverse Mohawk that looked worse when I had to smear Vaseline over the pink scalp burns in the middle.

These will not be the dating years. I repeated it like a mantra every time I got a good look at myself in a mirror. Then Carl became serious with a statuesque Scandinavian named Eva, a physical education major from Sweden, and the two of them coupled like wild animals whether I was nearby or not. I slipped away when my next check arrived. I'd heard from an old Burlingame friend that Gumbo had sold his car and headed to Europe for the summer. This meant his cottage would be empty and, inasmuch as he'd squashed my gravy boat with Louie, I was sure he wouldn't mind me housesitting for him.

The place was boarded up tight when I arrived and it took the better part of an hour to jimmy the back window. Ned had cut off the phone and electricity, of course, but I hadn't had those in the garages either and he'd at least left the water service on. I bought a case of Ernie's Black Label, a loaf of bread and a jar of peanut butter and made myself at home.

Ten days later I was passed out in the front room when I woke to loud hammering. I looked up from the couch to see Brad Lacy, Gumbo's harried landlord, nailing four-by-six boards across the door.

"Hey, Brad," I moaned. "Can you keep it down a little … I'm trying to sleep here."

He paused in his hammering, looked over at me with undisguised scorn. "Oh gee, High," he said, "so sorry to disturb you. And as long as you're awake, why don't you get the fuck out of here?"

"Why?"

"Do you see what I'm doing here, asshole? I'm boarding the place up so I can keep the likes of you and Gumbo out. Either grab your stuff and blow or I'll seal you in here!"

I looked around, saw I had two full bottles of bourbon left. "Go ahead," I yawned, laying my head back down. "I've got provisions."

The next thing I knew I was out on the front porch with my typewriter and bottles. *This is what comes from having a loser like Gumbo for a buddy,* I thought. I walked around the block until Lacy left, then returned and pulled an old chaise lounge from behind the cottage. Unfolded it near the porch and settled in. It was almost the Fourth of July and there was no reason I couldn't live outside until fall.

That's where Tony DeBola found me three days later. There was a steady rain coming down and I was still in the chaise, a soggy sleeping blanket across my legs as I drank warm Whiskey Sours and perused the newspaper. Around me were bottles, paperbacks and empty cans of cocktail peanuts.

It was five months since I'd seen Tony and it felt like another lifetime. He walked up to me, looked around in shock.

"High," he said, *"what the fuck are you doing!?"*

I tried to explain the last six months of my life to him, and the longer I spoke the more it seemed like I belonged in Gumbo's driveway.

"But Wilson," he said finally, "you're looking like a dead guy. And it's *fucking raining out you asshole!* Don't you see the disconnect here, that it didn't even occur to you to pull the chaise under the overhang where it's dry?"

"There's some alkie apathy at work here," I said, "I'd be the first to admit that."

"Yeah," sighed Tony, "I bet you would." He started to say something else, shook his head and walked off. Made it ten feet before turning around and coming back.

"Shit," he said, "I know I'm going to regret this."

"What's that?" I said.

"Taking you back to Arcata with me. Come on, High," he said, reaching down, grabbing my arm and dragging me to my feet. "I can't let you die of pneumonia out here."

"Wait a minute," I protested. "What the hell's in Arcata?"

"Humboldt State? Where I go to school? I'm out for the summer but I'm working as a gardener on campus and renting a house with another guy."

"Geez, I appreciate the thought, Tony," I said, "but I've decided not to trouble my friends anymore."

"Then you better quit drinking, dipshit. And believe me … I'm not inviting you to live upstairs with the real people. There's a dingy little washroom in the basement we call the 'Bat Cave.' I'll put you in there."

The basement? Damn, I thought, *that isn't charity … it's an insult.*

"In that case I accept," I said. I shook off the rain, grabbed my typer and the last bottle of Ernie's and followed Tony down the driveway.

Fate wasn't through with me yet.

Tony DeBola. When I think back on those Bay Area days and all the extraordinary characters I met there was no one I could count on like DeBola. Starting with that ride up the California coast in his '48 Ford I've known him for over forty years and he's never let me down. If he says he's going to do something, he does it; if I need him, he's always been there for me. He's my best friend and I truly believe I'd take a bullet for the guy.

But it didn't start out that way. After rescuing me from Gumbo's driveway Tony and I spent the night at his father's house, then headed north for Arcata the next morning. For some reason I'd bought a case of Dutch beer instead of whiskey for the drive, and inasmuch as DeBola wasn't drinking I was resigned to finishing it myself. Which wouldn't have been a problem if not for all the pissing. The more I drank the shorter the intervals between bladder emergencies, so by the time we reached Point something-or-other on Highway 1 DeBola was sick of stopping. I had my hand on my zipper and was threatening to waterfall right there in the cab when he finally pulled over.

"All right, asshole," he spat. "Just find a tree and do it!"

I eased out of the cab, walked to the edge of the blacktop and looked down. We were on a cliff a few hundred feet above the Eel River, with only a smattering of scraggly pines growing beside the road. I crab walked down to one and – with cars whizzing past behind me – stepped as close to the trunk as possible, grabbed a branch to steady myself, then reached for my zipper.

Except the branch snapped, plunging me through the tree and over the side of the cliff. I rolled off a couple outcroppings and then started bouncing, plunging down the rocky incline with a scream in my throat. I had maybe a second to realize that if I hit the giant boulder below I might live; if I rolled past it and plunged over the incline I was dead for sure.

Then I smashed into the rock back first and knocked myself out.

The next thing I remember is the far off sound of laughing. I worked my eyes open, looked up at the blue California sky. I couldn't remember where I was, then suddenly did and felt a surge of panic. Was I paralyzed? Were my bones ground to mush beneath the skin? I moved my throbbing head a little, discovered it was still attached to my neck. Used my scraped, bloody hands for a tentative survey of my body parts. I'd pissed myself, all right, and most of my clothes had been ripped off, and there were certainly places where my skin looked like raw meat … but not only was I alive, I didn't seem to have broken anything. It was a goddamned alkie miracle: being drunk and rubbery had saved my ass again.

Still what was that irritating sound? I looked to the top of the cliff – maybe two hundred feet above me – and there was that chunky fuck DeBola hunched on all fours beside the road. He was laughing so hard I thought he'd puke. He was so convulsed, in fact, that he was in danger of falling off the cliff himself. I raised myself to one elbow, then a knee, shook my right fist above my head:

"Hey DeBola," I yelled. "What's so goddamned funny!"

He tried to answer but collapsed in hysteria instead. Finally worked himself onto his knees and wiped his eyes. "JESUS, HIGH!" he yelled. "YOU ARE SUCH A FUCKIN' BUFFOON!"

"HEY SCREW YOU I COULDA BEEN KILLED OR PARALYZED, MAN!"

That just started him off again. I was suddenly, insanely *furious!* I wove to an upright position, started clawing my way back up the incline. I was shocked, concussed and bloodied, and there were places on that climb where for every yard I gained I seemed to lose two but DeBola's laughter – and the thought of choking the life out of him – kept me going. I don't know how I'd have made it to the top otherwise.

By the time I reached the edge of the highway, though, I was spent. I steadied myself as best I could beside the road, then slowly stood up and looked down. The only part of my T-shirt that was still intact was the neckline, right shoulder and sleeve. The rest of it hung off my back, as did most of my shredded jeans and a fair amount of skin. Plus I was so cut up there was blood running down my chest.

Based on the squealing brakes and near collisions, the shock to people driving by on Highway One was palpable.

"Come on," gasped Tony, still trying to catch his breath, tears streaming down his cheeks. "Let's get you in the truck before the sight of you kills somebody."

We hobbled up to the old Ford and he eased me into the passenger side of the cab. It wasn't until I leaned against the seat that I realized my back felt worse than the front of me (I still have the crosshatching of scars there). I groaned, reached over and grabbed one of those Dutch beers. Cracked it open and missed my mouth so the foam washed down my chest, mixing with the blood and grime and gravel.

"Now listen, High," said Tony, pulling onto the highway, "I want you to know that I take back what I told you in Gumbo's driveway."

"Huh?"

"About how I'd regret bringing you to Arcata." He looked over at me, started snickering again. "Hell, man … *it's worth it already you pathetic fuck!*"

And I couldn't help it, it was all so perfectly absurd that I started laughing with him until we had to pull over to the shoulder again … we were going at it so hard we'd covered the inside of the windshield with spit. A lifelong friendship was cemented right there because DeBola has always known the exact right chord to strike with me. I wouldn't have made it up that cliff without his laughter and I might have been scared to death in the cab without it. As it was the more beer I drank the more it seemed like just another shitty day at the office.

At least until we reached a roadside store, where a woman screamed and grabbed her children when I walked in. DeBola bought two large cans of antibacterial *Medi-Quik* along with some gauze and bandages, then took me out to the parking lot and sprayed me. When he had me thoroughly coated I held one end of the gauze so he could spin me in circles, wrapping me from head to toe like a mummy.

Then he stashed me back in the seat and we drove to his house in Arcata. It was a two-story ranch job that sat at the bottom of a grassy slope and his roommate (the owner of the house) was a law professor. When we pulled up he was bent over picking weeds in the garden below.

DeBola parked, walked around the front of the truck and looked down at him. "Hey Frankowitz!" he yelled. "Remember that Wilson High guy I told you about?"

Frankowitz sat back and looked at him. "No," he said. "I don't think so."

"You know," continued Tony. "The one you always say I'm exaggerating about?"

"Oh yeah … that fool. What'd he do now?"

229

Tony swung open the door, sending a cascade of empty beer cans onto the sidewalk with me right behind them, clinging drunkenly to the frame. I never should have released it, I was stiff with scabs beneath that gauze, but the alcohol had me convinced I wasn't as weak as I thought. So I let go, stepped forward to wave to my new roommate and tripped on the empties. Tumbled headfirst down the steep incline of lawn and rolled right into the fat bastard, cutting his legs out from under him so he flew into the air and landed back on top of me, further ripping my scabs.

"Hey Frankowitz!" yelled DeBola, raising his voice above my screams. "Meet Wilson High!"

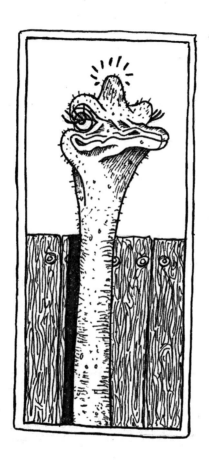

os·trich (ôs'trich) **n.** *struthio camelus.* Flightless native of central Africa. Largest bird in the world at seven – nine feet tall; can run at speeds up to 40 mph. Valuable livestock prized for meat, leather and feather products. Dumb as dirt.

When I owned emus and designed T-shirts for ratite owners I used to visit ostrich farms to photograph and sketch the giant birds. These terrifying, stately creatures can kill or maim in an instant with their powerful legs and talons, so the fence encircling them is always raised two feet off the ground. This way the keeper can roll to safety if attacked.

Even scarier, though, is how stupid the birds are. If you have one in a barn and the door he goes through is shorter than he is it's likely he won't duck but will, instead, keep banging his head 'til he's dead.

In this respect I'm much like an ostrich. When I was younger I thought booze and drugs would kill me but now I'm pretty certain it'll be complications from banging my head on doorways. For some reason I've always felt like a 5'10" guy in this 6'6" body, so unless I'm constantly vigilant I don't clear low doorways or, for that matter, much anything else. It amuses me to read about these NFL quarterbacks who retire because of a half-dozen concussions over the years. Hell, I've had *dozens* of them, and that's excluding the ones I've incurred falling *from* heights.

As a result the top of my bald head is extraordinarily sensitive and if it's banged at all – even lightly – I go into a weird, disembodied fugue state. It's the kind of consequence that's made me ambivalent about the height thing. I suppose it's possible that teachers, friends, employers – even strangers – have been as good to me as they have simply because I was taller than they were. That's what all the sociological studies on height would have you believe, anyway. But to me, someone who's always had the luxury of being taller than his peers, it's mostly just a subject I ignore.

Well, except when I'm in Amsterdam. Then I notice because the average height of a Dutch male is 6'1" and the women aren't much shorter, so I pretty much feel like a regular-sized guy over there. And occasionally in this country, when I'm crammed in an elevator with a group of shorter people, I'll be vaguely conscious of my maypole effect.

But generally speaking I think my indifference to the matter makes me seem shorter than I am. I've noticed over the years that a 6'3" person whose very conscious of his height will seem 6'6" or better, and that the reverse is also true. So my idea of the ultimate compliment is a friend telling me they'd forgotten how tall I was.

The Bat Cave in Tony and Frankowitz's basement was a grim concrete bunker with a blanket for a door, a cot in the corner and a wash basin on the wall. I had a chance to memorize every inch of it over the next week as I lay on that cot mending. I knew I'd done some internal damage because Tony was a Marine Biology major and had a stack of empty *Gerber's* baby food jars beneath the sink. I pissed in a series of them and my urine was black for forty-eight hours, then purple for a few days after that and, finally, a reasonable orange. The rest of me was strictly drums along the neurons. The deep bruises were everywhere and the scabs beneath the gauze kept sticking so I had to strip it off gradually or, alternatively, get drunk and start ripping.

Worst of all were the nutcracker headaches. DeBola would bring me down whatever he made for dinner when he got home from his landscaping job and gradually, after seven or eight days in the Cave, I'd recovered enough to limp my way upstairs.

Where I assumed the prone position on the living room couch. I laid there for the rest of the summer, drinking three six-packs a day and living off the weekly disability checks. Often I'd go all afternoon without walking farther than the bathroom or the fridge. These, when I look back, are in some ways the starkest of the drinking days. There was no more going out to look for women or friends or drinks ... now the boozing was an end in itself. It was a grimness that had little to do with falling off that cliff. It was more The Dread spreading through me, so even after a few beers there was still a gray pallor to the day. It got so bad that I started watching *Dark Shadows,* an afternoon soap opera about vampires, for comfort.

That was the last straw for DeBola. He'd come home from his job at four o'clock to find my now 260-pound carcass sprawled across the couch. I'd be covered in a sea of ashes, crumbs and empties, making a shushing motion to him lest I miss something Barnabas the vampire said.

So when Gumbo called and invited us to a river float Tony thought we could both use a change of scenery. The float was an annual event orchestrated by Ned on the property of Ted Grantham, another buddy of ours who owned an undeveloped lot on the Russian River. There was a giant bonfire and kegger on Saturday night, then on Sunday we'd all float down the river in tire tubes (often as many as 200 at once) drinking from kegs that bobbed atop wooden rafts.

It was a delirious affair for the participants and a horrific spectacle for onlookers along the river. Or so I presume. I went on three floats over the years and remember little of the Sundays and too much of the Saturday nights.

Particularly this time around. DeBola and I drove south from Arcata and arrived on Saturday afternoon. When I stepped from the cab I nearly knocked Carl Sampson over. Neither of us was feeling too social so we filled plastic pitchers with beer and took a stroll in the woods, catching up on our misbegotten lives. It turned out he had some LSD so I swallowed a tab, decided I needed to be farther away than that and took another one. We'd walked about a quarter mile when we came upon a large redwood chalet. It was surrounded by a fence with – of all things – a little guard shack at the gate. *What's to protect out here*, I wondered, then spotted a group of nuns behind the chalet.

"Hey look, Sampson!" I said. "Nuns!"

Just then a scrawny little rooster of a guy, his face mean and hard, came scurrying out of the guard shack. He had a shotgun in his hands.

"This is private property, hippies!" he spat. "Go back the way you came!"

"Whoa, gramps!" said Carl. "Just relax there … we're leaving."

We turned around, starting walking the other way. I could tell Carl had already forgotten about the place and I thought I had, too, except that – four hours later, when it was long evident that one hit of acid would have sufficed – I slipped into the woods and headed back towards the chalet. Was I looking for trouble? Did I want to see if I could creep through the dark forest without disturbing the guard? Was it really necessary to be carrying two pitchers of beer in the meanwhile? (I tripped and lost one of them before I'd gone ten feet.) Who knows? Drunk on an overdose of LSD the world is full of outcomes, most of them dangerous.

It was a moonless night and it took me twice as long to find the chalet in the dark as it had with Carl. I was sneaking through the last bit of woods, congratulating myself on having worn all black that day (right down to some grimy cowboy hat I'd found in Tony's basement), when I heard a low mumbling off to my right. The guard shack was dark and the chalet behind lit up with lights so I crept over to the fence and saw there were a dozen nuns kneeling and praying on a small hill inside the fence line. Above them was a four-foot-high statue of the Virgin Mary with Child, and above that an old, twisted tree.

Now for me, someone who saw religion as the poison in humanity's blood, the spiritual commitment of nuns (or, for that matter, anyone who gave their life over to a faith-based ideal) was a genuine curiosity. On acid and a bellyful of beer this bemusement morphed into aggravation, at least to judge by what happened next. I crept slowly along the fence line, imagining my fat ass moving with the stealth and cunning of an Indian scout, then because the nuns had their heads bowed in prayer I was able to slip over the fence and shimmy up the tree (it was bent at an angle above the statue, like an old Cypress). Then I inched out on a branch above the sisters without spilling a drop of beer from the pitcher. I was prouder of that than the nuns not detecting my presence (though I was sure the Mother Superior glanced up once or twice).

Now came the hard part. The statue had a two-foot-wide platform and my plan was to drop onto the front of it from my seven-foot perch in the tree, appearing as a sudden, monstrous apparition to the nuns.

Without spilling any beer, of course. I don't know what I was saving it for, and it hardly mattered once I was falling through the air, because just before I hit the statue I realized it wasn't concrete but some kind of papier-mâché construction. So my 260 pounds went straight through the platform and stuck there, toppling me, the statue and my now airborne pitcher down the hill. I rolled into the Mother Superior as I had Frankowitz a couple months before, sending her sailing over my head before I smacked into a second nun.

And the screaming … I'd never heard such carrying on and all I wanted was to have a conversation with the ladies. I extricated my feet from the smashed statue, stumbled upright.

"Now sisters!" I yelled, spinning around and grabbing drunkenly at individual nuns, trying to get somebody to listen to me, "I want to know why you think an omniscient entity needs supplicants!? Huh? He knows everything, He sees everything, what the hell does He want with you grovelers!?"

My audience herded themselves together, still caterwauling into the night, then made a sudden break for the chalet. I let them have a head start, figuring I could at least catch a fat one before they reached the door, but I underestimated what I must have looked like, dropping out of a tree all in black like that. Those nuns were *panicked* and by the time I caught up and stumbled onto the porch the last one had slammed the door behind her. It was a flimsy thing with glass panes so I smashed through one with my fist, reached in and undid the lock as the nuns scurried for their lives. It was quite a scene, a snapshot for a hedonist's headstone, and I paused just a moment to soak it all in.

Then I took three long strides and grabbed the heel of a nun burrowing beneath a couch. Had dragged her shrieking, convulsing frame into the middle of the room, ready to continue our "conversation," when I heard a gravely voice above me:

"HEY ASSHOLE! WHAT THE HELL'S GOING ON HERE?"

I looked up the winding stairway, saw it was the old guard from earlier in the day. He was dressed in pajamas and slamming shells into his shotgun.

I went from shithoused to sober in a flash. Looked down at my hands – soaked in blood and wrapped around that nun's ankle – and thought, *Sweet Baby Jesus, High … what the fuck are you doing!?*

I made record time sprinting from the chalet and down the steps. Unfortunately I was still ten yards from the fence line when the old watchman stumbled onto the porch.

"STOP BIG BOY!" he yelled. "STOP OR I'LL SHOOT!"

I lowered my head and tried a John Wayne in the *Sands of Iwo Jima* deal, bending low and crisscrossing back and forth in the clearing. I don't know if the comical nature of it made the old guy miss or he was just a lousy shot, but the first barrel took out part of the fence to my right and the buckshot from the second came so close to my head that – at least on acid – I swore I could *smell* it going by.

Then I was over the fence and into the woods, smashing ahead through trees and underbrush, oblivious to the branches smacking my face. When I felt I was a safe distance away I leaned against a redwood and gasped for air, letting the LSD/alcohol/adrenaline rush play itself out. Slowly, as my breathing returned to normal, I convinced myself that I'd imagined the whole incident or, alternatively, that it was simply

238

a prank gone awry. By the time I returned to the crowded party site, in fact, I was totally at peace with all religions.

Leave it to DeBola, Sampson and Hale to dampen my magnanimity. The three of them surrounded me while I filled a pitcher at a keg.

"Hey High!" said Tony. "We just heard gunfire in the woods! You know anything about that?"

"Come on," I said, taking a gulp from the pitcher, "I've never fired a gun in my life."

"No, *at* you," said Hale. "Someone shooting *at* you."

"Why do you guys always think the worst of me?" I asked.

"Just *look* at yourself," said Sampson. "How'd you cut your hand like that?"

I glanced down at my bloodied right fist. I wasn't sure on the acid, but judging by the cuts – and the scars that are still there today – it could have used some stitches.

But then something else came up and the matter was forgotten by all. There had to be two hundred revelers in the clearing and I was as surprised as any of them when – a half hour later, high above us on the winding switchback road that led down to the property – there came a procession of flashing red lights.

"HOLY SHIT IT'S THE PIGS!" yelled Gumbo.

Everybody started running but there was nowhere to go, it was either plunge into the river or the pitch-black woods. The air was thick with pot smoke, half the people drinking weren't twenty-one and virtually all of them were tripping on one substance or another. When they realized they couldn't hide they grudgingly migrated to the bonfire in the center of the clearing, either gulping their extra drugs or tossing them into the bushes.

The three police cars pulled into the east side of the clearing and the cops stepped out. They were led by a chubby, stern-looking character who must have been the chief. The officers slipped into the crowd while he stepped forward and looked us over. It was so quiet that all you could hear was the crackling of the fire.

"Listen up!" he said finally. "We're looking for someone from this very party site. He's about six-and-a-half feet tall, dressed all in black and wearing a cowboy hat."

I was standing way in the back with Hale and DeBola, and they both immediately looked at me.

"What?" I said.

"*What* is right!" swore Tony under his breath. "What the fuck did you do this time?"

"*Me?*"

"Who do you think they're looking for!" said Hale. "Johnny Cash!?"

Then it hit me ... that *was* me the chief was describing. As if to be sure I understood, Gumbo stepped forth from the crowd. "Well gee, officer," he said, "what did this big guy *do?*"

"Well, we think he tried to rape some nuns."

This was a jaded, dissolute Bay Area crowd, but even they reacted to that charge. Slowly, their stoned faces grim with resentment, they turned to look at me. The officers followed their gaze and the nearest one sidled up, slid my hands behind my back and slapped on the cuffs.

Dark Shadows my ass! I thought. Where was Barnabas when I needed him?

I've watched dozens of my friends' children grow up and whenever I query them as to why their kids (particularly their sons) are such strait-laced Dudley Do-Right types, they remind me about the "Zero Tolerance" era we live in. How the smallest, most innocent infraction can result in censorship and/or punishment now.

While as baby boomers we got away with damn near everything, even (ostensibly) trying to rape nuns. No one at the river float that night – myself included – seems to know what happened after the cops handcuffed me. We're all in agreement that I was dragged away, and I vaguely recall sitting in the back of the chief's car as we exited the clearing, but that's it. The next thing I knew DeBola found me in the cab of his truck the next morning. Did I convince the cops and nuns it was all a drunken prank gone terribly wrong? Was my good fortune so incredible that I even evaded the consequences of this outrageous act? Hell, was I having *delayed* blackouts now? I know I'd brought a hundred dollars with me and that was gone, so perhaps I'd paid some damages and been dropped off in the early a.m.

It wasn't really important. What was clear is that no one at the float was glad to see me, particularly the lightweights who'd swallowed their drugs in a panic the night before, or those who still believed

I'd raped some sisters. Such open hostility *might* have mattered if I weren't so hungover, but as it was I was lucky to simply float down the river without drowning. After Tony had driven us back to Arcata I mulled the matter over and it was evident that my alcoholic behavior had passed into a realm rife with danger and madness. If it hadn't been for the mollifying action of the acid that night ... who knows what might have happened.

So I decided it was a good time to give up the pretense of writing – finally admitting I was better *acting* like an author than actually producing the work – and return to school. Maybe take a dozen credits or so, get a nice, quiet work-study job, try to limit the hard drinking to weekends. The problem was finding a school that would have me. The first place I tried was Lower Columbia College, the junior college I'd attended on the basketball scholarship. I gradually developed a kinship over the phone with Dick Kent, the Director of Financial Aid, and after looking at my transcripts he offered me an Economic Opportunity Grant (still available to white guys in 1968) and a job in the college typing pool.

Three weeks later I boarded a Greyhound for Longview. I remember two Arcata friends – Crazy Reyes and Mama Roux, both of them long dead now – jumping on the bus at the last moment to bring me a present.

It was a pint of *Early Times*. I drank it after dark in the back of the bus, watching California disappear behind me.

I went to a fellow grower's house last week to test a *Northern Lights No. 5* and *Apollo 11* cross he'd grown (he's a Tea Party character and doesn't smoke dope himself). I call the guy "Harry Potter" because his masterly touch with plants goes beyond green thumbdom to pure and simple magic. I've been in dozens of grow rooms in my time and have looked at hundreds more in *High Times* and *Cannabis Culture* photos but I have never seen indoor plants as lush and thick as Harry's. I can create a hybrid and grow it out, for instance, and maybe manage 1-1/4 ounces dry weight when it's done; I give Harry a cutting of the same plant and he'll get 2-1/2 to 3 ounces in the same period of time. This depressed me to no end until one afternoon I walked into his back yard.

It was late August and there before me was a science fiction tomato plant. A single *Early Girl* variety that sat in a 10' by 15' planter and covered every inch of the space with giant, juicy red globes that spilled over the sides and onto the lawn. I tiptoed around it in awe. I grow tomatoes myself, as do most of my friends in Portland, and you could have fit *all* our plants inside that one box. I made my way to the end of it, clawed through the steamy, thick vegetation and saw that the stalk of the plant was nearly a foot in diameter.

Just then Harry strolled out of the house.

"Holy shit!" I said. "When did you plant this monster?"

"Oh, about three months ago," he replied. "But if you think that one's big, you shoulda seen last year's."

It was strictly *Ripley's Believe It Or Not* stuff … if he hadn't been a pot grower he could have been the human interest piece on every newscast in the country. What a relief to know that he – like his plants – was simply a freak of nature, that somewhere in his placid, tidy nature was a vibe that made plants thrive.

Along with better living through chemistry, of course. Harry grows his pot hydroponically, so the roots are bathed in chemicals twenty-four hours a day. Unlike my organic stuff, which smokes evenly, doesn't burn your eyes with nitrates and leaves no toxic burn in the back of your throat, Harry's bud (like most indoor pot) is about as tasty as your car's exhaust pipe. I asked him once if this bothered him any.

"Why would it?" he said. "I don't smoke it."

Spoken like a true Republican.

In September of 2001 I spent two weeks in Amsterdam with my friend Elaine. It was my eighth visit there (I usually stayed at an old English buddy's apartment) and probably my last. Not only did I feel I'd smoked all the coffee shop varieties at least twice, but I was so familiar with the city I'd lost interest in exploring it. The Dutch are a brisk, efficient people with extraordinary vitality (even their flowers radiate energy and well-being) but no one ever accused them of being friendly bastards. This was fine – I was over there getting high and having a good time, so personal invincibility was preferable – but after a decade of Northern European visits I felt the socialism practiced there bred flatliners: you'd meet selected natives, sit down and talk to them, share a joint or a drink and the more you learned about their lives the less it seemed like anything had ever happened to them.

I prefer some good ol' American lunacy myself. We've no safety net here so it barely matters whether you were born with a silver spoon in your mouth or nothing at all ... by the time you're done your life's been a screaming roller coaster compared to the average socialist citizen.

So I was actually relieved when we boarded a Continental Jet for home. We had seats in the back of the plane and left early in the morning for the Newark, New Jersey airport. Elaine had the window seat and I was on the aisle (a vain attempt to stretch my legs). When we'd been airborne for five hours I looked up at the little video screen that tracked our flight.

"All right," I said, "we're nearly halfway there! I'm not flying this far again, goddamn it. I get irritable as hell in these cramped little seats."

Elaine began to speak but was interrupted by the squawk of the captain's voice over the intercom:

"Attention, passengers. I am sorry to inform you that at this time there have been seven hijackings of United States commercial airliners. All air space over America has been closed until further notice. We will give you more information as we receive it but in the meantime we are turning this flight around and heading back to Amsterdam. We thank you for your patience and understanding during this emergency."

What!!??? "No way!" I yelled, jumping into the aisle and waving my arms. "Let Castro have the goddamned planes ... keep this baby headed for Newark!!"

A Dutch flight attendant rushed over and hustled me back to my seat. I was furious. The thought of sitting all that time with my knees under my chin for nothing – much less doing it *again* – was simply inconceivable.

So to be sure I added some guilt to my selfishness I was the first person that flight attendant came to when the crew learned details of the tragedy.

"Sir," she said, "apparently there were four planes hijacked by Arab terrorists. Two of them flew into the World Trade Center Towers in New York City, another hit the Pentagon and a fourth is unaccounted for. It's likely that thousands of people have died."

The Pentagon? Arab terrorists? So we were at *war* now? I heard a sob and looked over at Elaine, who'd burst into tears at the thought of all those innocent dead.

Great, I thought ... *the Empath and the Asshole*. I slunk down in my seat, started giving Arab-looking passengers the once over.

What to say about my junior college days? I'd end up at Lower Columbia a couple more times over the years, primarily because wherever I was and whatever I was doing Dick Kent would give me another chance. To vindicate his faith in me I always felt I should last at least one term and get a 4.0 grade average in the process. This wasn't as easy as it sounds (the staying through an entire term part, I mean). The grades themselves were little problem because I had the same routine in any class I was ever in, i.e., I took copious notes at lectures, then came home afterwards and typed them up in outline form. By then they were *mine*, even when I was drinking.

Three straight months of World Literature, Latin America History, Philosophy of Ethics and Physiology/Anatomy could seem like a prison stretch in that town, though. Fortunately I was kind of partial to its pulp mill grayness and sulphur stench. The reek was strongest late at night, when clouds held it low above the city. I lived in a $30-a-month room atop a paint store on Commerce Street and I liked to sit in the dark with my window open, sucking in the airborne poisons. There was a poignant melancholia to it all, a bit of a season-in-hell feel, and living inside a fart wasn't so bad when there was nothing happening, anyway. I had a couple of friends I saw on weekends and an older student separated from her husband who would fuck me standing up in the apartment house's hallway as long as I didn't kiss her. (We were out there, in a little enclave near the exit door, because she'd glimpsed the inside of my apartment; she probably still talks about it to the duffer she's doing now.)

Because that place on Commerce Street was the first of my "beer can bed" flats. When you opened the door to the apartment – which was essentially a large room with a bathroom and kitchen off to the side – you looked out on an ocean of beer cans and bottles that covered every square inch of the floor. Eventually, after several months, the only thing visible *other* than the empties was the mattress in the center of the room. That's where I lived, typing on a long board that rested atop mounds of cans on either side. I wouldn't drink while I was studying – which was generally late in the afternoon – and only drank before class in the morning if I had to. In between I had an easy typing pool job while saving the suds for the night time. This was my compromise: instead of confining the drinking to weekends I limited myself to beer. Enough of it to fill the room with empties, so when the neon *Hiller Paint* sign outside my window blinked red, it flashed pink off the silver cans. I never had a television or a phone and managed to lose every radio under the empties. My clothes consisted of two sets of flannel shirts and two pairs of jeans that I wore beneath the same old Levi jacket. I'd never been partial to drawers so I stuffed my clean underwear in a canvas bag and used it as a pillow. The dirty stuff … well, most of that went the way of the radios.

There were probably many problems with this mode of living but only two stand out. One was crawling to the bathroom in the middle of the night atop that sharp and noisy clutter. (I learned to make a path from flattened cans alone, then tried to keep it clear.)

The second issue was the odor. Normally the stench of the town offset it but sometimes, on a warm day when the wind drafted the sulphur reek north of the city, you could tell it was pretty vinegary in there. I tried to empty the containers before flinging them to a likely spot but it was evident I'd failed to finish and/or overturn my share. Plus there were discarded fast food bags and oily meat wrappers in the mix because I never cooked and after awhile you couldn't see the refrigerator and stove, anyway. (I brought home ice with my six-packs and put them in a cooler next to the mattress.)

It was the sort of crude but simple life that I liked to think set me apart from your average college student of the time or, for that matter, from any but the most execrable of bottom feeders. It felt so natural, in fact, that I only thought about it when I brought someone home and he or she took a look around and bolted.

By the time Thanksgiving arrived I'd pretty much stopped socializing. Then I received an envelope from Ned Gumbo in the mail. Opened it to the folded front page of *The San Mateo Times*. He'd scribbled, "Don't blame yourself, High!" above the bold headline:

MADMAN IN SHOOTOUT WITH POLICE!

Beneath it was a photo of Lonesome Louie Houston, clad only in shorts, flying spread-eagled through the air with a rifle in his hand and a plume of smoke at his back. He had a strange, startled look on his face, as if he'd just discovered he was Rocket Man.

No such luck, however. Apparently he'd shot out the windows of his neighbor's house in San Mateo, then demanded to talk to Mayor Alioto or Lyndon B. Johnson. He was speaking, he said, "from my Total Environment Room," where he was intent on killing himself if his demands weren't met. There was some gunfire exchanged, then the cops kicked in the back door while Louie was standing at the front one and shot him in the back with a tear gas grenade. He was propelled off the porch and onto the lawn, where he was dragged off to the Atascadero State Hospital for the Criminally Insane.

Jesus, I thought, *who could have imagined that the bus jump was only a warmup? Or that the King of the Cynics would involve politicians in his latest suicide attempt?* I toasted my old buddy as the beer cans blinked pink in the dark. Hoped that when they pumped him full of Thorazine he'd remember the good old days in Mexico.

When the fall term ended at Lower Columbia I bought a bottle of whiskey for warmth, walked out to the highway and started hitching south. I'd heard Gumbo was back in the cottage and thought he'd appreciate me spending the Christmas vacation with him. If he didn't … tough luck. (I hadn't forgotten the "one-pint-a-day" betrayal; Louie might have been in a decent mental ward by then if it weren't for Ned.) I made it down in about twenty-four hours and, just as I'd anticipated, Gumbo not only refused me lodging but tried to lock me out of the cottage at night. I took great delight in foiling his ploys so if I didn't wake him with my snoring he'd at least find me passed out next to the fireplace in the morning.

And there was a lot of passing out that sordid Christmas season, culminating in the Sunday afternoon Niner games. They were still playing at Kezar Stadium at the time and Gumbo and some other guys had a block of season tickets. We'd get together at eight Sunday morning to drink gin fizzes and by eleven o'clock – when we'd leave for the game, twelve of us squeezed into a couple cars – the only

251

reason we weren't killed is there was too much traffic on the road.

Plus most of the fans seemed as drunk as we were, and if not they would be by halftime. (I'd venture to say that when the Niners played at Kezar in the late 60s the fans in the stands constituted as many psychotically shithoused people as have ever gathered for a sporting event in the U.S.) The stadium seats were hard benches and banked steeply up from the field, so if you sat as high as we did you took your life in your hands trying to navigate the long, steep steps to the bathrooms. By the third quarter many men no longer bothered, simply pissing where they sat so long streams of urine poured into the lower rows.

It was a freakish alcoholic scene and the reason I took umbrage at Ned and the others claiming I was the worst rummy there. This culminated in the Philadelphia Eagles game shortly before Christmas that year. I was glad to see 1968 fading into the books and admittedly drank my gin fizzes a little fast that morning and yes, I did throw up on the shirt collar of the stranger in front of me, sparking a vicious brawl that nearly got us jailed, and there was, of course, the halftime hit of mescaline in a vain attempt to revive myself but that, as always, was no excuse for Gumbo's behavior.

Because when I came to after the game I was outside the stadium and Ned's voice was the first thing I heard. That was never a good sign but the way I felt was even worse. And why was I rocking back and forth? Why couldn't I move my body?

I shook my head and looked down. Somehow my friends had squeezed my now 280 pounds into a rickety metal shopping cart – and I mean *squeezed*, my hands and arms were pinned at my sides and my knees were under my chin – and I was being pushed along the sidewalk by Big Mac and Gumbo. I tried to talk but I was so cotton-mouthed I gagged instead.

In the meanwhile Ned's irritating voice droned on and on and on. It was obvious that he and Mac were very shitfaced:

"This sonofabitch gives drinking a bad name, Mac!" whined Gumbo. "That guy he threw up on was so big he coulda *played* for the Niners!"

"Yeah, Ned," slurred Mac, "but we still can't do what you're planning."

"Come on, man ... High's got more lives than a cockroach! You can't fuckin' kill him!"

I didn't like the sound of *that*. "Wha ... wha ... what's that?" I croaked, trying to lean my head back. "What're ya gonna do ... Gumbo?"

Ned gave his best, turd-sucking laugh. "So you're awake now, Wilson?" he crowed. "That's even better. Speaking for all your *ex*-friends let me tell you how much we enjoyed having to drag your fat ass out of the stadium! If it weren't for Big Mac finding this shopping cart we'd have left you in the park!"

"You ... should have," I moaned. Damn! That mescaline had been a bad idea. "Stop the cart and let me out, Ned!"

"Relax, Wilson," said Big Mac, "we're almost to the car."

The car? What had we driven to the game? Oh yeah, Ned's prized '56 DeSoto. I remember we'd parked it at the bottom of one of those steep San Francisco hills. Had I thrown up on it, too?

"Well, well," said Gumbo as we came over a rise, "there's the DeSoto right below us, High. You see it all right?"

"Uh huh, Ned, sure. Now let me out of here. You'll lose control of the cart on a street this steep."

"Lose control?" said Ned menacingly, and just like with the earache incident the year before I heard some scuffling noises behind me, a feeble protest from Big Mac, then the cart was on the edge of the hill and picking up speed. "YOU MEAN LIKE THIS, HIGH!?" yelled Gumbo. "IS THIS THE KIND OF LOSING CONTROL YOU'RE TALKIN' ABOUT YOU FUCKIN' ASSHOLE!?"

And then he shoved me down the hill.

Until I started this memoir I had no idea how much of 1968 I spent plunging from heights, but nothing in my experience before or since – and likely the ten lifetimes after this one – will ever equal the terror I felt speeding down that steep, bumpy street in a shopping cart, unable to move anything but my mouth.

And I'm talking the first two seconds only, because that's all I remember:

"AAaaaAAAaaGGGGgggGGGgggHHHhhhhhHHHhhhh!!!!!"

According to Big Mac I screamed right up to the moment the cart rammed a sports car on the curb halfway down, popping me into the air like a cannonball. I flew over the sidewalk, slashed through some thick bushes (which probably saved my life by slowing me down) and finally rammed headfirst into a stucco wall.

Mac explained this to me when I woke on Gumbo's couch four hours later. Ned himself was long gone, off to a Christmas in the Sierras with his parents. It was a reasonable retreat on his part: he knew "one pint a day" had melded into "attempted murder" and I'd be off to Longview by the time he returned.

But I'd be back for the little monkey … he could count on that.

POOR   OKAY   GOOD   VERY GOOD   EXCELLENT

From 2002 to 2004 I went north to Vancouver, British Colombia for three straight *Tokers Bowls*. These were four-day pot judging events put on by Mark Emery and his seed company. (There won't be any more of them: in 2006 Emery was arrested by the DEA and is doing a five-year stretch somewhere in the states). Essentially you paid $500 (before airfare and hotel) for twenty-four different kinds of buds and several days of marijuana-related activities, culminating in the Sunday selection of the "best in show" bud.

What made these particular judgings unique is the limited number of judges – 200 only, as opposed to the 1,500 to 2,000 at the Cannabis Cup in Amsterdam – and the hospitality of your Canadian hosts. For some bizarre reason (perhaps because B.C. is considered the "California of Canada"), they actually *like* Americans up there. So unlike the Amsterdam Cup that I attended in '95 (where the only thing you were given for your money was a judge's badge), from the moment you landed in Canada Emery and his gang worked overtime to make you welcome. Registration was smooth, you were handed a hemp bag full of rolling papers, pot postcards, lighters and matches, then a beautiful hand-blown glass pipe and "warmup buds" to last you until the two dozen contest buds – individual nugs encased in plastic with a letter printed on them – were hand-delivered to your hotel room (in a "Tokers Bowl" bowl, no less).

For the next three days you took over restaurants and cruise ships and hotels for such concentrated pot burnings that the smoke was thicker than fog. With twenty-four buds to judge in seventy-two hours the trick would seem to be testing eight buds a day over the three-day period. Except I liked to save Sunday mornings for a smoke out of the best varieties, so that left sixty hours, and when you factored in sleeping and eating and traveling and spaciness so extreme you *forget* to smoke, you're really talking about testing two dozen buds (nearly an ounce of pot) in a day and a half.

And it's not a wine tasting, of course. You're not swirling the smoke around in your mouth, then politely blowing it out. No, you're sucking 'til your eyes bulge, trying to *incinerate* the bud in pipes and bongs and cigars. I'd profile the average *Bowl* judge, for instance, as a thirty-five-year-old guy from Buttfuck, Minnesota who rarely sees *two* good buds a year, much less twenty-four great ones at once. This is pot he can't take back to the states and he's paid $500 for it so he's going to smoke every goddamn gram of it *plus* any other bud or hash he can get his hands on and fuck the consequences. (The irony being that they're often fleeing their local stateside weed because "you have to smoke it all day and night to get high.")

The only thing I'd change about the event is the music. Wherever we went for the evening there'd always be some loud rock, reggae or hip hop band playing, as if it were a drinking contest instead of a pot judging. So a group would take the stage, beseech a bunch of stoners who didn't know they were there to rock out, then start playing and – if it were early enough in the evening – maybe one couple would sway around the dance floor for a set or two before collapsing back in their seats.

Let me give you an example of some of *Tokers Bowl II's* contest entries, for instance, and consider how much dancing you'd be doing after smoking twelve of these a day:

> Dutch Treat
> Great White Shark

Rene
Sweet Tooth
Purple Skunk
Ultimate Indica
Blue God
Five-O
Hashplant
Mighty Mite
Shiskaberry
Honeypot
Burmese
Chronic
Blueberry

Even a hardened grower is lucky to be upright after that menu, much less dancing (assuming one could find a female to dance with). Stranger yet, at the third annual event they had magicians who traveled from table to table doing card tricks. It was like sleight-of-hand for blind people.

And if the contest pot didn't get you high enough Mark Emery (a very generous, very personable guy) would come around with selections from his personal stash. Or, more devastating yet, someone would pass you a bong of bubble hash. A couple of lungfuls of that stuff and you could kiss discrimination good-bye.

(Bubble hash – for those who don't know – is basically made by wrapping one vinyl bag around the inside of a five-gallon bucket, followed by another four bags – one on top of the other – with various sizes of mesh on their bottoms (they're stacked smallest to largest gauge). Then a pile of "shake" (small buds and leaf) is thrown in, and the balance of the bucket is filled with ice and water and blended with a mixer for twenty minutes. The result – as each bag is lifted and the water drained off – is a wafer of trichomes (resin) on the bottom. The lower you go, the better the grade of hash. It's called "bubble hash" because when laid on top of pot and lit, it *bubbles down* into the weed.)

I'm not much of a hash fan myself, believing that the difference between pot and hash is the difference between flying and floating. I also took the judging of the twenty-four entries seriously. (It's why I was there, of course, looking for something – hell, anything – that'd ratchet up the highs.) First I'd roll each bud into a joint and mark it with its individual letter, carefully noting its resin, density, general appearance and bouquet. Then I'd light it and assess relative harshness and taste before waiting ten minutes or so for the high to kick in. A positive entry in my judge's notebook might look like this:

V. Striking dark green and blue hues; thick, "chunky monkey" bud; classic fruity bouquet with slight ammonia backbite and even matte of resin. Something of a moderate choker (slightly hashy), with a smooth, climber high that hints at sativa in the line and just misses.   4.5

The judging was done on a scale of 1 (poor) to 5 (excellent). At first I thought this an unusually broad criteria – how much weight should I give to taste and bouquet, for instance, as opposed to appearance and high? – but then I thought about it some more and realized there's nothing that evokes the K.I.S.S. principle ("keep it simple, stupid") like a pot judging.

Most of my fellow judges took this literally. They were okay for the first couple hours or so, maybe even the first day, when it was still easy to make discernible notes, but after that their tally sheets devolved into scribbles on napkins.

There's some merit to this approach: you don't want to be carrying *Bowl* notes around if busted by the local gendarmes. The Vancouver cops are reasonable about cannabis usage but an international pot judging in their neighborhood is a bit much. So the *Tokers Bowls* were basically underground affairs (none of the judges were told where to meet each day until the last possible minute). In 2003 a couple from Texas were popped smoking contest bud in their car and not only did the police arrest them but they found the girl's tally sheet. Unfortunately for her, she made the kind of detailed notes I do. She later described sitting in her cell, listening through the bars as the cops in the squad room read her stuff out loud:

"Get this: 'Induces "nostril flare" from its hydroponic burn!' NOSTRIL FLARE ... can you believe it!?"

"How about this one: 'Minty with a hint of lemon in its thick resin – makes a GREASY CHICKEN kind of joint!'"

Big Mountie yuks all around. And the most interesting part of my fellow judges' *seeming* confusion is that when it came time to vote we all pretty much agreed on what was the best and worst pot. It was the question most often asked by friends when I returned, in fact, i.e., how can you tell one high from another when you're that fucked up to begin with?

It's like any sport I told them: you gotta practice.

When the *Bowls* were over it didn't take long for reality to set in, though. You'd stroll through the departures door at the Vancouver, British Colombia airport and find yourself elbow-to-elbow with GI's and German shepherds. If one of the dogs sniffed you, then immediately sat down, it meant you smelled of pot. This was not a debatable, legal conclusion and the dog wasn't there to set you up *unless you lied about smoking*. Then the inference was you had something to hide and your bags and person would likely be searched.

This was not a problem for me. I saw my fellow Americans' stuff being pawed over and had a ready answer when my dog's handler asked if I'd smoked weed during my stay:

"Every possible second," I told him, and was passed right through.

I repeated that the second year, then in 2004 there were no soldiers around and I figured I'd sail through customs without a hitch.

Unfortunately they knew the dates of my visit corresponded with the *Bowl* so the agents tore through my satchel and suitcase with a vengeance. It was irritating but I wasn't worried ... I'd packed and repacked those bags to make sure none of the contest pot made the trip south with me. After customs I was passed onto the security checkpoint and had my bags rifled again because the x-ray machine spotted mustache scissors in my medicine kit. Finally I straggle up to the boarding gate, wait in line with my boarding pass only to be picked for the *airline's* random luggage check!

By then I was pissed but what can you do? I flew home, my friend Elaine picked me up and dropped me off at my house, and when I reached the front porch I set down my canvas satchel, unzipped its long front pocket and reached for my car keys.

I pulled them out all right, along with a fat green contest bud (marked "B"), still glistening in its plastic baggie. All three agents pawed through that same pocket and here I make a blind stab and draw the dope out immediately.

It was awhile before I breathed again. I'd like to be grateful for this oddly selective luck of mine – the kind that keeps a body out of jail while postponing the grave – but I've never known who to thank.

I hitchhiked back to Longview on the first day of 1969. (With the way I looked and felt after my alcoholic Christmas it took nearly forty-eight hours.) The first thing I did when I hit town was pick up my $300 Economic Opportunity Grant at the financial aid office. I cashed it, paid the landlord her $30 for the month of January and was standing at my apartment door, key in the lock, when I looked up to see a uniformed policeman walking down the hallway.

"Are you Wilson High?" he asked.

Jesus, I thought ... *I can't have done anything yet, I just got here.* I quickly pulled the key out of the lock and pocketed it; no matter what came down, my situation would not be improved by the cop seeing my beer can bed.

"Yeah," I said, "I'm Wilson High. What's up?"

The officer stopped in front of me and handed me a sheath of checks from a folder he was carrying. "This is the third time I've come by here looking for you, Mr. High," he said. "Did you write these personal checks to Ray's Market?"

I leafed through them. They were mine all right, I just didn't remember writing so goddamned *many!* Which wasn't half as disturbing as the red INSUFFICIENT FUNDS stamp on each of them.

"Yeah," I sighed, handing them back to the cop, "they're mine."

"And you realize, Mr. High," he said, "that kiting checks is a felony?"

Actually I didn't; all of a sudden the calamitous year behind me was looking a lot better. "Well, no," I said, "and I've never written a bad one before, officer. Hell, I don't remember writing most of those, me being an alkie and all."

"That's no excuse, Mr. High."

"To say the least."

"I'll tell you what. You give me the $187 you owe the market for the checks and penalties, and I'll take the money to Ray and we'll call the whole thing square."

Part of me ... just for a moment ... mulled over who was doing who a favor here and why? (A *cop* to strong-arm deadbeats? Pay up or go to jail? This was small-town bill collecting at its best.) Mainly, though, I was just embarrassed. I wasn't a thief for chrissakes. I was a drunk who'd take handouts from a Lonesome Louie or the state – and maybe drink more of Gumbo's liquor stash than I should – but I tried not to steal from people. I dug the $187 out of the grant stash, exchanged it for the wad of checks and a lecture. Watched the cop walk away as I tabulated my remaining bills versus the amount of money left in my hand and realized, to my growing horror, that my alcohol budget for the rest of the month amounted to three-and-a-half bucks.

Which I promptly spent on a six-pack and a package of baloney. I sat drinking and eating them as the sun set on my sea of cans. I remember the night vividly because I knew it was time for the Hard Things, for seeing if I actually had what it took to quit drinking. It seemed like a ridiculous matter to contemplate at twenty-one, but the belligerence and near-death experiences of the past year were starting to wear on me. Throw in bad checks written in blackouts and I was headed for the grave, the madhouse or jail, maybe all three.

When I see people I haven't seen in years and they marvel that I'm still alive, much less that I ever quit drinking, I like to tell them something they can smirk about later, i.e., "I just wasn't self-destructive enough."

Oddly enough I mean it: I've always wanted to live. I wasn't sure I *would* under the circumstances – and I realize now, 45 years later, that tons of dumb luck is the only reason I did – but all through the psychedelics, the uppers, the downers, the booze, the pot and the d.t.'s, my brain was being protective of me.

This notion, absurd on the face of it, is why those old friends (much like the reader) can afford to smirk. Yet if it weren't true, why was I being *forced* to consider sobriety at such a tender age? The deteriorating attitude and tolerance, the near fatalities and check kiting, these were incentives to quit; The Dread I felt before I drank in the morning ... that was the *reason*. I'd had the comas as a kid, panic attacks when I tried to do too much as a high school senior, plenty of bad acid and even worse Methedrine ... but throw them all together and they were barely a warmup for what woke me those hangover dawns.

Scared sober, in other words, is the only kind of sober I would ever be. If it hadn't been for the terror instituted by my brain, the early onset d.t.'s as opposed to the cottonmouth, headaches and nausea typical to a drinker my age, I wouldn't have been sitting there thinking about quitting. I liked the oblivion of alcohol WAY too much for that.

Plus I was broke and had a new term of school starting in that cold, creepy mill town ... what better time to hang up the bottle for awhile? Part of me even looked forward to the test: I couldn't remember the last time I'd gone two straight days without booze.

So I registered for my classes and things went pretty well for a week or so. That apartment was vaguely less comfortable but what the hell, there was less crawling across it to pee so I barely noticed the clutter. And there was no question I slept better once I was back on solid food and regular hours.

But then, inevitably, I got bored. I was ashamed to admit it even then; it seemed so pathetic that a bright guy with an inquisitive mind, presented with the myriad possibilities of the world around him, couldn't find a constructive way to amuse himself.

Ennui is the enemy. That was my mantra then and forty years later it not only hasn't changed, it's still kicking my ass. When I thought it more likely I'd levitate than stay sober I went to a pay phone and called Alcoholics Anonymous. I'd been given the number by my friendly small-town banker, who like the cop was disappointed by my check writing habits. I figured I'd use it sooner or later and was curious about anything that might help.

So an hour later I'm sitting in a coffee shop with my potential sponsor, Ralph X. He was a pale, fat, big-headed guy who used to be a teacher and jittered as he spoke. His hands, his lips ... there was a lot of wobbling going on and the coffee and cigarettes kept him amped. He listened to the quickest synopsis of my story I could manage, then started telling me about "one day at a time" and the Serenity Prayer and all the while I'm thinking, *Man, this guy needs a drink bad!*

He must have noticed my attention waning. "You know, Wilson," he said, motioning to the waitress to top off his coffee again, "I've never heard of a twenty-one-year-old seeking help before. It's really quite remarkable in someone who's barely the legal drinking age."

"I suppose. How old are you, Ralph?"

"Thirty-five. And I'm considered the young guy in the group."

"Really?"

"Those stories of yours ... I mean I'm not doubting them or anything, God forbid I'd never do that and that's the point ... drinking makes us do terrible things. But ... well, for someone your age you've lived a pretty ... eh, well, *exaggerated* life, shall we say?"

"You think I'm bullshitting you, don't you?"

"Oh no no, it's just …" He suddenly reached across the table and grabbed my elbow. "You know what I could have done with my life if I'd quit drinking at twenty-one, Wilson!?"

"Easy, Ralph," I said.

"Didn't you say your apartment was around here?"

"Right up the street."

"Let's go there and talk some more. You got any Coca-Cola?"

He bought a six-pack of Coke and we climbed the stairs to my apartment above the paint store. As I was opening the door I apologized beforehand for the state of the place.

"I mean there's some cans spread around, stuff like that," I said.

Ralph scoffed. "Don't worry about it, Wilson," he said. "I'm sure I've seen worse."

I shrugged and opened the door just far enough that I could climb over the high wall of cans. Then I slid down to the mattress in the center and waited for Ralph.

It was some time before his big head poked over the pile in the doorway. "Oh my God," he was saying. "Oh my God …"

"So what do you think, Ralph?" I asked, yelling over the clatter of cans as he struggled for a foothold. "Am I an *AA* kind of guy?"

"The meeting's at seven sharp!"

**THOMAS WOLFE
(1900-1938)**

Alcoholics Anonymous had been an inevitability in my life for years and that first meeting made it worth the wait. It was held in a large room at a local church and there must have been thirty people there, most of them male, middle-aged mill workers (the exceptions being Ralph and Dan X. – the city editor at the local newspaper – and his wife).

But other than the stories the most intriguing part to me was the amount of coffee and cigarettes consumed. I remember leaning against the wall at the 1995 Cannabis Cup in Amsterdam and a producer for *60*

Minutes asking me how I could stand all the smoke in the room.

"Obviously," I said, "you've never been to an AA meeting."

They're probably all non-smoking gigs by now, but back in 1969 there was still no national panic about cigarettes or, for that matter, alarmist articles in the media about the dangers of caffeine.

Not that either would have made much difference to those Longview rummies. Like me they'd been fucked on the booze deal so they were going to work that addict Jones any way they could. We sat in a circle of folding chairs as one after another of them shared stories from their drinking days. I couldn't remember when I'd laughed so hard and would have been having a high old time if it weren't for that wife of Dan X's. Whenever I looked at her she'd be staring back at me with the oddest expression on her face, as if she were vaguely terrified of me. It was pretty disconcerting (looking as bad as I did I was used to women ignoring me), but then it was my turn to speak and I jumped up and told the tale of my night with the nuns in Guerneville. Ralph had urged me to tell everyone why I'd come to AA, and if that yarn didn't sum it up nothing would.

It must have worked – well, the LSD part got a lot of blank stares – because everyone greeted me effusively afterwards and exclaimed over how wonderful it was that a young person was seeking help. I was a real inspiration they said, a shining beacon in the dark alkie hell.

And all I could think as I shook their hands was: I want a long shitfaced ride like you had, buddy, and you and you and you.

Then it was only me, Dan X. and his wife. Ralph had introduced me to him before the meeting and he seemed like a nice enough guy. Now that he had the wife with him, though, he looked a little nervous.

"Colorful story you told there, Wilson," he said. "And don't let the 'higher power' part of AA fool you. You can surrender yourself to whatever power you want."

"As long as it isn't booze."

"Ha ha … that's right." About then his wife, still doing her seeing-a-ghost act, elbowed him in the ribs. "Oh, and Wilson … this is my wife Katie Sue."

"Pleased to meet you," I said, but when I took her hand she jumped as if shocked.

"You know," she said, gasping, "I bet you had brain fever as a boy!"

"Huh?"

"A brain fever! Did you have one as a child?"

"Well, actually," I said, "I had two of them."

"Aha!" she exclaimed. "I knew it!"

I turned to Dan and chuckled. "Is this part of the AA deal?" I asked. "You bring your wife along for fortune telling?"

"Eh, no," he mumbled, "not exactly."

"And you say you're a writer," she continued. "I bet you write standing up, with the paper on top of the refrigerator."

I did like to type that way, at least before the advent of the beer can bed. "Now how'd you know that?" I asked.

"Because you're the reincarnation of Thomas Wolfe!"

I looked at Dan X. and he wasn't laughing. "Thomas Wolfe?" I said. "The 30s writer, *Look Homeward, Angel* and all that?"

"Exactly. Growing up in Asheville, North Carolina we lived right next door to the Wolfes and my sister and I used to sit with Tom all the time. I'll never forget the unusual way he used his body and hands to tell a story and it's *exactly* the way you do it! Why, being in the room with you was like seeing him in the flesh again. And not only that … he died of a brain fever!" She gasped and her voice caught in her throat as she lunged forward to hug me. "Oh Tom!" she wailed. "Are you back? Is it really you?"

I looked over her head at her husband and we exchanged the alkie eyebrow lift that indicated we could both use a stiff one right about then. He because of her and me because of the past life she'd picked for me.

I couldn't think of a writer I liked less than Thomas Wolfe. The guy was a total windbag.

If ol' Katie Sue saw me on the streets of Longview today she'd still think I was the reincarnation of Thomas Wolfe and I'd still be hoping she was wrong. I didn't mind the thought of having lived before … hell, I loved the idea … but if I'd done it as that hulking overwriter then being a drunk this go-round was my punishment: it was hard for me to read a paragraph of his stuff, much less a full page.

And I had more than enough problems in present time, starting with that tender age of mine. I represented the AA old timers' booze-wasted youth: like Ralph they looked at me and speculated on the lives they'd have led if *they'd* quit drinking at twenty-one.

Unfortunately for all I wasn't the torchbearer type; I was also no more likely than they'd been to pull off youthful abstinence. Maybe *less* so given that it was 1969. My fellow boomers had bulging eyeballs all across America and I'm sitting in mill town church rooms, listening to old drunks reminisce?

It was a nice try – and it wouldn't be my last – but it was simply too soon. I could feel my resolve eroding as the weeks and meetings slipped by, how "quitting forever" had gradually morphed into "giving my mind and body a rest." Plus the general AA message was little help because I couldn't understand what good it would do me (when it came time to sidle up to the bar) to know there were other addicts wrestling with the same temptation. This was sad, of course, but it wasn't comforting or helpful, nor was it anymore useful to my sobriety than turning my life over to some fantastical "higher power."

But the idea of staying sober "one day at a time" … now that I liked, that I could use and did. It's what got me to the six-weeks-on-the-wagon mark, and when I felt myself hanging by my fingernails I decided dropping out of school and getting a job would lessen my overall stress.

Or maybe, subconsciously, I just wanted to earn enough to pay for the bender ahead. I found if I sat on that beer-can bed long enough – trying to dissect which of my devious alcoholic stratagems was really in play – I'd end up frozen with inertia.

So halfway into the winter term I dropped out of school. Hired on at a local pulp mill as the No. 2 Cleanup Man on graveyard shift. This entailed cleaning up different spills around the mill and driving the old dump truck when it filled with waste. It was a sleepwalker's kind of job and the relative solitude suited me.

271

I would have had more of it if I weren't as big as I was. I must have been quite a sight in my Levi jacket and overalls, a silly little hard hat perched atop my head: in a way, in fact, I was simply a fatter, hairier version of my volunteer fireman self.

Except now I was often covered with mud. This was an offshoot of my stubbornly walking to work every night, a rainy four mile trek from my downtown apartment. There were few sidewalks along the way and vehicles were treacherously close to me the last couple miles. These were basically fast-moving mill worker trucks that either didn't see me or, spotting me, swerved through puddles to spray my hippie ass. This irked me for awhile because it made the first hour of work ... until the mud on one side or another of me dried ... much harder to do.

But then I started drinking again and barely noticed. On that first fall from the wagon I initiated a pattern I'd repeat in the years ahead, i.e., I didn't really need an excuse, so I didn't pretend to have one. My only consideration was that there be nothing glamorous about the first pop of booze. So on a Saturday morning I went to a seedy lounge that opened at 6:00 a.m., studiously avoiding the faces of the other rummies as I gulped down a shot.

There's nothing worse than a "making up for lost time" bender. I shiver to remember that one, the way I'd forgotten all my AA buddies by 9:00 a.m. I recovered just enough to return to the mill on Monday, then worked hard at staying only slightly buzzed during the day – reading mystery novels and smoking local ragweed – before hitting taverns to drink "reasonable sums" at night. This was more doable than it sounds because of that four-mile walk. It was a cold, damp, *vicious* winter in Longview that year, and though it seems preposterous now, I never got around to buying rain gear, much less a decent overcoat. So there were many occasions when I stepped out of a downtown tavern at 10:30 p.m., saw the sleet blowing sideways on the street and thought, *Shit, I'll never get there this time, they'll find my frozen ass in a ditch.*

But I always made it. That's what I liked best about booze, of course … I'd try anything on it. What's more my size and appearance earned me the nickname "Animal." Which in turn helped disguise my drunkenness: nobody got close to me and they all assumed I was a hippie, not a rummy.

Then I jeopardized my disguise by coming in particularly soused one cold night in March. I was out sweeping wood chips beside the truck, leaning into the icy wind to keep myself upright, when the foreman found me, told me to go get the payloader (a small bulldozer) and clean up a chip spill under the chemical tanks.

This was excellent news. I liked operating the payloader and it was so noisy it'd keep me awake. I was halfway across the yard when the foreman called to me:

"And don't forget, Animal! The gas gauge is broken so you gotta eyeball the tank before you start up!"

"Yeah yeah," I yelled, "I got ya." I walked to the locker room first, sat down to take a crap and passed out on the toilet for twenty minutes. Came to even groggier than before and splashed cold water in my face to little effect. Finally lit a cigarette and headed out for the payloader. Somebody on swing shift had used it for the same job and I was halfway into the cab when I remembered to check the gas. I slid down, walked to the back, unscrewed the cap to stare into the tank.

Or eternity, perhaps, that being what I saw when the lit cigarette in my mouth ignited the fumes. The resulting explosion burned off every hair on my face – beard, mustache, eyebrows, eyelashes – and torched the hair beneath my hard hat on both sides of my head. I stumbled backwards, threw off the hat (revealing – unbeknownst to me – another smoldering half-Mohican) and pawed at my face. Was I blind? Was the skin on my face charred?

No, my mug felt seared but intact, and I could definitely still see. Which was less reassuring than it might have been when I looked around and saw what I'd done. Not only was the gas tank still burning, but the flames were reaching six feet in the air and licking the bottom of a huge tank overhead.

Written on its side – flickering in the firelight – were the words DANGER—HIGHLY FLAMMABLE.

I'm ashamed to admit that for the first time in my life I actually began running in circles. I was so shithoused, so confused and so freaked out – all at the same time – that I couldn't decide whether to run for help or run for my life. By the time I realized I could do both that overhead tank was turning pink. I screamed and took off for a shed across the yard. Inside were a couple millwrights having a cigarette and – though I couldn't see myself – their reaction when I stumbled inside told the story:

"Jesus Christ!" said the guy nearest the door. "You been to your own barbecue, buddy?"

"FIRE!" I yelled. "FIRE IN THE PAYLOADER!"

I ripped the extinguisher off the wall, turned around and ran back towards the fire. I could hear the two millwrights clomping along behind me and we were still fifty yards away, converging with a couple other groups, when a third millwright came strolling by the payloader. He looked at the geyser of flames like it was something he saw everyday, casually bent over and picked up the discarded cap. Screwed it back on the tank and extinguished the flames instantly.

Then he continued into the night without a backward glance.

Myself and the other two guys stumbled to a halt in the middle of the yard. "Goddamn," I gasped, "I thought if I did that the tank would explode ... or implode ... or something horrible!"

"How'd that fire happen, big guy?" one of the millwrights asked.

"Well, eh, ..." I tried to think fast. Was there any *plausible* explanation for what I'd done? "Well, you see, I was checking the gas level in the tank ..."

"With a match!? You checked the gas with a match!?"

"No no, I didn't say that! It was just I forgot I had, you know ... a lit cigarette in my mouth."

"Oh! Well hell, pal ... that's much better!" The two of them had a good laugh over that, then the one who'd made the barbecue crack drew closer and peered at me. "Hey! I didn't recognize you without your beard and long hair! Aren't you the one they call 'Animal!'"

"Yeah yeah."

"Well shit, *no wonder* ..."

More big horselaughs. After that someone changed my nickname to "Highly Flammable." (Get it? Wilson *High*. Real millworker humor.) I'd be walking along Commerce Street in the afternoon and it was worse than the "Hormel" gig. A mill worker cruising in his GTO would spot me and immediately start honking.

"HEY, HIGH! HIGHLY FLAMMABLE! WHAT'S COOKING, MAN!?"

Or: "PAINT ON SOME EYEBROWS, HIGHLY FLAMMABLE! YOU'RE SMOOTH AS A BABY'S BUTT!"

And why wasn't I fired from the mill? Well, irony of ironies, with the powerful union they had drunkenness was the only infraction you could be dismissed for and virtually the only thing I was never accused of. This was before drug tests, mind you, and a foreman told me they were sure I was under the spell of some weird, exotic substance.

I didn't have the heart to tell him it was just booze.

It disappointed me, too.

RAILCAR

As might be expected, the more I drank and the longer I worked, the more trouble I got into at the mill. The final incident came two months after I'd begun. I'd been promoted to "No. 1 Cleanup Man" (by virtue of attrition), a job that entailed driving a little stand-up railcar on the tracks behind the mill. I'd scoot along until I found an open car full of wood chips, carefully couple up and drag it back along the tracks to a pit surrounded by huge pincers. Then uncouple and walk to the control room, where I'd direct the metal arms to first squeeze around the car, then lift and turn it like a toy, spilling the chips onto conveyor belts below.

When the car was upright again I'd re-couple and steer it to a different track in the yard. It was an easy job for all its responsibilities and I tried to keep a tight rein on the pre-work drinking for the first week I did it. Then I had a couple days off and ran into a girl I'd known in my basketball days. Neither of us was looking too good but she had some acid and was living in her parents' cabin on Toutle Lake so one thing led to another and we spent two desperate days and nights drinking and rutting in the woods. When it was time to return to work I should have called in sick or at least eaten something first. Instead I stumbled to the control room just as graveyard shift began and hadn't unloaded two chip cars when I knew I'd made a mistake: the alcohol and psychedelics buzz wasn't going to last, I was crashing hard and beginning to see fleeting phantoms in the air. This forced me to find the bottle of vodka I'd hid behind a shed for just such emergencies. A couple pulls smoothed the rough spots for awhile, then I started getting groggy just as Ben Fleer, one of the foremen, showed up at the control room. I'd seen him approaching from across the yard so barely had enough time to pop a mint in my mouth and take a rag to the booze sweat on my face and neck. (Not that he would have noticed necessarily: I still looked like a guy who'd sucked a blowtorch.)

Fleer was the youngest of the foremen and we got along pretty well. He told me the mixers needed some white pine in the pulp mix so I was to drive to the back of Yard G and pull up the designated car.

"'G?'" I mumbled. "Do I know where that is?"

"No," said Ben, unfolding a slip of paper, "that's why I made a little map for you. See here? That's 'G' right beyond the third lot."

I stood as far away from him as I could and nodded assent. Took the map from his hand and walked outside. The hookup car I used was just big enough for me to stand in, kind of a closet with windows that sat atop two big wheels. I had an electric engine gear box with Forward and Reverse on it and an air brake at my feet. Once I was inside Ben clamored onto the stairs beside me, grabbed the handhold and leaned in.

"Out where you're going no cars have been moved for awhile so the tracks get *really* icy!" he said. "Make sure you keep it slow and use the brake a lot ... you want to be *crawling* when you reach the cars at the other end."

"Uh huh," I muttered, fighting to keep my eyes open. Fleer jumped off the car with a wave and I started down the track. It was pitch-black out there and I found myself nodding off every time I lowered my chin. I tried speeding up the car so the cold air whistling through the cab would keep me awake, and when that didn't work I tightened down my hard hat and rested it against the wire mesh window, hoping the fierce vibrations would help.

Instead the *clackity clack* of the tracks only made me groggier. The next thing I remember is Fleer shaking my arm an hour later. I thought for a moment that the car had filled with wood chips somehow, then realized I was laying face down in a frozen mound of them. I felt like I'd been run over.

"Ohhhhhhh shit!" I moaned. "Jesus."

"High!" said Fleer. "Damn it, High! Are you okay?"

I wiped off a swath of chips that had frozen to some drool and blood on my mouth. Sat up slowly, seeing first eight of Fleer, then four and finally two. My head was ringing and the whole left side of my body ached. It took a minute but with Ben's help I finally stood up and looked around. The car I'd been riding in was derailed and laying on its side a good ten feet away, the window pulverized and the cab bent at a 30-degree angle.

"Wow! What the fuck happened here?" I said.

"You don't remember, High? I drove out here when you didn't come back and found the railcar like that and you laying here unconscious. I thought you were dead, man."

"I do remember heading out here ..."

"As best I can figure it," said Fleer, "you hit that stationary line of cars going way too fast."

I glanced back and forth from the twisted hookup car to where I'd landed in the chips. Cautiously rotated my left arm and bent the leg on that side. Like my hip they seemed plenty bruised and swollen, all right, but it didn't feel like I'd broken anything.

Then I removed my hard hat and checked it out. It looked as if someone had taken a sledgehammer to the left side of it.

"Whoa," I murmured, "check out this dent. I should be dead *at least!*"

"It's a fuckin' miracle, High," said Fleer. "What do you think happened? Were you going too fast and hit the cars before you realized where you were?"

"No, I was drunk and I passed out," I sighed. "Hell, I'm drunk now. I was drunk when I burned up the payloader for chrissakes! Can't you guys smell it on me?"

Fleer leaned toward me and sniffed. "Well, actually," he said, "not to be rude or anything, *Animal,* but not only does this paper mill reek but ... well, with you there's a lot of competing odors going on."

"Uh huh. I quit, Fleer. I mean you'd have to fire me, anyway, now, so this will make it easier on everybody."

To his credit he didn't feign disappointment. He drove me back to the mill office in his truck, had me write out a blurry statement for the accident forms, then gave me the name and number of the mill doctor and told me to see him first thing in the morning.

"Don't blow this off, High," he said. "There could be something seriously wrong with you."

We both had a good laugh over that one, then we shook hands and I limped back to town. I was scared and sore and confused. The life-threatening incidents were drawing closer and closer together and my drunkard's life was spiraling out of control. It was inevitable, of course, but that didn't make confronting it any easier.

Because improbably enough I hadn't hit bottom yet, there were still darker holes to crawl into. Perhaps if I hadn't spent the last week emptying the apartment of debris and had hobbled in there that morning to a cold beer can bed ... maybe that would have assured me I had nowhere to go but up.

But I doubt it. Instead I realized I could squeeze everything I owned into a pillowcase and be on the 7:00 a.m. Greyhound heading south.

I made it with minutes to spare.

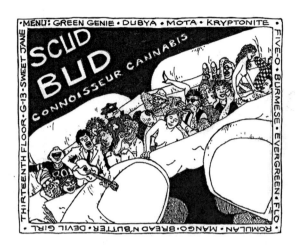

Marijuana is conspicuous by its absence in a lot of my booze-soaked yarns and that's because I always considered the pot and alcohol mix the most wretched of highs. It was vaguely doable if you smoked first, I suppose, then drank beer or wine moderately afterwards, but reversing the order ruined both drugs, the way Europeans do when they mix marijuana or hash with tobacco.

Not that it was *easy* to say no to a joint when I was half in the bag from booze, or even that I ever did. But it was 1981 (when I had that first crop in Bolinas) before I started smoking everyday. In the twenty-five years since I'd guess I've gone what? six or seven days without pot? At first glance that may seem like excessive toking, but though I puff four or five different *kinds* of dope during a 24-hour period, the sum total rarely exceeds a joint. I burn less weed than any longtime stoner I know, in fact. A number of male friends who come by – most of them semi-retired, all of them infinitely more successful than I am – smoke twice as much as I do. They seem to have no governor where weed is concerned; I'll roll and light a joint, try to put it out after a

281

half-dozen hits and they'll snatch it from my hand to keep puffing. *Where's the discipline, boys?* I think. *That's nothing but overkill.* Of course, I'm the one who had a brownie for lunch.

Maybe the concussion played a part, or even being in shock and not knowing it (drinking whiskey under the circumstances was certainly a crucial factor). But about the time I boarded that Greyhound south I lost control of the game. Faithful readers may believe that happened two hundred pages ago and I wouldn't argue with them. It may, in fact, be putting too fine a point on it to suggest I'd weighed any consequences since that morning in Canby's bathhouse.

Yet I felt like I had. This was all part of the ever-evolving dance, wasn't it? Wasn't the thing with me and booze just like the old rock-'n'-roll anthem:

> *"We shall see*
> *which one will bend."*

If so I was finally and unequivocally bent: I had more of my faculties in Mexico than I did on that bus. Or buses, as the case may be. I was thrown off the first Greyhound for drunken belligerence somewhere south of Roseburg, Boregon, boarded another in Grants

Pass and made it as far as Yreka, California before being ejected again. Then nothing for four days. I don't know where I went or what I did but I spent (or had stolen) all the money that wasn't hidden in my shoe, lost half of a front tooth in some altercation or another, and was passed out on the steps of Dick Hale's Berkeley apartment when he found me late the afternoon of April second. Taped to my shirt was a note in somebody else's handwriting:

Buy gun. Load. Spread newspapers.

I had no idea whose sentiments they were or how I'd ended up at Hale's place. What's worse, he was in law school and newly married. Smelling, drinking and looking as I did (I had a lot of hair on the top and back of my head, but everything else was coming back in patches and the left side of my face was as bruised as my mouth), he shuffled me to another friend of ours, Dove Harlow, who was a student at Cal and rented half of a two-story duplex in East Berkeley.

Harlow was an old buddy and offered to put me up temporarily while I looked for work. It was certainly a grave error on his part, but only one of us knew it at the time.

Because right then my life was me in that railcar: it was time to take the hit. Time to see what would happen if I got after it, if I just drank booze 'til I couldn't drink it anymore. All or nothing, win or lose, the last big roll of the dice.

The question was … how to do it with only a hundred bucks to my name? The answer: *Olde English 800*. (Thirty-five years later I still flinch typing the words.) It's a Blitz-Weinhard malt liquor that's also known as "acid in a can" because of its strong, sudden, extremely delusional effects. The legend was (and probably still is) that you could drink half as much of it and get twice as drunk as you would on other malt liquors. I'd never tried it myself, only watched guys test it on two different occasions at Gumbo's place. Both of them had a single half quart before loudly proclaiming the liquor's ineffectiveness and horrible taste, then going out and crashing their cars a half block away. Ned and I could actually hear the second crash, and instead of running to help he jumped up, hustled into the kitchen and poured the remaining *Olde English* cans down the sink.

"What are you doing, fool?" I yelled. "I coulda used those in emergencies."

"Exactly why I'm getting rid of them, High," he said. "You on *Olde English* is something I *never* want to see."

Later I'd run into black winos in those Union City bean fields and wonder why they walked around with a single can of beer in a bag. How drunk could you get on one can of beer?

Eventually one of them drew back the paper, showed me the ugly brown and gold can inside. "Hell dis ain't beer, kid," he said. "Dis be da Ollldddddee English."

I settled in at Dove's – which consisted of claiming a filthy old white overcoat that some prior roommate had left behind – then went down the street and bought two cases of *Olde English 800* half quarts. I figured if the stuff was half as toxic as its reputation that'd last me a month.

It was closer to six days. At the end, according to Dove, I wasn't even bothering to refrigerate it. Was I insane … or was it the *Olde English?* And wouldn't a person *have* to be mad to drink more than a six-pack a day of that poison?

Absolutely. Except for shooting up and licking toads I've tried damn near everything and *Olde English* was easily as scary an opiate as I ever ingested. After the first half quart I lost all ability to reason; after the second I lost any inclination to do so. Of the next five days I remember little but how badly I felt wherever I woke up in the morning … usually on a neighbor's lawn or the loading dock of a warehouse down the street … and how quickly a can of *English* would cure me of all interest in the matter. Other than that I have only brief, intensely insane snapshots: a Chinese girl sucking my cock, a gloomy Oriental grocery store, a dark bar, some thin black guy punching me hard in the face.

The rest is thrown together from Harlow's descriptions and a photo he sent me years later. (I still have it around here somewhere; it's paper clipped to that note Hale found on my chest.) In the Polaroid it's a bright, sunny day and I'm standing in front of Dove's duplex in that shabby overcoat. The sleeves barely reach my wrists and the shredded hem stops just above my knees. (This is particularly apparent because I have no pants on.) I'm wearing black leather gloves, lumpy steel-toed mill boots and a *Yankees* baseball cap. In my right hand is a long, thin butcher knife, in my left a crushed *Olde English* can.

There is so much grime and blood on my face and coat that they're damn near shiny from it. On the back of the photo Dove wrote: "Pigpen, the 300 lb. slasher. 4/4/69"

It was my twenty-second birthday; at that point Harlow and I both presumed it would be my last. He says I'd appear early in the morning – while he was studying for exams – and demand to know what he was doing in *my* apartment. Then I'd have a quick couple cans of *English,* pull the butcher knife out of the overcoat, grab a six-pack and disappear. No one knows what I did during the day or night, where my pants went to (I kept my underwear on, apparently), or whether the blood splatters on my bruised face and coat were mine or other people's.

In most towns I'd have been arrested and jailed, even hospitalized on sight; in 1969 Beserkeley I was just a bigger-than-usual freak. I like to think I was prescient about that, that I knew it was the one place I could play out the game without incarceration, but if so I nearly miscalculated. After five days of *Olde English* and hot dogs (Dove says I often had *Der Wienerschitzel* wrappers falling out of my pockets), I woke up the sixth morning behind a Safeway store and was as queasy as I'd ever been in my life. I threw up off and on for an hour and couldn't tell if the puke was full of blood, rusty *Olde English* or both. When I could finally stand I wobbled the three blocks to the duplex and barely made it up the steps to the second floor kitchen. I remember sitting at the table there ... Dove across from me with a textbook and a bowl of cereal ... and my hands shaking so hard I couldn't pop the top on a warm *English* half quart.

"It'd be easier if you took the gloves off," said Dove.

"Eat your cereal, butt fuck!"

"And I'd appreciate your taking it easy on that dreck today, High. You had your birthday but tonight's *my* twenty-first. I'm having that big party I told you about."

"Party?" I finally got a finger under the pop top and pulled it off. Smelled the *Olde English* stink as I lifted the can.

"Jesus, High, you've turned into a goddamned animal! Have you looked in a mirror or smelled yourself lately!? You're scaring the hell out of me!"

"Party?" I repeated, gagging down the syrupy malt liquor. (You didn't sip *Olde English*, you glugged it.)

"Yeah. Hale will be here, Milltown, some of my Cal friends, even your buddy Gumbo."

That cut through my alkie fog like a laser. "Gumbo?" I said. "Gumbo's coming?"

"Yeah, he called last night. He heard you were here, says you owe him ten bucks for some calls you made at his place. He's coming to collect."

Leave it to Ned to bring me back to the real world. I was suddenly so angry that the tremors in my hands felt like they belonged there. I drew the long butcher knife out of the lining of my coat, admired its grimy edge.

"Oh he's going to collect all right," I muttered. "He's gonna get *exactly* what he deserves!"

I spent the rest of the day planning Gumbo's demise. I might have had misgivings at first, but they passed with the second can of Olde English and a grim review of Ned's treacheries. There was the obvious stuff, like me freaking out on acid and him pouring a bottle of Novocaine in my ear, or the way he ruined my sweet deal with Lonesome Louie or, worse yet, pushing me down that steep San Francisco hill in a shopping cart.

But what my *English*-addled brain remembered were things like the vacuum cleaner. There were several instances where Gumbo, having awakened to find me passed out on the cottage carpet, extracted his revenge by tiptoeing outside, retrieving or smashing some beer bottles, then bringing the shards inside and spreading them carefully around my head. Next he'd plug in his loud, antiquated vacuum cleaner – knowing, as I've indicated before, that above all noises in the world I hated the sound of vacuum cleaners – then gently roll it over to my closest available ear ... and flip the ON switch.

I'd wake screaming, my sweet alkie stupor shattered by the skull-exploding noise, and *Schadenfreude* Ned would howl in triumph.

Why had I waited so long to remove this nasty little bastard from circulation? Surely no jury would convict me ... hell, I'd be doing a public service. The question most asked about Gumbo was "Why's no one ever killed that sonofabitch?"

So went the delirious workings of the last of my mind as I nursed four cans of *Olde English* through the early afternoon and evening. I wanted to *remember* the sensation of sinking a butcher knife into Ned; the only question was whether to carve him slowly, stretching it out for me and the other partygoers, or just give him one in the ear, the way he liked to do to me.

And it's so difficult to write about it now, so hard to think about myself on the day I touched bottom. What I remember most is how *gray* everything was. I sat in a far corner of Dove's living room in an overstuffed armchair, empty *Olde English* cans flung around beneath me, as I slowly tapped the butcher knife on one gloved palm or another and waited for Gumbo to arrive. I remember Dick Hale coming up and saying something, and Jay Milltown trying to communicate with me about my drinking, but according to Harlow the worst part was the dozen people I didn't know. All friends of his who'd dropped acid or eaten mushrooms in anticipation of a loving, hippie birthday party with their soul mate Dove.

Only to come on in the company of a drunken, barelegged brute in an overcoat and gloves. Who'd curse at them and wave a butcher knife if they got too close.

"Friends who were there still remember it," Dove likes to say, "and they all agree it was a terrifying night."

I'd put it in my Bottom Ten, too. Especially when Ned finally arrived. Unlike everyone else, who approached me warily if at all, Gumbo not only marched right up to me ... he kicked the armchair.

"Hey High!" he said. "Where's my ten bucks?"

"Ten bucks?" I growled.

"Yeah. You made a bunch of long distance calls over Christmas when you were staying at my place."

"Those were to *you,* asshole, telling you what I was going to do to you for shoving me down the hill in a shopping cart!"

"So what? I want my ten bucks!"

"YOU LITTLE PRICK!" I squirmed around trying to rise from the chair but Hale, who'd been on the boxing team at Cal, was there in a flash to shove me back down. He dragged Gumbo away and I sat there, seething and cursing under my breath, as the little asshole squeezed between Dick and Milltown on a couch.

Every couple minutes he'd break off from whatever conversation he was having to look at me. "Hey High!" he'd yell, grinning from ear to ear. "Where's my ten bucks?" Again and again, maybe a dozen times over the next hour: "Hey, High! Where's my ten bucks?"

You know, now that I finally write about it, maybe I knew what I was doing after all. Here I am in the midst of some alcoholic/psychotic break and Gumbo is not only *pimping* me ... but milking it for all it's worth.

Finally I'd had enough. I pretended to get up to go to the bathroom, then halfway across the room lifted the knife over my head and charged the couch, shoving freaked hippies out of my way and screaming at the top of my lungs:

"YOU'LL DIE NOW GUMBO YOU WORTHLESS LITTLE COCKSUCKER!"

In my memories I'm flying across the room. Harlow says, however, that I was so catatonic from the *Olde English* that it looked like I was stuck in molasses. And Hale, who stood up and waited for me to arrive at the couch – then casually dropped me to my knees with a single punch to the head – confirms this: "A slow motion Pillsbury Doughboy, High."

Anyway, while I was crawling around on the floor, trying to rub my jaw and retrieve an *Olde English* can that had rolled out of my pocket, Hale proposed that Ned and I settle our differences on the front lawn. This met with unanimous approval from the other partygoers and the next thing I knew Milltown was helping me down the stairs to the street.

"Don't do this, Wilson," he told me. "You're not going to stab Gumbo. You're so fucked up you couldn't stab yourself. Let me get you some help, man."

I told him to fuck off, spent the next ten minutes performing just as he predicted. Essentially Gumbo would do a little dance in front of me, taunting me, and I'd lunge for him with the butcher knife, miss by a foot or two and fall flat on my face to the cheers of the black guys and their girlfriends who lived in the other half of the duplex. They called me "The Hulk" and littered the lawn around Gumbo and me with copies of *The Incredible Hulk* comic books.

Finally I threw away the knife, just tried to grab Gumbo and crush him to death. But he easily evaded me and, before long, too exhausted to stand and reeling from the whirlies, I fell on my back and passed out.

I woke maybe an hour later, still laying face up on the lawn, comic books all around. I rose to my knees, crawled to the nearby bushes and took a piss. Laid back down and stared at the April sky. I'd never felt so empty in my life; it was like I wasn't there at all, as if I'd finally been reduced to a contour drawing.

For the first time I couldn't see a tomorrow with me in it. I was broke, crazy and strung out on my own poisons, hating booze for failing me so young even as I cursed it for taking so long to kill me. I finally, reluctantly, dragged myself to my feet and began the slow walk up the steps to Dove's place. I took a left into the closet at the top of the stairs, where I had my last six-pack of *Olde English* stashed, popped open a half quart and had it halfway down when I heard the singing:

"Happy Birthday to you, Happy Birthday to you ..."

What was this? I stumbled to the dark living room doorway, looked through to the dining area. The entire party, their faces lit by the flickering candles on a huge, four-foot long birthday cake, were gathered around the dining room table and singing to Dove.

Of all the horrible things I did as a drunk the one I'd truly take back is what happened next. Not that it was the worst or anything ... hell, I'd just tried to kill a guy with a butcher knife, might, in fact, have been doing the same to other people all week.

No, it was the simple, utter pettiness of the act, the pathetic *smallness* of it. I stood there unnoticed in the doorway, looked at all those stoned faces lifted up in song, Dove beaming away at the head of the table, and thought, *Fuck this! Nobody gave a damn about my birthday! Where was my happiness, where was my sweet little birthday cake!? I'm twenty-two and my two-bit life is already over!*

I roared at the top of my lungs – alerting everyone to The Hulk's return – then charged the dining room with my head down. The hippie couple nearest me screamed and jumped out of the way as I leapt at the end of the table, sailed past the stunned partygoers and landed face first in the cake with a giant *Splat!*

I beat my arms and legs up and down even as the frosting squeezed into my ears.

rogue (rōg) *n.* (1) scoundrel. (2) person of a low, unprincipled, tricky nature. (3) Ned Gumbo.

After all the years and all the wars Gumbo and I remain good friends. This surprises a lot of my other pals – both those who know Ned personally and the ones who've met him through my stories – and as explanation I usually offer the tale of "The Raincoat Section."

Our friend Ted Grantham has had the same 49er season tickets for thirty years. He inherited three of them from his father and they're aisle seats on the 50-yard line, about twenty rows up from the visitors' side of the field. He has a regular group of guys he goes with but every once in awhile one of them can't attend and he invites Ned or, five years ago – because I happened to be in the Bay Area for a couple days – both Ned and myself.

It was a warm September Sunday and the Niners were playing the Cowboys. I sat in the aisle seat with Ted next to me and Gumbo beside him. As the fans around us (many of whom have been sitting in the same section nearly as long as Grantham has) settled into their seats, there were two things I noticed immediately: (1) they all seemed to know Gumbo, slapping him on the back and trading insults as soon as they spotted him; and (2) they were all wearing light rain gear even though there wasn't a cloud in the sky.

I asked Ted about this. "Is there rain predicted for today?"

"No."

"So these people in the seats around us ... why are they wearing rain gear?"

Ted laughed. "Just wait," he said. "You'll see."

As the game began – the Niners were winning but the details on the field escape me – Gumbo began working on the large thermos of coffee and rum (mostly the latter) that he'd smuggled into the stadium. By the time the second quarter began he was screaming insults at Roger Staubach, the former Cowboy quarterback who stood behind his old team's bench:

"FUCK YOU AND YOUR GOD, STAUBACH, I WENT TO THE HALL OF FAME IN CANTON AND SPIT ON YOUR PLAQUE YOU COWARDLY CHRISTIAN COCKSUCKER!"

The usual stuff, most of it escalating as the game proceeded. By the start of the third quarter Gumbo was fully shithoused and when there was a big play on the field he jumped up, threw his arms into the air and cheered. This wouldn't have been otherwise noteworthy except the cup of rum and coffee was still in his hand and the contents sprayed on everyone around us.

Where it dribbled harmlessly from their plastic hats and raincoats. I looked over at Ted and he grinned. "When I know Ned's coming to the game," he said, wiping rivulets of rum from his own face, "I call the other ticket holders and alert them."

"And they not only put up with it," I said, "but wear raincoats to boot? Because they *know* he'll get drunk and spray 'em with booze!?"

"Yep."

"Instead of calling security, you mean, or beating the shit out of the fool themselves."

"Right."

"But that's incredible."

Ted laughed. "What do you mean, High?" he said. "You tried to *kill* the sonofabitch and you're still his buddy."

I looked down the row at Ned. He'd filled another cup to the brim and after a long, sloppy gulp toasted me with it.

"Friends to the end, High," he slurred. "Friends to the end."

The morning after The Hulk episode was easily the grimmest of my young life. I woke on my back in the living room, still covered with cake crust. Both of my arms had fallen asleep so I had to flop around like a seal before wrestling myself to my knees. The room tilted, spun around and righted itself as I began a slow, wobbly crawl to the hall closet. Twice I lost my balance and fell over but I couldn't wait for the use of my arms, not when there was a can of *Olde English* looming. When I finally got there I was relieved to find the door ajar. I nudged it open with the top of my head, then pitched forward and smacked the cold hardwood floor with my face.

It was almost worth it ... there in front of me was the prize, the last two half quarts of *English* only inches from my bleeding nose. I was desperate to drink one; I wanted to shut out the previous day's images and the whole sick life piling up behind them. Except I still had no feeling in my hands. All I could do was stare at those ugly cans and moan.

And just like that I started weeping. Great, desperate, gulping sobs that racked my body and echoed off the walls of the closet in a terrible wail. Where was this sudden sorrow coming from? Was it not being able to open those cans, or the way I looked, the way I felt, the way I'd feel when those two half quarts were gone and I had no money to buy more, even the way I'd embarrassed Dove?

Most likely all of the above. I was wrapped in a fetal ball and banging my head on the floor when Milltown found me. Apparently he'd slept in one of the spare bedrooms because the next thing I knew he was clutching my shoulder and shaking me.

"Jesus Christ, High," he said, "are you all right?"

It was a couple minutes before I could catch my breath and stop sobbing. By then Jake had sat me up me up against a wall and the feeling had returned to my extremities. I pointed a trembling hand at the *Olde English* cans.

"Give me one of those!" I gasped.

"No way," said Jake. "It's six in the morning and those cans are *warm*, man! That poison is undrinkable cold!"

"Milltown pleaazze ... I'm begging you here."

"Look at yourself, High! You're a bloated pig, you stink, you've got cake all over you, your hair is growing out at weird angles all over your head, your nose is bleeding, you walk around in an overcoat waving a butcher knife and I just found you crying hysterically in a closet! All because of fuckin' booze. You HAVE to quit drinking, man!"

"Right after those two cans," I croaked. "Seriously."

Milltown sighed, reached over and handed me one of the malt liquors. I ripped it open, tipped it back and drank half of it down. Turned away to belch.

"Wilson," he said, "you've gone totally around the bend. Do you understand that?"

I lifted the can, took another long pull. Leaned back and fought

297

to keep it down as the foul contents swirled in my stomach. "Yeah," I said finally, "I know."

"So what're you gonna do about it? You gonna get some help?"

"I don't have ten cents to my name, man."

"Oh hell ... there must be some kind of free detox ward."

I stood up, hobbled to the bathroom for a long leak, carefully avoiding the mirror over the sink. Came back and sank into a living room chair across from Milltown. "Yeah," I said, finishing the can, "there's detox wards, all right. They're called drunk tanks and if I can't find a way to *steal* alcohol I'll probably end up in one. Now leave me alone, Jake ... okay? I appreciate your concern but I've got some things to think about and I wanna watch the sun come up."

He muttered something underneath his breath and took off. I fancied it my last sunrise but that was just The Dread talking. There was no doubt I liked taking chances and I certainly could work up a rage but suicidal? Not consciously ... I felt more pathetic than sad.

Which narrowed my options considerably. Even if Harlow didn't throw me out I was duty bound to leave after my shameful performance of the night before. Which meant finding a bush or garage to crawl into at night while looking for a job during the day. Except then I'd have to find some regular clothes and ... the real kicker here ... dry out.

I guess when it came down to it I was simply too scared to quit drinking. Several times lately I'd vomited blood in the morning but that worried me less than the little withdrawal probes that preceded the puking. Portents of terror and doom so frightening that only hair of the dog could vanquish them. I'd spent a long time hiding from those demons, protecting a sanity that booze had pretty much destroyed, anyway.

It was a quandary as old as opiates and I've often wondered what I'd have done without Milltown. I'd finished the second can of *Olde English* and was staring dazedly out the window when he ran up the duplex steps and burst into the living room.

"Wilson," said Jake, "I found a place that'll help you!"

"Huh? Where's that?"

"Herrick Hospital. I saw their number in *The Berkeley Barb*, called them up and hey! it's a really nice place, High. Not only that, alcoholism is covered by the State. You've worked in the last six quarters, haven't you ... enough to get disability money?"

"Well, yeah," I said. "But this Herrick ... what is it exactly?"

"A psychiatric ward," he said. "You'd have to commit yourself for thirty days observation."

"A mental ward? You mean ... a nut house?"

"Yeah."

I thought about it for awhile. "Damn," I said finally, "do you think they'd take me, are you sure I'd qualify?"

"I told you," said Jake. "State Disability will ..."

"No no ... do you think I'm *crazy* enough?"

Milltown looked me up and down and laughed. "Are you shittin' me, High," he said. "That's the easy part."

Carl Sampson called this morning. I was thinking about him as I wrote the *Olde English* episode yesterday, he being the only *white* malt liquor alkie I've known. After the *English* I couldn't stomach the stuff myself, but Carl drank it for years. In black bars in the worst parts of Oakland, no less, on a series of benders that stretched over a thirty-year period.

Then when he was living at that dive motel in Vegas this winter he quit. I've seen him twice since he moved to Sisters to work for DeBola and in both instances we spent a lot of time talking about alcohol. It surprised me that he missed it as much as he did because: (1) like me his quitting was a *fait accompli,* every time he got drunk he'd suffer a neuropathic condition that left his arms and hands numb; and (2) he's a binge drinker, the kind of guy who goes 90 days without a drop, then does nothing but drink for a week or two straight. I've always thought boozers like that had an advantage over the rest of us, that during their long dry spells they've already *practiced* life without alcohol, so when it comes time to quit they should be better at it than a regular drunk.

Which is ridiculous, of course, if you need the silly poison you need it and addicts either quit or die. Still I suppose I could have taken Carl's interest in the subject a bit more seriously. The first thing I thought when he called this morning, told me he'd put together a stake and was heading south (returning to salesman work somewhere because his hands were too numb for hard labor) was that the breezy mountain cabin and cold grout on the tile jobs had affected him physically.

Then after he hung up I wondered if he might be drinking again. The possibility didn't sadden me – I'd be drinking myself if I could, and Carl's neuropathy won't let him booze for long – but that serious physical problem not deterring him longer than it has ... that'd surprise me a little. I guess I think anyone suffering that badly from alcohol abuse would quit as readily as I did (particularly someone of Sampson's fortitude), but that's as silly as the notion that it's easier for binge drinkers to quit: I forget how many times I stopped and started before the door was finally slammed shut FOR me.

Plus I was young with a wide open future ahead. Sampson is sixty-three and somewhere around Klamath Falls by now, everything he owns in the back seat of his twenty-year-old Mercury and five hundred bucks in his pocket. With his hopes stretching no further than warm weather ahead.

Milltown was right: after a good look at me no one at Herrick Hospital
questioned my madman bona fides. (If they'd had any doubts they
vanished once I pulled the butcher knife from the overcoat and
waggled it at the doctor.) After an hour examination, signing some
papers and saying good-bye to Jake, I was hustled into an elevator by
a couple of large black orderlies. They took me to the fourth floor and
through a series of locked steel doors to the mental ward office, where
after further processing by a nurse I was ushered into the main room
and told to wait until my bed was ready.

I could have been in the lobby of a nice hotel. The floor was
tastefully carpeted and the furniture comfortable and modern. I went
over to the nearest couch and sank down in the soft green cushions. Lit
up a Camel and thought, *Damn! This might turn out to be easy duty*

after all, I should have signed up for sixty days!

Then the shrieking began behind me. "POWER TO THE PEOPLE! POWER TO ME! I'M THE REINCARNATION OF ELDRIDGE CLEAVER AND JUSTICE IS MINE!!!"

Eldridge Cleaver was dead? I turned around, saw a maybe twenty-year-old skinny black kid with a giant Afro and wild, rolling eyes.

"IT'S PAYBACK FOR CLEAVER! IT'S TIME FOR THE HONKY MIND BUTCHERS TO DIE!"

The guy was spraying spit and working himself into a serious frenzy but no one seemed to notice.

Well, no one but me, anyway. "Hey shut the hell up, asshole," I yelled. "I'm trying to enjoy a smoke here."

But he acted like I wasn't even there. Bent down, started glancing around as if he were looking for something, then focused on the mental ward office. It was a 10' by 15' cubicle of glass that allowed the staff and patients to look out on each other. At the moment there was a group of doctors inside and the Afro character seemed to concentrate on them. Suddenly he emitted a bone-chilling scream, swung a folding chair over his head and charged the glass. It was apparent he meant to smash through it and those were the characters with the *pills* in there. I waited until he was parallel with the couch and running at full speed, then jumped up and right hooked him deep in the gut.

It felt good to connect after all those drunken swings at Gumbo. Eldridge and the chair went down in a heap and I'd barely sat back down myself when the two orderlies charged out of the office and grabbed me. One of them turned his back to the office to block the staff's view while his partner gave me a quick jab in the belly.

"Jesus," I gasped, feeling the *Olde English* bile rise in my throat. "What's wrong with you guys?"

"Why'd you punch our schizoid brother here, High?"

"He was gonna smash the office glass with that chair. I did everyone in there a favor."

"Oh, you idiot," said his partner. "That isn't glass … it's foot-thick shatterproof plastic! Willie charges it everyday."

"Oh." They stepped back and I looked down at Willie. From the vomit on the carpet it was apparent he'd had scrambled eggs for breakfast.

"Sorry about that, Eldridge," I said.

He didn't respond and the orderlies hustled me off to a little room in the corner. There was a bed beside the wall and one of them handed me a backless gown, told me to change into it, then pile my clothes by the door and get into bed.

They left me alone as I stripped off the overcoat, then the boots and gloves and soiled underwear. It left a mess of cake crumbs and black, flaky stuff on the carpet, so I got down on my hands and knees and swept the whole mess under the bed. Stood up and slipped beneath sheets for the first time in a year.

It felt good. So good it was hard to stay awake. I'd begun to nod off when the door opened and the same doctor who'd admitted me earlier walked in with a clipboard.

"Well, Wilson," he said, "how are you doing?"

"Okay. This place is deluxe."

"Uh huh. Well, we'd rather you didn't punch your fellow patients anymore? Another incident like that one and you'll be asked to leave, I'm afraid."

"Sorry, Doc," I said. "I'm still a little shitfaced."

"That's why I'm here, Wilson. You indicated earlier that you had great fears about the withdrawal process and were afraid to detoxify without tranquilizers."

"Pretty much, yeah."

"So it's a Sunday, I'm the only doctor still on the ward and I'll be going home in a couple hours. Would you like me to leave sedatives with the nurse? Something to help you out when withdrawal begins?"

I had some cottonmouth going but I made myself swallow, then forced the word out: "No," I croaked.

"*No?* But I don't understand, I thought that's what you wanted."

"I did, but I just changed my mind. I'm in a safe place here and I've been running from this withdrawal thing for years now, Doc. Why not just go for it, see if the demons are as bad as I've made 'em out to be."

"I strongly advise against that, Wilson. Remember ... you're still inebriated now. If you actually experience the delirium tremens they can be very serious, even fatal. And from what you told me about how long you've been drinking and the symptoms you've suffered so far ... well, you're young, but the withdrawal process could be very severe nonetheless."

"Yeah," I sighed, "but I'm going for it, anyway."

"I'm not sure you understand me: if I don't leave you something there'll be no doctor to prescribe *anything* for you before tomorrow morning. You'll be completely on your own here."

I yawned, nestled down in the pillows. "Go enjoy your Sunday, Doc," I said. I pretended to fall sleep but watched instead as my last chance for the Easy Way walked out the door. When all was said and done I couldn't resist testing myself, I was an all-or-nothing guy even with my sanity hanging in the balance.

I passed out before I could regret my decision.

There'd be plenty of time for that later.

Almost eight hours after I'd fallen asleep in the hospital I woke from a feverish stupor and looked around. For a long, wonderful moment I had no idea where I was.

Then reality hit me at the same time as the withdrawal. I lurched for the bedpan on the stand beside the bed and puked into it. Orange, putrid stuff, maybe blood, maybe *Olde English* ... probably a little of both. I rose shakily to my feet, went into the bathroom and poured the whole mess into the toilet. Flushed it away, took a long, hot piss as the ticking started. *Tick tick tick. Tick tick tick.* Like a watch, except the sound was inside my right ear, then slid behind my right eye. *Tick tick tick. Tick tick tick.* Or wait ... now it was *click click click*. It felt like my optic nerve was chewing itself loose from my brain! I stumbled to the sink to slap some cold water on my face, made the mistake of catching my image in the mirror.

I'd avoided looking at myself for weeks and it was probably the one thing I'd done right. I was so bloated my eyes were tiny slits and the parts of my face that weren't bruised and purple were covered with pustules of acne.

And that was the good news: worse yet was the hairdo. The fuzz on the sides of my head had grown only an inch or two, leaving a tangled mop on top that hung over my ears in greasy, cake-encrusted strips. The image that came to mind, in fact, was a pig in a popcorn wig. I stuffed my head under the faucet and ran cold water over it until a copperhead snake popped out of the drain to nip at my tongue.

Right away a pattern was established that I hadn't foreseen in my trepidation over the d.t.'s, i.e., what else could a cartoonist with hallucinations expect? The more imagination you have, the stranger it'll get when the floodgates open. I sank to the tiles on the bathroom floor and let the usual scary moments flash by. All had terrified me in their time and now they were nothing, pathetic trifles that paled against the madness ahead. I began to sweat and shake, finally curled into a fetal position and lay on the cold floor. In time the sporadic hallucinations turned into a steady stream and I found that – though I couldn't stop them – I could effectively *change* them. If my teeth turned into termites, for instance, I'd blink my eyes and shake my head until an alternate vision appeared, maybe me underwater with electric eels chewing my balls.

None of it slowed the burgeoning backdrop of Dread, though. As its icy fist squeezed tighter and tighter I found myself grateful for physical distractions; every new tremor got my full attention in hopes of mitigating the mental horror. I was finger-painting a nosebleed – actually smearing my last name on the hospital smock so I wouldn't forget who I was – when I sensed a new danger overhead.

It was a giant spider hanging upside down on the ceiling. A vile, fetid thing that stunk of menace but seemed no worse than the hallucinations that preceded him ... except I couldn't make him disappear. I employed the blink-and-shake half a dozen times to no effect. In a panic I scuttled across the tiles and out of the bathroom, crawling to the edge of the bed and elbowing my way on top of it. I took

307

a glug of water from the pitcher on the night stand, laid back on the pillow and tried to control my breathing so I wouldn't hyperventilate.

Scritch scritch. Scritch scritch. I looked up and the spider had followed me across the ceiling. I tried the blink-and-shake again. Nothing ... he was still there. Suddenly I was whimpering in terror. There was no way that spider could actually exist, of course, but if I couldn't make him go away then my mind was truly gone! I'd passed into a psychotic never land!

"Ohhh Willlsssson ...."

The spider spoke. He sounded like a snide Arthur Godfrey.

"Ohhhhh Willlssoonn ..."

I glanced upward, my mouth wide open as I gulped for air. What had happened to all the oxygen in the room?

"Time to pay the piper, Wilson," snickered the spider, as he twisted his abdomen around and shot a bolt of webbing down my throat.

I knew the foul filament couldn't be real, so why was it choking me? I grabbed at the ends of it – frantically pulling, stretching and clawing with my hands – but it felt like I had a coil of rope stuck in my windpipe.

Scissors! I needed a pair of scissors to *cut* the webbing out! I slid off the bed, tried to stand up but my legs were so wobbly I kept falling down.

So I gave up and crawled to the nurse's station. Out the door of my room, across the carpeted lobby, around tables, chairs and couches like a mad rat in a maze.

If it hadn't been two in the morning I might have encountered other crawlers on the way. As it was the lone nurse on duty seemed surprised to see me. I popped my head up in front of her, began a frantic banging on the glass as I pointed at my mouth.

"HAHWAH NEED TUPARAN SCISSORS SNORT SNORT CUT THROAT MMWAGAH!"

I figured I'd annunciated pretty clearly for a guy with a web in his windpipe but the nurse's only response was to push a red button on her desk.

I never saw the orderlies. They hit me from behind, wrestled me to the floor and pushed my arms through the sleeves of a straitjacket. Then they cinched me up and dragged me to a room at the end of the hall.

"You could have done it the easy way, High," one of them said, panting. "You could have been shot up with enough Librium to knock out a horse but noooo! you were gonna fight the pink elephants yourself!"

"I TAKE IT BACK!" I screamed. "GIMME SOME DOWNERS YOU COCKSUCKERS!!!!!"

"Too late, pal," grunted his partner. They unlocked the room's large metal door and shoved me inside. I hit face first, tumbled onto my back as the door slammed shut behind me.

When I'd finally crawled to my knees and shimmied up against a wall I looked around. It was a padded cell for chrissakes. I was wrapped up in a straitjacket and locked in a padded cell!

Well, I thought frantically, *at least the spider and webbing are gone.*

Scritch scritch. Scritch scritch scritch.

I've sometimes wished I could remember who I was before those brain fevers as a kid. Did I write, draw and think slowly? Could I read a Hardy Boys book over a period of days instead of burning through it in a couple hours?

I have similar considerations about my psyche before the Herrick d.t.'s episode, because who goes insane and comes back the same? And was my delirium (and oversensitivity to alcohol in general) a consequence of those very same fevers, a matter of my brain protecting itself from another deadly intruder?

It doesn't matter, I suppose: where the mental storms raged that morning there's only echoes left. It's the one part of delirium I'm grateful for, the fact you *are* delirious and hence don't remember much after the first hour or so. All I know for sure is that the spider and the hallucinations that preceded him were just the "alkie aura," a benign bell in my head that signaled the *onset* of the d.t.'s. Once I was inside that padded cell the real action began. I screamed, I cried, I died or went crazy twice a minute while rolling furiously from one end of the room to the other, trying to cocoon my sanity with movement.

Because staying sane – remaining a me that I *recognized* – was the hardest part, the object of my pitiful search for an anchor in the cyclone. By the time two orderlies retrieved me at eight in the morning I was hoarse and too weak to walk. They extricated me from the blood- and vomit-soaked straitjacket, showered me down in the bathroom and dressed me in a new gown. Then slung my arms over each of their shoulders and hustled me back to my room. Once I was under the sheets they raised the bars on the side of the bed so they could secure my wrists with leather straps.

"Downers," I croaked. "Gimme … downers."

"Hold on," said one of them. "No patient here's ever gone through the kind of withdrawal you have. The entire staff's on their way to see you."

Ten minutes later there they were … the psychiatrists, the psychologists, the nurses, the physical and occupational therapists – there might have even been a receptionist or two. Fifteen people encircled my bed and stared at me like a zoo exhibit.

Which was oddly appropriate, given that they, in turn had the heads of different animals to me. I saw a rhino, a giraffe, a wolverine, a weasel, a panda bear …

"Mr. High," said the orangutan closest to me, "we heard you've had quite a night."

"Downers," I gasped.

"You're feeling down?" asked the rhino.

Who were these fools? And were they truly even there?

"I can see you're still having tremors, Mr. High," continued the orangutan. "Are you still hallucinating, too?"

"Of course, …" I croaked. "You're … an orangutan!"

"Really?" He seemed quite excited by that. "And what about my colleagues? Do you perceive them as different sorts of animals?"

"Ye … yess."

"What am I?" said the rhino.

"And what do you see me as?" chirped the cheetah.

I closed my eyes, marshaled the little strength that remained in me as I jerked upright. "SHOOT ME WITH DOPE YOU FUCKIN' CLOWNS!"

That – along with a seizure that made my left arm and leg flop uncontrollably – finally got me 500 milligrams of Librium in the ass.

It knocked me out immediately. I slept for ten hours and when I woke the frightening hallucinations had turned into cartoons on the back of my eyelids. Tom and Jerry, Sylvester and Tweety Bird, Mr. Magoo, Heckle and Jeckle ... all I had to do was shut my eyes and I could watch full-length animated cartoons of my own design (in Technicolor, no less) with whatever sound or special effects I wished to add. It was quite extraordinary, really, the perfect mix of withdrawal and antidote, a peek at how the d.t.'s might be with the anxiety element removed.

I appreciated the interlude ... the rest of me felt like road kill. I spent one day being fed with a needle and another slurping Jell-O and soup like an old man.

Except I was twenty-two years old, of course, and it's why different members of the staff kept coming in to check on me. I was their project, a drunk in his twenties seeking help was a real anomaly at the time. This was as discomforting to me as the earnest, "Go get 'em, son!" empathy of my AA fellows. I wasn't there because I *wanted* to quit drinking, for chrissakes, I was there because I physically *had* to. Even today my stock response to how I sobered up is, "It wasn't me ... it was the d.t.'s."

If it were up to me I'd be the shithoused clown at the bar next to you, the guy George W. Bush should have been.

The withdrawal episode pretty much eliminated that notion, though. I wasn't naïve enough to think I wouldn't drink again, but there'd certainly be less hiding from the consequences now. I'd have to be more judicious, pick my spots like a junkie probing a vein.

Around day three the last of the cartoons vanished and I came face-to-face with Lesson No. 1 for mental ward alkies, i.e., once you sober up you're just a regular guy in a nut house. Depressives, schizophrenics, borderline psychotics, failed suicides and pill poppers … Herrick had them all.

Not that they much noticed each other. Take my roommate Ed, for instance. I'd been moved into a two-bed room with him once I'd recovered from withdrawal. He was a high school teacher who'd flipped out in the middle of class and been receiving electroshock treatments since. When he was awake (which wasn't often), he stared blankly ahead and drooled. He might have been the perfect roommate if his glacial slowness hadn't driven the sober me crazy. After a few days I found myself standing him up and *shoving* him into his clothes in the morning, then helping him eat and even doing a rapid brushing of his teeth at night so he wouldn't spend an hour in front of the mirror.

Which is to say mental ward life more or less agreed with me, everyone there being in far worse straits than I was. Plus the grub was excellent and every four hours the real Feeding Time came, one nurse or another hunting you down with a paper cup full of pills. A lot of it was just B-12 and other vitamins, but I campaigned with the shrinks to keep a host of exotic downers on my menu, stuff they might hesitate to use on older patients.

In the morning there were group therapy sessions, in the afternoon private meetings with your assigned psychiatrist. I don't remember the name of mine, much less his face, only that I found the sessions lamer than the ones my coach sent me to in high school. I was certainly as neurotic as the next guy, and I loved how booze transformed me from moody introversion to garrulous extroversion in a flash. But I couldn't be convinced that the reason I was alcoholic – be it psychology or nature or genes or a combination of the three – was a particularly significant issue when it came to my quitting. In that regard my approach was the same as it had been that morning in Canby's bathhouse:

THE CREED

I was alcoholic.
Being a drunk is ultimately a miserable,
self-destructive life.
There's no reason to spread the pain over a lifetime.
Get it done young. Suck that booze tit 'til you're
killed or cured.

It may have been "The Existential Alkie" approach (my personal favorite, though therapists would give it many labels over the years), but my earnest plea to them never wavered, i.e., show me something better. I'm nearing the end of this game, I'm playing out the hand as best I can, so what are you offering that's better than gambling with death and insanity?

Nothing more useful than AA's "one day at a time," that's for sure. And the longer I spent fleshing out my personal philosophy the more acute the irony of the d.t.'s episode: here I'd spent all that time avoiding the delirium tremens, when, in fact, they represented my best chance for scaring myself straight.

So I had much to think about during the remainder of my stay at Herrick. In the meanwhile I had a steady stream of curious friends, all of whom were weirded out by the mental ward atmosphere. You had to be prepared in there, you could feel a hand on your shoulder and turn around to see the sutured neck of Martha, who tried to cut her own throat with a can opener, or maybe have to deal with Frannie, selling you an imaginary ticket for the Alcatraz tour boat.

Not to mention the vitriolic Eldridge and a chorus of creepy schizo moaners. It got so strange in the lobby one afternoon that I ignored protocol and took Sampson and his girlfriend Elsa to my room. We'd no sooner stepped through the door, though, blithely chatting amongst ourselves, then I realized the technicians were giving Ed a shock treatment right there on his bed. He was bent like a bow, eyes bulging and teeth clamped down on a leather bit, as they shot the juice between his ears.

Bzzzst bzzst ... crackle. "Hey get out of here, High!" yelled one of the techs.

I hustled Carl and Elsa back into the hallway. "Jesus," I said, leaning against the wall. "I hadn't seen that before."

"That was terrible, Wilson!" said Elsa, hugging me. "They're not going to do that to *you,* are they?"

"Actually," I said, "I may have already done it to myself."

The next time the two of them visited they offered me a place to stay when I left the ward. (Translated into "Sampson Speak" this meant they were joining a commune and I was welcome to come along.) I was reluctant at first but what the hell ... what *was* I going to do without a cent to my name and the torturous prospect of sobriety hanging over me? Maybe a hippie commune was a reasonable alternative.

So when my thirty days were up I helped Ed dress for the last time and headed for checkout. Staff and various long-term inmates who had no idea who I was gathered to say good-bye. When an orderly opened the door to the outside world I raised my right hand and waved. I was wearing a dead schizo's shirt, green hospital scrub pants and my ugly steel-toed boots.

In my left hand was a bag of prescription drugs.

"I'll be back!" I said.

315

Carl and Elsa lived in a ramshackle, two-story house on Dwight Way. I was only there for a week, but in that time the place was jammed morning, noon and night with freaks and their dogs. It had more fleas than a kennel and the only time people circulated was when someone upstairs had a drug they'd run out of downstairs. In order to sleep I had to find an unoccupied closet or crash with the mutts in a van outside.

It was definitely not the ideal scene for a guy struggling to stay straight. All I had going for me was the utter strangeness of sobriety, a novelty that wore off fast. I was tempted to pop some of the pills they'd given me at the ward but ended up trading them for food and cigarettes instead. Mostly I just sat in corners that didn't include stereo speakers. Occasionally Carl and Elsa would come around, or stoners who liked to hear d.t. stories, but I was usually by myself. There were plenty of women in the house but with my hair and clothes I looked like a guy who'd *escaped* from Herrick so I wasn't getting any of that. To amuse myself I would watch other young people drink; try to pick out the potential drunks in the crowd, then contemplate how many decades it would be before booze became a serious problem for them.

Because that was and always will be my bitterness: not sadness, not self-pity, just anger at the goddamned economy of it all. Where was *my* long run, where was my alkie second wind? Quit drinking at thirty? I could have handled that if I had to … maybe even twenty-eight in a pinch. But *twenty-fuckin'-two!* This was outrageous to me.

One day a time, I told myself over and over, *one day at a time,* even as my peers writhed around me in a psychedelic daisy chain.

Carl, Elsa and I were waiting for the organizers to pick out a site for our commune. They returned from their search on the sixth day, claiming they'd located the perfect place, "a beautiful cottage with an acre of land high in the Santa Cruz mountains."

Or at least that's the way Dusk and Dawn (the co-organizers, along with Dharma and Donna) described it.

"Shack in Corralitos" was more like it. We piled into the obligatory Volkswagen vans the next morning, drove south to the California coast. Dusk was steering the wheezy beater I was in and as we came around the bend off Highway One he jammed down the accelerator, told us the cottage was straight ahead.

"Wait 'til you see it, guys," he gasped, choking on a hit of hash. "Real country living."

He turned up an unpaved street, hung a left and there was our Walden West: old whitewashed boards, broken windows, collapsed steps, a yard with knee-high yellow weeds and an overturned mailbox.

We stepped out of the van for a closer look.

"Pretty cool, eh?" said Dusk. "A place we can truly make our own."

Most of the others (there were nine of us altogether, I could never get the names straight) nodded their heads in agreement and I thought well, there's other shacks around and a street full of Mexican kids out front, so to these guys getting back to nature means the wind blowing through your windows.

Sampson came up and put his arm around my shoulder. "Are you thinking what I'm thinking, Wilson?" he asked.

"From the nut house to the outhouse you mean?"

317

"Something like that," he said, and we both laughed a little too hard.

When I use the word "commune" to describe what we had in Corralitos I simply mean that's what we called it. In truth it was just a shack full of lazy hippies who wanted to live off the land and thought spring in the mountains would be a good time to try it. We moved in with our stuff – or everyone else did, anyway, all I had was the clothes on my back and a few cartons of cigarettes – and it was real sixties basic: a mattress here, an herb jar, Timothy Leary poster and incense holder there, three couples taking the bedrooms so Carl and Elsa were left with one corner of the living room and me the other. Which meant that just like the old days I was ten feet away from Sampson's roaring grunt fucks. Someone gave me a blanket to spread atop a threadbare rug and I curled up, prayed for the sleep that never came.

The first morning the nine of us gathered in the living room for a strategy session. Pipes of grass and hash were passed around while we plotted our communal strategy: planting a garden and pooling our cash ($208 total) now that the rent was paid for a couple months, then making crafts to sell, fixing the shack plumbing so we could actually take showers and go to the bathroom indoors, etc. That would take care of the first week.

"But before that," said Dusk, "I think we should drop some acid."

"That's a great idea," said Sampson. "It'll be like a housewarming!"

So my communal buddies dumped the lump, establishing a pattern they'd maintain throughout our Corralitos stay. We straggled outside eventually, began digging the garden plot on the south side of the shack. I was only going through the motions and did twice as much as the rest of them. Somebody would finally get far enough down in the weeds to turn over a spade of ground and everybody else would exclaim and gather around it.

"Look at the earthworms! That's a good sign, isn't it?"

"And the soil … see how black and rich it is?"

"I feel like an early settler, out here with my pioneer brothers and sisters!"

Group hugs all around while I wandered off to the shade of a cherry tree. Before an hour passed I was alone out there while the rest of them fucked each other in the shack. Sampson was making so much noise that the Mexican kids stopped their game of baseball in the street, gathered around the broken fence out front to giggle into their palms.

The first week at Corralitos passed, then the second, and the garden plot was no further along than the broken pipes in the bathroom. It was easier to take sponge baths and shit and piss outside, then gather in the living room periodically to smoke (yelling over the stereo about what everybody would be responsible for the next day) than it was to fix things. We could do it because we'd brought enough dope for a month and only ate brown rice and vegetables.

Or everybody else did, anyway. I was pretty much living on ketchup and rice while envying the two German shepherds their beef-flavored kibble. This left me the odd man out when you threw in my lack of a woman and the fact I still hadn't done any drugs – I was just as intent on imprinting my brain with how bad sobriety felt as I was in remembering the terror of the d.t.'s. – so I began to spend less time at the shack and more in the surrounding countryside, often walking alone for hours at a stretch. (I enjoyed the damp, cloying fog in the morning hills best, the way I could only see a few feet in front of me. It seemed like an appropriate metaphor for my life at the time and, I suppose, is probably still suitable.)

Ambition would have helped, along with a need to prove something to somebody. But the booze cruise wasn't done yet and that made fantasizing about the life I'd never lead a bigger joke than it would have been otherwise. Mostly I just smoked and walked the dampness off my schizo shirt and scrubs. I'd return to the shack in the late afternoon, when everyone but Sampson was exhausted from sex and idleness, and retire to my living room corner to read through a box of musty *Reader's Digest Condensed Books* I'd found in a closet. It sounds like a grim, dark time but I remember it with surprising fondness: just six weeks before I'd been clinging to sanity so the chance to sit around and do nothing while I healed was a genuine blessing.

But all good things come to an end – especially when you're broke – and after a steady stream of visitors from Berkeley and assorted trips to the store the commune coffers were empty. Sampson heard that a cannery in Santa Cruz was hiring and I went with him to check it out. The vans were broken down at the time so we hitched the twenty miles and were hired on immediately. It seems the spinach crop was in and to get it out they were hiring anybody with two legs and a pulse. The foreman was reluctant to put me in the frozen foods section with only those flimsy green scrubs for pants, but that's where bodies were needed so Carl and I were given rubber gloves and little white caps, told to stand across from a couple Mexican women. They'd grab frozen packages of spinach from the conveyor belt at their sides, stack them twelve to a tray and slide the tray across rollers to us. It was our job to lift and stack them on the racks behind us. When these were full they'd be dragged to the refrigerated railcars in the yard.

It seemed simple enough but it was 30 degrees in there and other than trying to kill Gumbo I hadn't exercised my upper body in months. So I was shivering the first hour and exhausted the second from lifting those icy trays. By the time the 12-hour shift ended I could barely make it to the highway with Sampson.

"You know, Wilson," he said, waiting for me to catch up, "you're not in very good shape, man."

"Fuck off, Jocko," I moaned. "You think I went to Herrick to work out?"

"Well I thought you'd fall over in there. Maybe you should take tomorrow off."

I thought about the rice waiting for us when we got back to the shack. Contemplated how good it would be to sink my teeth into a nice, thick rib eye.

"No," I said, "it's time to return to the real world, Sampson."

It wasn't easy but I worked the next two weeks straight, telling myself it was for the burnouts back home (lighting the morning's tenth bowl of hash) but knowing the real reason was the lure of a good meal. When Carl and I were finally paid I cashed the nearly six hundred dollar check, gave him four hundred of it to hand over to the commune, then bought two thick steaks, a loaf of bread and onions and hitched back to Corralitos. My roommates were digging into a cold vegetarian's delight – sickly plates of seaweed, cauliflower, sesame seeds and the like – as I threw the steaks in a frying pan, loaded sliced onions on top of them and cranked up the burner. As the smell circulated through the shack I had to listen to the usual litany from the other room:

"Burnt flesh! Bad karma!"

"That steer's adrenaline is sizzling with the meat, Wilson, ready to poison *you!*"

I let the zucchini eaters jabber as I flipped the steaks in their hot, bubbling juices and buttered half a loaf of bread. When everything was ready I left the steaks and bread on a table in the kitchen and went outside for a good long piss. I was ready, damn it, I'd been fantasizing about those rib eyes for weeks.

Then I walked back inside to see Ulysses and Olympus, Dusk and Dawn's giant German shepherds, finishing off my plate of meat. I was speechless.

Dusk and the others, sitting against the living room wall with their rice bowls, looked over at me.

"What is it, High?" said Dusk.

"Your ... fucking dogs ... just ate my steaks!"

"Wow! Sorry about that, man."

"But they're carnivores, too," said Dawn. "Be cool and share."

"Yeah, they probably did you a favor, Wilson," said Elsa.

I just looked at them. Walked in, retrieved what was left of the bread, grabbed some rice and took my place beside the wall.

The next time a joint came by I grabbed it and sucked 'til my eyes watered.

I was gone from the commune a couple days after Carl and I quit at the cannery. He and Elsa were heading north to visit DeBola in Arcata, but I'd caused that character enough trouble and hitchhiked to the Bay Area instead. I got a room in a Burlingame boarding house and a job a few days later as a carpenter's assistant. I had no skills that didn't include a sledgehammer but they were hardly necessary, it was a Hillsborough remodel job that progressed at a leisurely pace. I tore down walls, banged nails, carried materials from one place to another and mostly just bullshitted with Carrie Williams, the wealthy woman of the house. She was twenty years older than I was but we became fast friends immediately and remain so to this day. She'd make lunch for old Ed the carpenter and me, even bring us lemonade on our breaks, and as long as she was paying the bills nobody seemed to care how long the job took.

The rooming house had been a vague attempt at avoiding the Burlingame Hotel's corrosive atmosphere but little by little over the next six weeks I began to drink on weekends. First it was only on Friday nights, then gradually Saturdays because I was so hungover from Friday and eventually, of course, Sunday mornings, where I'd try to moderate the withdrawal from the previous two days. It was no longer a matter of my needing a binge or excessive drinking to suffer the d.t.'s … they'd become as regular as cottonmouth now. It was scary but effective aversion therapy and the very thing that should have limited me to weekends the rest of my working/drinking days.

At this point my parents were also living in the Bay Area, having returned from Portland the previous fall. They were still pretending there was hope for me so introduced me to a friend who owned a San Leandro paper mill and by the second week of June I was working there as a Press Assistant.

I'd done a similar job in the Longview box plant. Essentially I stood at the front of the long press that printed colors and labels on boxes and fed them in stacks – cut but unfolded – into the hopper. It was only moderately difficult work and allowed me to put my brain on cruise control, doing whole shifts without really being there.

I was living in a sleazy motel five miles east of the plant, a distance I chose to walk everyday as opposed to using my '52 Green Cadillac. It was an odd old car that Gumbo had found for me. At first sight you might think it was payback for trying to kill him a couple months before, but the two of us had so much natural animosity that The Hulk incident was just another link in the chain. The quirky thing about that Cadillac, as Sampson reminded me when he was here, is that I was the only one who could start it. It had a touchy ignition button on the panel that had to be poked in a precise way (when the accelerator was halfway down) or the engine wouldn't turn over. I did it without thinking but remember now that I could never teach anyone else to do it.

(Not that friends were clamoring to get behind the wheel. My vehicles were interchangeable with the little rooms I lived in, so they were filled to the brim with empty bottles, cans and fast food containers. I pretty much drove garbage trucks around, actually.)

The Caddy had a hole in the radiator so I used to pour that

"Radiator Plug" gunk in there, a sludge made of tiny rubber divots. They were supposed to plug the hole but instead just slowed the leak enough that, if I were careful, I could make it over the San Mateo bridge on weekends without overheating.

The walk to work didn't amount to much ... it was summer and plenty warm. As for the motel it was cheap and rundown and will always hold a special place in my heart. My room was the last one in a dark back alley and only the toilet worked steadily (hot water and/ or a shower was a twice-a-week long shot). When I first moved in I went to turn on the TV and the knob fell off in my hand. *Perfect*, I thought, *I won't be bothered by distractions in this dump, I'll be able to concentrate on the reading and writing in peace.*

I "wrote" in a lot of rooms like that in the late 60s and early 70s but don't like to dwell on it because I rarely finished anything but the odd letter to friends. The rest was barely started or half-finished novels, autobiographical sketches, short stories and notes. I found some of them in the attic the other day. It was crap then and after 35 years in a box it's still crap (quite literally, in fact, stinking from a horse stall I used to live in), but it was surprising to see that something had survived that part of my life.

I also read novels, biographies, newspapers, discarded magazines, cereal boxes, anything I could get my hands on. Except for the worst of the drinking days (in places like Mexico with Lonesome Louie) I generally read at least 300 books a year and still do. My basic pace is 100 pages an hour and whether it's great literature or trash it all washes down the drain the same. I'm not boasting because there's little admirable about it, it's just the way my personal scanner operates. So when I'd be working a steady job like that box plant and trying not to drink during the week I did a lot of reading and writing when I got off at night.

Because I sure as hell wasn't sleeping ... five hours a night was a big deal. I'd lay low during the week and try to save my energy for Saturday night, when after six days of work I'd steer the Caddy across the bridge to wherever the party was that night. I was usually half-baked by the time I arrived and liked to take psychedelics as a counter balance, waking up all over the Bay Area on Sunday mornings. Sometimes I got lucky with college girls but usually I blew it by passing out or, worse, offering a prospect a ride home.

The whole summer passed like that and other than the way I felt on Sundays I had no serious complaints. Then one Saturday night, after a particularly wild party at Gumbo's cottage, I decided – for some drunken reason – that I should drive back to San Leandro. I'm not claiming I never drove drunk: myself and most of the people I knew in the Bay Area drove drunk constantly. It's just that I *tried* not to, particularly after an evening of LSD and vodka.

But my good sense was nowhere in sight that night. As I left Burlingame at midnight and steered south on El Camino Real I thought I was doing pretty well. I was drunk and vaguely hallucinogenic, sure, but I was on top of it, I'd driven under worse conditions and made it. Plus I was going so slow that I could feel all the bumps in the road, something I never experienced at regular speeds.

Then somewhere around Belmont I happened to look over at a Happy Pies Restaurant on my right. The first thing I noticed was how close it was to the road ... I was damn near scraping its outer wall with the Caddy. The next was how startled the people inside looked, as if they'd seen a ghost. *What's that about?* I wondered, just as I felt a bump and crash and a newspaper rack flew across the hood and banged the windshield.

Holy shit! I was driving on the sidewalk! How long had I been doing that!? I pulled a left onto the street itself, realized one of my front tires was flat even as I saw the flashing red lights behind me. First one squad car pulled up, then two more, all of them with their sirens blaring.

It seems I'd been driving on the sidewalk for awhile. I pushed open the door of the Caddy, wobbled onto the street with my hands extended.

"Just cuff me, boys," I slurred. "I'm totally shitfaced."

They took me to the county jail for booking and after the fingerprinting had me puff into a breathalyzer. By then I'd decided I wasn't so drunk after all, that in fact I'd been rash in my admission to the cops. I was trying to convince the one leading me to the drunk tank of this when his buddy behind the machine called me back.

"Seeeee," I said, "I'm not really drunk at all."

"High," said the Sergeant, "breathe into the tube again."

I did, expelling a noisy rush of air as I fought to stay upright. The Sergeant peered down at the results, shook his head.

"I thought so," he said, "I just couldn't believe it."

"What?" I laughed, triumphantly. "Not drunk after all, eh?"

"Buddy," he said, ripping off a sheet of graph paper and showing it to me, "according to this … you're legally dead!"

"Huh?" The other copper laughed, gave me a good shove in the back as I stumbled to the tank.

When I was writing about my reading and writing habits back in the day I was reminded of the absence of art during that period. It's another of the vagaries of an all-or-nothing nature, how someone who had drawn or cartooned virtually every day from ages two to eighteen could suddenly not only quit for twenty years ... but rarely even doodle in the interim. As if all that early stuff was me interpreting life, and once that interpretation morphed into experience I *became* a cartoon.

I know I always chalked it up to burnout myself, the mountain of drawings, posters, cards, little books, calendars, etc., that I drew for other people growing up. It was entirely my own doing, of course, I thought so little of my gift – considering it more gimmick than talent, as if everyone would cartoon if they didn't have better things to do – that I literally can't remember ever saying "no" to someone who asked for a drawing.

I read now about all these graphic novelists who were tortured bastards as kids, so abused by their families and peers that they retreated into a fantasy world that traps them even now. I could have used a little of that action. Instead I got *Leave It to Beaver:* a loving mom, an adoring father, three smiley jock brothers and all those weekends on ski slopes and lakes (at least until dad lost his business) … and became a fat drunk, anyway.

I suppose graphic novelist *might* have been better.

Of all the things that happened to me during my drinking years I have the hardest time remembering how I got *out* of jails. This is because I wouldn't have alcohol around in the morning so along with the generally sour patina of drunk tanks there'd be the alkie aura action: hallucinations, swirling panic attacks, accelerated heartbeat and difficulty breathing. It was in just such places, in fact, that I first learned to mask the madness. I believed that the degrading nature of withdrawal meant it should only be done in private; when I was caught out of my rathole – and jails were as caught as you got – I was forced to adopt protective measures, to learn how to go insane without anyone noticing.

To be a WASP Master, in other words, to look like a regular guy while my brain dribbled down my throat. The sheer *publicness* of my Herrick Hospital display had offended my sensibilities and would not be repeated. Instead I learned to blink-and-shake behind my eyes while staring straight ahead, keeping my nostrils slightly flared and mouth partly open. I know because it was a look I practiced in the mirrors of my little rooms. It is not an easy thing, staying cool while you're losing your mind. Take a couple hits of bad acid, wait until it peaks, then go chat up your Republican parents ... that'll give you a vague idea how weird it gets.

Still in the years after Herrick anyone around me while I withdrew would simply think I was constipated. It was Gumbo, of course, who came up with the best description of it. Not long after that drunk-driving incident I'd slept off a good one and was filling a glass of water in his kitchen when he walked in and saw me.

"Well," he declared to the other guys in the room, "there must not be any booze around. High's got his *dead sailor* look!"

After that it was a big joke among my Bay Area friends but again ... you had to catch me not holding any booze first, and that was a rare event. I woke from some of the worst drunks imaginable, the previous twenty-four to forty-eight hours a total blank, and could still remember where I'd hid enough hooch to get me on my feet the next day.

What I recall from the post-drunk-driving morning is getting an early September court date, along with a preliminary assessment of the damages (mostly crushed newsstands). When added to the towing and car storage fees the incident cost me $800 before I even went to court, a sum that pretty much equaled my savings for the summer.

I didn't have wealthy parents to help me through school but I did have Dick Kent, that Director of Financial Aid at Lower Columbia College. After a couple days back at the box plant I started thinking (like I always did when fall approached) that if I was going to be broke I might as well be in school. I called Dick, was given the usual promise of an Economic Opportunity Grant and a work-study job if I could make it up there for registration on the eighth of September.

My court date was the seventh. I worked at the plant right up to the day before, returned to the motel to pick up my portable typer and a paper bag full of underwear and socks, then drove to Burlingame and gave the Caddy to Gumbo. Except for the radiator it ran like a charm and I was sure he could clean it up, fix the starter, bang out the dents from my sidewalk cruise and make himself a few hundred. All I wanted in return was a place to sleep for the night. I had two hundred dollars to my name and since I'd paid all the damages associated with the episode I was hoping for no more than $150 fine.

That was the maximum penalty for drunk driving; when the judge threw in reckless driving the next morning the fine rose to $300.

"Okay," I sighed, reaching in my pocket. "But I've only got $200, Judge. I'll have to mail you the other hundred later."

He and the bailiff had a good laugh over that one. "Mr. High," said the judge, "you're lucky you didn't kill someone that night. You'll find a way to get $100 in the next sixty minutes or you'll do thirty days in the County Jail."

"What!? But I have to be in school tomorrow!"

"Good-bye, Mr. High."

I was taken to a little room off the courthouse and given a single phone call. I lit a cigarette, buried my head in my hands and thought about it. This was serious business ... who could I count on to show up with a hundred bucks in the next hour? When it finally hit me it was such an imposition that it was hard to make myself do it, but I thought about no free grant and thirty days in the slammer even as the second hand on the big wall clock ticked away.

Finally I gave up and called Carrie Williams, the woman who owned the house I'd been working on with Old Ed. Nia, her Japanese maid, answered, and I told her I needed to talk to Carrie immediately.

"She very busy," she told me, and I could hear the clamor of people and plates in the background.

"This is an emergency, Nia," I said. "I have to speak to her now."

"H'okay." She put the phone down and I lit another cigarette, listened to that infernal ticking. Wondered if they put a giant clock in there just to make losers like me sweat.

"Hello?"

"Carrie," I said, "this is Wilson."

"Oh hi, Wilson. How are you?"

"Not so good. Listen, I'm at the County Courthouse, I've just been fined $300 for that drunk driving incident, I only have $200 and if I don't come up with $100 in the next ... forty-five minutes ... I'm going to jail for thirty days. And I'm supposed to be in the Northwest tomorrow for the start of fall term."

"That ... sounds just like you, Wilson."

"Yeah yeah, real funny. So can you help me out here? I mean I hate to ask this obviously, but could you bring me that hundred bucks? You know I'm good for it."

"Well, I would, Wilson," she said, "but I'm having a cocktail party for Shirley Temple Black at the moment."

"Shirley Temple?"

"Yes. She was just appointed Ambassador to the United Nations, you know."

I laughed in spite of myself: I was getting reamed by the Good Ship Lollipop. "Never mind," I said, "I shouldn't have bothered you."

"I'm sorry, Wilson, maybe ..."

"No no, that's all right, I'll figure it out. Thanks anyway, pal."

I hung up and the bailiff across the room shrugged.

"No money?" he asked.

"No money," I said, and he took me to a holding tank behind the courthouse where I was shoved in with the rest of the clowns. A half hour after that a green jail bus pulled up and we were all handcuffed, chained one to the other in a line and shuffled out to the yard. I was literally one guy away from the bus steps when Carrie's big Buick screeched into the driveway. She jumped out in a silk dress and pearls, wobbled a couple steps in her high heels, took them off and ran the rest of the way, waving a hundred dollar bill over her head.

She handed the money to the bailiff and – after paying off the clerk and collecting my typewriter – drove me to the Greyhound Depot in Burlingame. We were pulling up in front when I thought, *Hell, how am I going to pay for the bus, I've only got 80 cents to my name.*

I looked over at Carrie and it was like she read my mind, handing me still another Ben Franklin. "Thanks, Carrie," I said. "This is as nice a thing as anybody's ever done for me. I'll repay you when I can."

"I don't care about the money, Wilson," she said. "Just stay sober."

I looked at her.

"Well," she laughed, "how about you put me in your book someday instead."

Done.

I cited jumping in Dove's birthday cake as the one thing I'd change about my drinking years but that obviously isn't true: I was just as saddened by the number of times Dick Kent extended me grant money and I repaid his trust by dropping out of school. Yes, I graduated from college eventually, and there's little doubt that it was loans and grants and work-study jobs that made it possible, and I know Dick forgave me (and realized I was a risk to begin with) because of my drinking problem ... it's just that I always expected better of myself.

Because I shouldn't have been back in school to begin with. I had no particular interest in it and the longer I went and the more I used up the few classes that interested me the less reason I had to continue. It wasn't like I had a profession in mind ... at sixty-four I'm *still* waiting for that light bulb.

But Kent believed in me and worked hard to keep me on board. When I arrived in Longview in September of '69 the first thing he did was tell me about ESARF.

"ESARF," I said. "What the hell's that?"

335

"It stands for Evergreen State Alcoholic Recovery Foundation. They've got their headquarters down in Vancouver but they're buying buildings in cities all over the southwest part of the state. Making them into recovery houses, in fact, a place where alcoholics can live together and build a sense of community, maybe help each other out with their problems."

"Huh."

"And the exciting news is they're opening a recovery house right here in Longview. I heard their local representative speak at a Lion's Club meeting the other night and, well … I hope you won't think this presumptuous of me, Wilson, but I told him your situation and he said that if you were willing to help out around the place … paint, wash walls, mow the lawn, et cetera … he'd give you a room for free."

Great, I thought, *my own special interest frat house.* "Sure, Dick," I said, and got the details and my grant check from him. Walked the two miles to the address on Tanner Avenue and saw the place long before I reached it, a huge, dilapidated old building that must have been a rooming house once. As I drew closer I saw a dark-haired, cadaverous character hunched over the steps. He wore thick glasses and was pounding a nail into the bottom of a handrail.

Or trying to, anyway … he hit the step more often than the nail and seemed relieved when I interrupted him.

"You must be Ken Donski," I said, walking up and extending my hand.

"Yeah, man," he said. "And you're the kid Kent told me about? Wilson High?"

"Yeah."

"What kind of name is that?"

He had a voice like gravel and was so skinny and desiccated he could have been a corpse. I guessed he was fifty or sixty years old and they'd been hard years, there was no doubting that. I couldn't stop staring at him.

336

"What?" he said finally.

"Sorry," I said, "but you look like one of those Pennsylvania coal miners you see in the old photos."

"The fuckin' lungers? The grimy guys with bulging eyes? The assholes who look like they're gonna die any second?"

"Exactly."

"I'm a different kind of underground, Wilson. I shot heroin for forty years."

"*Forty years!*" I exclaimed. "I didn't know that was possible."

"Fuck yeah! Compared to booze junk's a goddamned preservative!"

We bonded quickly. Here was a guy who'd gone through a lifetime of withdrawal, an old hipster who'd chased the dragon in dingy little rooms from Rhode Island to Nevada. After dozens of failed attempts he'd quit using three years before and was now working for ESARF.

He was better at it than the Herrick staff just by virtue of his credibility. I'd sit up late at night listening to his horrific yarns of a life lived on death's blade. Clinics, penitentiaries, junkie girlfriends, shit jobs, overdoses, straightjackets, gunshot and knife wounds ... it seemed Ken had seen and done every horrible thing imaginable.

And survived it all. It gave me hope for my Existential Alkie approach. In the meanwhile, as the first official tenant of the recovery house my deal (and the rules) was simple: I would get a free room and use of the community kitchen as long as I helped with the painting and yard chores and didn't use drugs or alcohol. The local Alcoholics Anonymous chapter would be holding meetings at the house soon and when it did I was required to attend.

Other than that I was on my own. It was a good arrangement because Ken had as little interest in the lawn as I did and painting the second floor hallway was nothing to me. The house was monstrous and there were ten bedrooms and a bathroom up there. I picked the smallest room in the darkest corner for my own and spent most of my time studying World Literature or Philosophy, whatever took my mind

337

off the ennui. Ken was very helpful in that respect. When the weekend came around and I'd tell him I was dying to go out and get blasted he'd slap his hands and encourage me.

"I'm *used up!*" he'd croak, the perennial Viceroy hanging from his lower lip. "If I were your age trying to quit something? With all the drugs available now? I'd never make it, kid."

He was the first person who'd put my youth to use by challenging me that way. He'd act like I didn't have the guts to make it, so I'd dig down and find another day of sobriety just to prove his skinny ass wrong.

In the meanwhile there were the twice weekly AA meetings. It was great seeing all the rummies from the year before, and I was used to being Thomas Wolfe to Katie Sue, Dan X's wife, but those meetings were really long and – between the studying and my janitor work-study job – I didn't have three hours to give away at night. I appealed to Ken for an occasional AA waiver – there were no other tenants in the house so who would know? – but he thought the fellowship was good for me.

"You're the brooding loner type, High," he said, "same as I am. Being around people who care about you and share your problem is important. That's the *point* of these ESARF houses."

It's true I had few friends on campus, but when I wasn't drinking or stoned I rarely sought the company of other human beings, anyway. I did hook up with a woman named Karen, a thirty-five-year-old, divorced mother of six who was desperate enough to fuck me in my room, but I wasn't that friendly a person sober and – if I considered myself a peripheral character *before* the mental ward stint – I felt like an alien now: the difficulty of being a twenty-two-year-old alkie worked both ways.

But I was trying. So when the end of October neared and all the AA chapters in the surrounding towns had a Halloween Party in Rainier, Boregon (just across the Columbia River from Longview), I agreed to go to it with Ralph X., my AA sponsor from the year before. We drove over in his beater Renault and it was something about the two of us in the front of that little car, a couple of fat losers making the seats squeak as we chain-smoked Picayune cigarettes ("The Pride of New Orleans") and sucked on cans of Coke ... that made me flip the switch. The "fuck it" switch, the idea of *how could drunkenness be worse than this?*

At first I tried to pretend otherwise. The party was at a barn outside of town and after parking we walked in on hundreds of alkies and their long-suffering families. Most of the latter were wearing brave smiles and, I imagine, trying to forget the bad ol' days, when the punch would have some extra pop to it. Now the wives and kids sipped it while the ex-boozers burned through coffee and cigarettes. As I moved through the crowd and members of the different chapters came up to greet me – I was still the twenty-two-year-old prince then, the one young drunk in the tri-county area seeking help – all I could think was:

"Which are you drinking, the water or the wave?"

It was a quote from John Fowles' novel, *The Magus,* and in the two years since I'd read the book it was the first time I'd remembered the phrase. Now I couldn't get rid of it, it was rolling around my head like some wretched *Steely Dan* song. Was this an omen? I went over to the punch bowl in the center of the room, looked at the pallid fruit floating on top, then the jack-o'-lanterns and little Twelve-Step placards all around and thought ... *I'm going with the wave, baby.*

It was a two-mile slog in the rain back to town. I stopped at the first grocery store I came to, bought a gallon of *Chablis Blanc.* I'd never been a wine guy but I had two dollars on me and there was no State Liquor Store around so wine it would have to be. I found a warehouse porch that was sheltered from the downpour. Sat in the dark inhaling the wet stench of the pulp mills across the river. I don't recall how much of the gallon I finished, maybe half of it or so, before I left it there for the next guy and wandered back to the AA function. I was just going to sit in Ralph X.'s Renault, kind of wait the party out, but once I was finally at the barn, saw the lights were still on and heard noise from inside, I decided fuck it, if I can hide the d.t.'s from people I can sure as hell hide a sip of wine or two.

So I went in through a side door. There was a ceremony going on, various alkies marching to the microphone to accept sobriety awards. The crowd was cheering them on and I slowly drifted to the back of the room, keeping to the shadows and walls until I found a pole to lean on. I had a vague suspicion I should have taken a piss before coming in and it grew to a certainty as more and more alkies took the stand. They were being acknowledged for six months sobriety, or one year, two years or whatever, and once they got hold of the mike they didn't want to give it up until they'd thanked everybody they could think of. That was fine, if I'd been sober for a couple years I'd have something to say about it, too, I supposed, but I *really* had to piss. There was only one men's room and it had a long line from all the caffeine being consumed and the way I smelled I didn't want to get near anyone, anyway.

I glanced around. I was in the dark at the back of the barn and there was no one within ten feet of me. Maybe with enough noise and people's attention elsewhere I could piss where I stood.

I gritted my teeth, waited for the right moment. It came when Dan X. accepted his three years of sobriety award. He was a major windbag and I figured I could easily empty my bladder while he rattled on. I eased out my dick and let go a torrent behind the pole, a burning hot piss that filled the cracks in the floor and ran under my boots.

I was gasping with joy and weaving a little unsteadily as Dan thanked everyone, made a joke, then said something to the effect that what really kept him sober was the young people in AA.

What was that? I tried to ease the pressure on the spigot so I could hear better, made out something about "the ones who have the guts to confront their problem early like we should have!"

There was a roar of affirmation from the crowd and I turned up the pressure again, trying to *push* that piss out.

"Yessir," roared Dan, getting really worked up now, "young people like Wilson from our Longview group! Where are you, Wilson, you were in the back there awhile ago. Come up here and take a bow, son!"

Fuuuuuuuuuuuuuuuuuuuuucccccccckkkkkkkkk!!!!!!! I shut off the valve, shoved my dick back in my pants and zipped up. Turned around slowly hoping no one had spotted me yet ... only to look out on dozens of smiling, expectant faces.

"There you are, Wilson!" boomed Dave. "Get out of that corner and into the light where we can see you!"

I eased out of the shadows, my boots squirshing while I held my fat thighs together. I hadn't sought a Higher Power my whole time in AA but I started to then. *Oh shit, Lord!* I prayed, raising a hand to wave as the clapping began, *I need your help now ... I can't fuckin' hold it!*

I took another jerky step or two, then the dam burst, hot piss running down my leg and out the cuff of my jeans.

"Hey!" yelled some fat kid. "He's pissin' his pants!"

"And he's drunk!" yelled somebody else. "He's fallin' over back here!"

All of a sudden the only sound in the room was the waterfall down my leg. *So much for the young alkie faction,* I thought, as Katie Sue jumped up from her seat and wailed.

"Oh Thomas!" she cried. "What have you done now!?"

The males in my family have always been suckers for dogs. We had a long succession of them growing up, everything from boxers and collies to spaniels and shepherds. There were no leash laws back then and certainly no pooper-scooper brigades. Instead the dogs were allowed to run free until they, in turn, were run over by cars. I'd venture we lost four mutts that way and another two or three to hereditary diseases before a tough little beagle made it into our teens.

My brothers continue to raise dogs while I've respected our canine companions by not doing so. Only once did I weaken, when I was twenty-eight years old and drifting through the Bay Area. Somehow I ended up at a ranch in Half Moon Bay with Ned Gumbo, where he, a plate of hash cookies and a bottle of rum convinced me I needed a ride to Seattle and a Scottish Deerhound puppy (in about that order). Or maybe it was that he'd only give me a ride if I took one of the puppies.

I know he spoke of those dogs in hushed, reverent tones, how they had a long and glorious heritage and only royalty could possess them in ancient Scotland et cetera. It was true as far as it went, I suppose, but that's why Ned owned them: he considered Deerhounds the ultimate chick magnets. He'd stuff two or three dogs in the open bed of his power wagon, then drive to wherever the girls were and park at the curb. If you'd never seen the breed before – and most people hadn't – it was difficult to walk by his truck without remarking on them.

"It's better than a personality, Wilson," he used to tell me. "First you've got the perfect conversation piece; second you're a caring, sensitive guy just by association with the dogs; and third … well Christ! you own Deerhounds! obviously you're a man of taste and refinement, too!"

By the time midnight arrived I was sure I'd told Ned I wasn't interested in a puppy *or* a ride to Seattle. Six hours later I came to in the back of his speeding truck. The sun was barely up and he'd affixed a camper shell so I was only partially freezing. I groaned, tried to gauge the hangover ahead. Gradually became aware of two distinct sounds: one was a soft whimpering off to my left, the other a vile screeching from the cab area.

I checked out the whimpering first. The sweet, doe-eyed, ungainly creature on the blanket beside me had to be my puppy. Gumbo had named him Jowett (after one of his shyster cars), but he seemed so sad and vulnerable that I changed it to "Bukowski." Wrapped another blanket around him, sat up and looked through the back of the cab at Ned. He was, as I suspected, alone in there, screaming at imaginary enemies as he sped along at 100 miles an hour.

I peered even closer, saw the plate of hash cookies on the seat beside him. It was empty, so there was no percentage in distracting the fool. I hunkered down, drew Bukowski closer and gave him a hug.

"It's hard to believe, pal," I said, "but you may actually *be* better off with me."

If only that were so. Once in Seattle we moved to three different places in two weeks before holing up at Nearly Normal Jimmy's house in Bellevue. Bukowski was six months old by then and would have been hard to house-train under normal circumstances. As it was he was always shitting in one room or another. I tried to discipline him but knew my aimless lifestyle (the very reason I'd avoided pets in the first place) was the main culprit.

Well, that and his sweet face. Like his namesake, Bukowski was a very unusual-looking character; it was obvious Ned had given him to me because he was that rare, non-regal, ugly Deerhound. His knobby head was too small for his long legs and body and his coat dull and scraggly even for a puppy. Plus he had little monkey eyes and wasn't too bright.

Which only made me love him more, of course. Maybe not enough to go out and get a job so we could have a place of our own, but enough that it broke my heart when he disappeared one day. I'd gone to the back door to let him in and he was nowhere in sight. A search of the neighborhood proved fruitless so I called the pound the next morning and sure enough, they'd picked him up on Nearly Normal's street.

Jimmy and I drove over to bail him out but I refused to pay the additional, $20 fine for an unleashed dog. The humane society officer claimed Bukowski had not only run out of Jimmy's yard and barked at him, but chased his truck, too. This was preposterous.

"My God!" I told the clerk, "this is a *Deerhound!* They don't chase other dogs, much less trucks or people! And the idea of him barking like a common cur ... well, it's too outrageous to contemplate! If that officer scooped up my dog he had to come into our yard to do it!"

Maybe I'd been listening to Gumbo too long, but I meant every word of it: Bukowski may have been an ugly Deerhound, but he *was* a Deerhound. So two weeks later I went to court to fight the ticket. I'd found a five-dollar bill on the sidewalk the day before and Jimmy and I had celebrated with a case of *Rainier Ale*. We were late getting to the courtroom the next morning and ran up the hallway to an elevator. Slipped inside with a group of other people. As the doors slid shut I saw a black guy in a suit come running towards us.

"Hold the door!" he yelled. "Please hold the door!"

I was the closest and should have obliged him, I suppose, but I felt like a gravel truck, as if I were all hard, rough edges. I started to lift a hand, then dropped it back to my side.

The black guy lunged and squeezed two fingers through the doors. Pushed his way inside and glared at me all the way to the fifth floor.

Ten minutes later Jimmy and I were seated in the courtroom when the bailiff stood up. "Please rise for the Honorable James Richardson," he said.

I watched the judge walk in. It was the black guy from the elevator.

"Say, Nearly Normal," I said. "You got a twenty I can borrow?"

After that I admitted what I'd known all along and started looking for a better home for Bukowski. It took a few phone calls, but eventually my farmer brother Ben – who'd seen and admired Ned's Deerhounds – agreed to take the dog if I could transport him to his Northern California spread. I did that by talking Doc Willard, an old college buddy who was unemployed at the time, into driving us down there in his van. (I promised him we'd head to Lake Tahoe afterwards; it was mid-May, the prime hiring time for the Stateline casinos.)

So one morning before dawn we rolled onto I-5 South and were at Ben's farm north of Sacramento twelve hours later. He had another dog named Ulysses and the idea was that Bukowski, bred over the centuries to chase deer, would teach him how to hunt.

The next morning Doc and I pulled away as Bukowski watched us from Ben's front porch. I was doing the best I could for him but it didn't stop me from sobbing uncontrollably. It's still the most poignant moment of my young life, the instant when all the things I'd never be rose to smack me in the face.

I got a job in the slot department at Harvey's Casino and a room in a rundown motel off the highway. Doc drove back to Seattle, stopping at the farm on his way to give Ben the particulars.

Two weeks later the motel manager knocked on my door, said I had a long distance call at the office. I walked over and when I picked up the phone it was Ben. *Aha!* I thought. *Probably calling to thank me for Bukowski*.

"Wilson?" he said.

"Yeah?"

"I just want you to know I'm going to shoot your dog."

"What!? Why!?" Ben was a no-nonsense farmer: if he said something, he meant it.

"I have never seen a more useless living thing. Do you know what he does all day?"

"Uhhhh … nothing?"

"Exactly! I'm only sure he's alive because he eats the food I put in front of him. Otherwise he acts like a goddamned library lion."

"He's a Deerhound, Ben. That's what they do … they're ornaments."

"What about the deer hunting?"

"Has he seen any deer?"

"No, but there's plenty of other crap around. Rabbits, pheasants, gophers, squirrels …"

"Deer only. If a deer comes through your yard you'll see one of the world's great predators at work. 'Til then … well, you're stuck with a library lion."

"I'm shooting him."

"Wait! Let me call Gumbo first, see if he wants him back."

Ben said he'd wait forty-eight hours and, surprisingly, not only was I able to track Ned down, but he agreed to drive over to the farm and pick Bukowski up. (He may have been a third-string Deerhound, but he wasn't going to let some farmer shoot him.)

He returned him to that Half Moon Bay ranch where, ironically, the neighboring farmers shot him. Three different times over the years: twice in the body and once in the right back leg. He kept confusing their cattle and sheep for deer, yet not only survived *their* attempts on his life, but also nature's.

Because before he died at fourteen (twice the normal life span of a Deerhound), he'd been recognized in the breed's newsletter as The World's Oldest Living Deerhound.

'Atta boy. Turns out you were regal after all.

It's only since I've been writing this memoir that I realized how many times I made an ass of myself in Longview, Washington. The firehouse episode, the burning payloader, the runaway railcar, getting drunk at the AA party and pissing myself ... all of it while squandering a free education.

After the Halloween party I was down the road in twenty-four hours. I had a hundred dollars in my pocket and a vague notion of returning to the Bay Area eventually, but made a point of stopping in Portland first. My brother Joe, one year my junior and a senior at Portland State, lived in a downtown apartment and managed a tavern in Beaverton called "The Spigot."

I was there to see him but after a couple days in my company he decided it was the tavern I was really interested in. He might have been right ... I've never had a relationship that's less fathomable to me than the one I have with Joe. My optimistic slant is that because we were born fourteen months apart, even shared the same room until we were teenagers, that there must have been a time when we were close.

But that may be an illusion on my part ... sometimes you're just the older brother and that's the end of it. The much taller older brother in this instance, the one whose passion for books and art was countered by Joe's for sports and cars. Our main source of conflict, in fact, may well be how alike we are, the way we both inherited the Irish in the family so not only do we compete for the storytelling limelight, we often have differing versions of the same event.

There's no arguing that Joe's fashioned a successful career from his blarney, though. He's had his own bar and restaurant in Lake Tahoe for twenty-five years now, whereas The Spigot was his first management job and I was the black sheep brother who'd disappeared into a bender while he was still in high school.

So his trepidation at my sudden appearance was natural. That's why I was there: to reconnect, to be the big brother Joe had never had. Just as soon as I spent my last hundred bucks on a series of drunken nights with old high school pals, that is, coming home early in the a.m. to pass out on the floor of his kitchen. When the money was gone I was browsing the Help Wanted section of the newspaper, more interested in quick cash than a job, when I spotted an advertisement in the corner:

MONEY PAID FOR BLOOD
EARN UP TO $10 A WEEK!

I thought about it. If I was staying with Joe and grabbing the occasional free lunch at The Spigot (he quickly learned not to let me drink in there), I could stick to cheap wine and *live* on ten dollars a week.

I walked down to the blood bank and discovered that you only earned the ten dollars a week if you donated plasma, i.e., had a pint of your blood taken out, the plasma removed, then the blood reinserted with a creepy, cold chemical added. Or you could give a pint of blood outright and wait two weeks between donations.

I went the plasma route just once. The blood they returned to me gave me the chills and the whole process took too long: sitting there with needles in you and looking around at the other donors was pretty depressing. This was the 60s, before all the sophisticated hepatic tests they have now, and there were a lot of guys in there that looked worse than I did. This is another step down I thought, four years ago I was an All-City basketball player, an Honor Roll student and Class President in this town. Now I'm a fat drunk hawking his blood for wine.

I got over it soon enough once I was outside with the money. I bought a couple gallons of *Gallo*, brought them back to the apartment and drank them over a couple of days. When Joe realized I was selling my blood to avoid working he knew desperate measures were called for.

"Wilson," he said, "I want you to play on my flag football team at the college."

I laughed, lit another cigarette. "That," I said, "is the worst idea I ever heard."

Three days later I was lining up at defensive end on a muddy Portland State field. It seems ludicrous to suggest I did well at it because not only was I an alkie dirtbag but the league was a difficult one with guys on other teams who were much bigger and tougher than I was.

But under all that fat I was still twenty-two and an athlete. Not the jock my gung-ho brothers were maybe, or even as competitive as most guys my age, but along with being stronger than I looked I had an uncanny knack for grabbing flags.

Plus like most males, Joe and I connected best on a playing field. He was the quarterback on offense and the cornerback behind me on defense (the same as when we were kids) so he'd give me directions and I'd go where he told me. It took a whole quarter of that first game before I threw up, and two more games before I could make it through four quarters without laying down, but by then the team was 6-0 and I'd actually curtailed my boozing. It wasn't easy but Joe appreciated it and on the second weekend of December we played an undefeated squad from another division for the league championship.

They were a mostly Samoan fraternity and it was a vicious defensive football game. I had my nose bloodied by the giant asshole blocking me before the first series of downs were complete. My only satisfaction was twice rubbing off him to grab the flag from the halfback's hip on sweeps (which just got me another shiver in the mouth on the next series).

At the end of the second half I was barely standing and had never so wanted a game to end. The weather was cold and icy and we were leading 7-0 with thirty seconds remaining when their best wide receiver beat Joe in the corner of the end zone for a score. Now it was 7-6 and they were lining up for the extra point that would tie the game. Joe signaled for a time-out, called the other defensive lineman over while I sat on the grass and moaned. I wasn't sure, but I thought that huge Samoan had given me a concussion.

Finally Joe walked over and bent down next to me. "Listen," he said, "you got anything left?"

"What's it look like?" I gasped.

"So we don't want a tie game and an overtime here. I'm the one who was beat on that play, you know."

"Yeah, yeah ..."

"So I want you to line up at right tackle. Pete and Travis are going to do a stunt and, if it works, you should be able to squeeze into the backfield and block the kick. I'm counting on you, Wilson, you're our tallest guy."

I grinned in spite of myself ... that's what he used to say to me in the varsity basketball huddles. I struggled to my feet, dragged my ass over to the right tackle spot. *At least I'll be away from that monster on the other end,* I thought; *let Travis take one for the team.* The ball was snapped, he and Pete did their stunt and, magically, the center moved to help block them as I took three long steps, left my feet in the best leap I could manage and *Thunk!* the kicker whacked the ball right into my chest. I'd done it, I'd blocked the kick, and the rest of the team jumped on me and the ball as we rolled triumphantly in the grass.

Afterwards there were beers all around and I woke up the next day with brain bayonets. I'd barely had a glass of wine when Joe came out and dragged me to his car. He had a shift to work at The Spigot and insisted on treating me to a lunch. It was a large, two-level tavern with a bar, booths, tables and a dance floor on top and a long stretch of pool tables below. A light snow was falling as we arrived and Joe made me a sandwich, then went behind the bar to help Tim Olson, a guy we went to school with. He's a wrestling coach at a high school in Portland now and lives a few blocks from me. I see him occasionally on my walks and the last time we hooked up he recounted what he saw that day:

"Your brother was so proud of you," he said. "Not only for blocking that kick but the fact you'd cut back on the drinking. I mean up until then he'd been really disappointed in your ass. And why not? You weren't just a drunk, you know, you were such an intense, fuckin' *psycho* drunk! Anyway, he makes you a sandwich and you eat it and your face is all swollen and puffy from the game and I wanted to give you a beer but Joe said no, the last thing he wanted was you fucked up in *his* tavern.

"So we got real busy and I didn't know where you went off to until maybe an hour, an hour-and-a-half later, when this Jeff guy comes to the bar. He's a semi-regular, and he says 'Hey Joe!' then motions to the lower level. 'Is that big fucker down there your brother?'

"Joe looked out at the pool tables and there you were sitting against the wall with your head down. 'Yeah,' said Joe. 'So?'

"'Well,' said Jeff, 'I'm not trying to be an asshole or anything, and everyone else down there is afraid to say anything because, you know, we really like you, Joe.'

"And you know zero bullshit, hardworking Joe ... we got things to do in there and the drink servers are backing up so he tells this Jeff guy to cut to the chase and Jeff says, 'Well, when one of us gets up to take a shot at the pool table, your brother drinks our beer!'

"'What!?' said Joe, just as we look down there and sure enough, some old guy stood up from his table and as soon as he figured out his shot and bent over the table, you jumped up, grabbed his half-full pitcher of beer, tipped it in your mouth and believe me, you didn't just drink it, High ... you splashed it all over your face and shirt in the process. I'm telling you, it's hard to look at you now and think of the clown taking that beer shower because, really, it was so goddamned *outrageous!*

"In a place Joe was responsible for no less. He literally *leapt* over the bar, ran down to where you were, grabbed you by the collar, then told me to take over while he pushed you outside. I heard later that he what ... took you to the highway and threw you out?"

"Something like that," I said.

Actually he let me go back to his apartment first, pick up my portable typer, then he took me to the highway. It was snowing and I had nothing but a jean jacket that was as soaked with beer as I was. Joe hadn't spoken since we left the tavern; this was the worst to him, that I'd somehow usurped the High family honor by making a fool of myself in a tavern.

We stopped beneath an overpass and he reached in his pocket, pulled out a twenty-dollar bill and tossed it to me.

"Thanks, Joe," I said. "I'll pay you back."

"Oh you already have," he said. "And big brother?"

"Yeah?"

"Don't come back, okay?"

"Oh," I said, shivering as I stepped out into the cold, "you can count on that, pal."

It was fifteen years before I stopped in Portland again.

I blocked that %#$@&%$* kick, though.

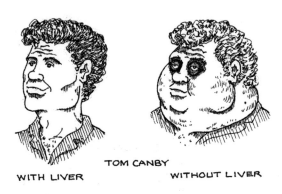

TOM CANBY

WITH LIVER   WITHOUT LIVER

Gumbo called the other day to tell me Tom Canby had slipped into a coma and been rushed to an intensive care unit. After all these years of waiting he'd finally climbed to No. 3 on the liver transplant list and now it looks like he'll die before he gets one.

"Oh don't be too sure, Gumbo," I said. "They've counted him, you and me out before. As a matter of fact … do you know the quantum physics theory that maintains there's actually infinite dimensions beyond this one, all of them slightly different from each other?"

"No."

"Well, trust me … if it's true, this is the only one where the three of us are still alive."

And sure enough, this morning Canby woke and asked for solid food. He comes from that old White Russian stock that lives as long as rocks: his grandparents were so ancient they had to be dragged to the grave and his mother, as I've mentioned earlier, made fourteen suicide attempts before succeeding.

And even that was just luck.

I've been disappointed over the years by the lack of mobility in my friends' kids, particularly the ones that finished high school and didn't continue their education. They hang around Portland in dead-end jobs when, at the very least, they could be bumming around the West Coast, trying out other cities and states, getting a little perspective on the show.

But I suppose it isn't that easy anymore, is it? Not only could I always find cheap places to live when I was their age, but the jobs were *everywhere*. Many of them were horrible, low-paying factotum tasks, I'll grant you, but they were also temporary and if you didn't like the one you had you just walked down the street and got yourself another one.

Actually, now that I think about it, maybe that was just me; except for Sampson none of my other friends have had 50 full-time jobs. I know I was looking for something better than usual when I arrived back in the Bay Area. I had a terrible cold from hitchhiking in those beer-soaked clothes and Gumbo, perhaps because it was nearly Christmas, was feeling providential and let me sleep in the crawlspace above his bar. I spent the holidays cocooned in there, fighting fever and congestion and living on soup.

It kept me sober, though, and with a new set of Goodwill clothes and a bit of a hair and beard trim I was ready to look for work in January.

Hopefully some kind of office job. I picked up the *San Mateo Bugle* Help Wanted ads and it turned out the paper was looking for a copy boy. I arranged an interview and, as usual in those circumstances, the woman in charge of personnel was dubious: I was a little old for copy boy action and most of my previous jobs had been blue-collar.

Then I aced the spelling test and typed over 110 words a minute and she hired me on the spot.

It was my job to get to the newspaper at five every weekday morning (it was a two-mile walk from Gumbo's cottage) and pull and clip the copy off the UP and AP ticker tapes. I'd hang it on hooks for the appropriate editors, then spend the rest of the shift checking typos, running errands for City Room guys or sitting at my desk reading. It was moronic work and I was paid accordingly but I liked the early hours and enjoyed the hard drinking, hard smoking company of the editors and reporters. (It was the only job I ever had where my co-workers looked worse than I did in the morning.)

Well, other than Fridays, anyway. I was trying to stay off alcohol between Sunday and Wednesday and confine my drug activities to pot and mescaline. Then one Tuesday afternoon in early February I came home to the cottage and climbed into my crawlspace for a nap. Gumbo was out of town at the time and after a two-hour snooze I woke at quarter of three in the afternoon, splashed some water on my face and left to visit Carrie Williams. Once every week or two I'd spend the afternoon with her and her kids, then stay for dinner afterwards. It was a nice, civilized interlude in my otherwise twisted days and was definitely the closest I came to home-cooked meals.

That Tuesday I stayed later than usual, though, and returned to Gumbo's place around 10:00 p.m. It was dark and cold and walking up the driveway I heard the murmur of voices in the back yard. I figured friends had broken into the cottage and were having a party (I'd done it often enough myself over the years) and was irritated that I'd have to throw them out to sleep.

Then I rounded the corner of the house in front and looked out on a large cluster of people. Jeanie Kelly, one of Gumbo's ex-girlfriends, was cradling something in her arms and gasped when she saw me. She ran over, grabbed me around the waist and hugged me.

"Oh Wilson!" she said, "I feel so bad for you and Ned!"

I was baffled. "Why?" I said. "What's up?"

She stepped back and pointed towards the cottage. "Ned's place! The way it burned to the ground like this!"

I followed her hand and suddenly realized that yes, you could see right through Gumbo's scorched, crumbling cottage to the neighbor's fence beyond. Jesus! My heart sank as I ran through a personal checklist. Had I been drinking earlier? No. Had I cooked something and left a gas burner on? No. Had I left a cigarette burning? No. Had I left the gas heater going? Yes, but I always did that in the winter. So did Ned.

"What the hell happened?" I said.

"The fire department said that sometime around three o'clock the gas heater exploded."

Minutes after I'd left for Carrie's house: if I'd been asleep in my crawlspace I'd be toast.

"But not all's lost, Wilson!" said Jeannie, brightening.

"Oh yeah?"

"Look!" she cried, shoving the bundle at me. It was an old plastic satchel of mine that had melted around some papers inside.

"Your manuscript is the *only* thing that survived the fire, Wilson!" she said. "It's a sign ... you must be destined to be a writer after all!"

I didn't tell her it was just some old *Western Civ* notes.

357

EMUS

After the cottage burned down I rented a room at The Town & Country Hotel. It was just up the street from my old digs at The Burlingame Hotel but appreciably upscale: it cost thirty dollars a week instead of twenty and catered to mostly working drunks.

Of course, just like at The Burlingame I was the only tenant under forty years of age. That and the desperate ambiance of those places was unsettling to my friends. Most of them visited at least once but I can't remember anyone – even Gumbo or Lonesome Louie – doing it twice. They treated those hotels with the same trepidation they did the mental wards and I couldn't understand it.

Unless it was my room that bugged them: I still wasn't good at throwing empties out. Anyway, it was while I was working at *The Bugle* and shortly after I moved into the hotel that I heard from Lonesome Louie for the last time. The publisher of *The Bugle*, Thomas Tapton III, was a wealthy, high society character who looked like

Alfred Hitchcock with hair. I'd only seen him once – a fleeting glance in the executive offices when I had to deliver something to a secretary up there – but the word was that he rarely appeared in the newsroom.

Then one morning in early March, when I was trying to stay conscious after an all-nighter on peyote, Tip Wade, the assistant City Editor, rolled across the floor on his chair.

"Jesus Christ," he said, "look sharp, High! Mr. Tapton's on his way down!"

"Really?" I yawned. "Why?"

"No one knows ... that's what's scary."

All of a sudden the generally raucous newsroom quieted to a murmur as newsmen and editors straightened their ties and stubbed out their cigarettes. I heard the Managing Editor saying something in the hallway, then the portly Tapton breezed into view, took a regal left into the newsroom ... and marched straight to my desk.

I looked at the gut under his silk vest, slowly worked my way up to his face.

"I presume you're the Copy Boy?" he asked.

"Yessss ..."

"Mr. Wilson High?"

"Yessss ..."

He reached into the pocket of his suit, removed a photograph and made a great show of handing it across the desk to me, holding it between his thumb and forefinger like a used condom. I reached up and took it from him, saw it was a picture of a desert shack encircled by barbed wire.

"If you flip the photo over," said Tapton, "you'll see it's actually a postcard addressed to you."

I did as he suggested, tried to read the smeared handwriting on the cardboard:

To WILSON HIGH (Thieving, Cocksucking,

Motherfucking, Beaner Buttfucking Copy
Boy Piece of Shit!)
c/o THOMAS TAPTON the TURD!
San Mateo Bugle
12 Railway Road
San Mateo, CA

Jesus! I recognized Louie's scrawl and cleared my throat to say something, but Tapton held up his hand and bent over the desk instead.

"Perhaps, Mr. High," he said, giving me a good blast of martini breath, "you could receive your … *personal* mail at home from now on."

"Absolutely," I said. "I don't know how this person even knew where I …"

But he'd already spun on his heel and left, strutting back to his perch amongst a slew of lackey head nods.

How *had* Lonesome found me? I picked up the card and read the message:

Dear High:

This is my latest Total Environment Room. I live here hoping the heat will kill me before I do. You're the only Friend I ever had.

Be Brave … you're next!

~ Louie

Tip Wade rolled over and looked at me. "Well?" he said. "What was *that* all about?"

I slipped the postcard into my pocket, shook my head. "Believe me," I said, "you don't want to know."

And for a long time neither did I. I thought about Louie often in the decades ahead but always presumed he'd killed himself because (1) he seemed determined to do so; and (2) he never contacted me again. Then in May of 1996, when I was driving around the country with my friend Elaine, selling those ratite shirts I'd designed, I ended up at an Emu Convention in San Angelo, Texas. I drove around town for awhile but couldn't remember any of the streets and didn't recognize anything but the hotel I was living in when the mayor threatened to bust me. Once we were settled in our motel room I took out a local phone book and looked up HOUSTON. I remembered his parents' names – Lawrence and Sandra – and the sister, Gail, and sure enough, there was a Sandra Houston on Lancer Drive.

It was a difficult call to make. 37 years had passed, but if the mother remembered me she was more likely to call the police than speak to me. And I was, of course, slightly embarrassed to present myself as the Wilson High she'd known in the 60s. I was a crazed, alcoholic drifter then, and now ... well, now I drove around the country in a beater truck selling bird shirts.

I made the call. Louie's mother answered and when I identified myself as an old friend of Louie's she was very excited. "Really?" she said. "He had so few and I haven't heard from one in a long time."

I cleared my throat. "And Louie himself?" I asked. "Is he ..."

"He hung himself in 1971, Wilson."

"Ahhhh ..."

She gave me directions to her house and insisted we come by so Elaine and I drove over there. Sandra must have been ninety years old by then but she welcomed us in and wanted to know everything I could tell her about Louie (a sanitized version with no mention of my "advance against royalties," of course). At first it was evident that she didn't remember me (her husband had been dead for twenty years and Gail was married and lived in Washington, D.C.), but as time went

361

by I wondered if it wasn't simply Southern manners: whatever had gone on all those years before I was still the rare soul who'd cared about her son. She brought out old family albums and Elaine and I looked through photos of the young Louie (in a Little League Baseball uniform of all things) and even clippings from various city and state spelling bees he'd won.

Then all the albums and articles stopped when he was thirteen years old. "He was always an odd little boy," said Sandra by way of explanation, "but when puberty came so did the blackness. We lost him forever then."

"The last time I heard from him," I said, "he was living in a desert shack."

"Oh yes," she said, "but he was back with Claire at the end. One day he told her to go out and run some errands, that he wanted to be alone so he could hang himself."

Elaine just looked at me. "That sounds like Louie," I said.

"Well, he tried," said Sandra. "He put a rope around a rafter in the cabin where they were living, slipped the noose around his neck and stepped off a chair."

"Oh I'm soooo sorry," said Elaine.

"Except the rope broke. When Claire got home Louis was still laying on the floor, a big rope burn on his neck. He was so angry."

It was obvious what side of the family Louie got his West Texas scrappiness from. "Don't tell me," I said. "The next day he got a stronger rope and did it right."

"Yes," she said. "That was the end of my Louis."

"I'm sorry," I said.

"But not surprised."

"Actually, the only surprise is that he made it 'til '71."

"I think you're right." Then she sat up straight, asked if we'd like to hear Louie's favorite song as a boy and went over to the piano. She started playing a gospel tune while I laid back on the couch and remembered her boy: hiding me in those lockers at the airport, standing in that Mexican bar with his .45s blazing, doing the Diogenes bit with his stopwatch on Burlingame Avenue, signing his Buick over to me before hopping beneath a bus ... I hadn't expected to see his like again and, for all the crazies I've known since, I never really did.

Then it was time to leave. Earlier Sandra had given me an 8x10 photo of Louie that still hangs on the wall in front of me. He's sitting on the steps of the cabin where he hung himself with his cousin Ned at his side. Ned has a big grin on his face and Louie ... well, he looks like his own executioner, the way he always did. Elaine and I hugged Sandra good-bye, thanking her for her generous hospitality, then she stepped forward and slipped a small plastic envelope into my hand.

It was a bag of marbles. "What are these?" I asked.

"Those were Louis' when he was a boy," she said. "I thought you should have them because, well ... he ended up *losing* his marbles, didn't he?"

Maybe she remembered me after all.

That spring of 1970 was when I first began to rationalize my heavy psychedelic use as "practice." Since the Herrick Hospital withdrawal I'd probably had a dozen hallucinatory-stage incidents from booze and The Dread, if anything, was getting worse.

Which, in turn, made it easier to use acid, mescaline, mushrooms and peyote with impunity. No matter what situation I put myself in after I ate them it wasn't going to be half as strange or terrifying as the d.t.'s, so I kept pushing the envelope until I was popping mescaline at work. Could I sit at my desk (much less run errands) without gnashing my teeth and gulping? Could I speak to other people in the newsroom without dissolving into a rant? These were the kind of obstacles I faced on d.t. mornings, so why not practice them when I was high?

Well, the best reason was the erosion of personal discipline. I know, it sounds like I've never had any (particularly when I still eat so many marijuana brownies per year), but other than the fear of madness the only thing keeping me sober was determination: on psychedelics that disappeared in a flash.

So gradually I drank more and more during the week until I needed a beer or two at four in the morning just to make it to work. Or I'd wake still drunk from the night before, think I was fine until 9:00 or 10:00 a.m., then shrivel with the shakes as the booze wore off.

I was slipping into the same old cycle and I didn't have the heart for it anymore, it was too hard to fool myself at that point, to imagine a night before that was worth the morning after. So one Thursday evening, when I'd gone to the happy hour at a bar called The Lava Pit with Gumbo and Big Mac and drank eight or ten Salty Dogs, I stepped onto the street afterwards and was shocked to see it was still light out. I thought it was ten, maybe eleven at night, but when I looked at the clock in the store next door it was only 7:00 p.m.

And there I was dead drunk; I didn't know how I'd make it the six blocks to my hotel without falling over.

So I stumbled twice as far to the Mills Hospital Emergency Room, where I told the doctor on duty about my Herrick Hospital stay and convinced him I was a suicidal alcoholic who needed further treatment.

Or something like that. It was hardly difficult to get yourself committed to the California mental health system at the time – particularly if you'd worked long enough to earn disability payments – and I could always play the youth card in a pinch. I was given a check-in time of eight the next morning at the Agnews State Hospital in San Jose and walked up El Camino Real to Poplar Avenue, where Carrie Williams' house was. It was nearly midnight by then and I snuck into her back yard, found a heavy towel in the bathhouse and wrapped myself in it. Laid down on a chaise lounge by the pool and passed out.

I woke at dawn to Carrie, still in her bathrobe, shaking my shoulder. "Good God, Wilson," she said, "you scared me half to death, I thought it was some bum sleeping out here!"

I shook my head and sat up. "Jesus, Carrie," I said, "it *is*."

"Well, what are you doing here? Did you get thrown out of your hotel or something?"

"No, nothing like that. Actually … I just need a ride."

"A ride? To where?"

"Agnews State Hospital."

"I don't understand," she said, sitting down on the chaise next to me. "Do you need to visit someone there?"

"No, that's where I'm committing myself. To dry out, to try to get squared away. I've been drinking a lot again."

She looked aghast. "But to Agnews, Wilson?" she asked. "My God, that's a *horrible* place! It's positively *medieval!*"

"That doesn't matter," I said. "Will you give me a ride?"

This was the tricky part. I was asking her to help me instead of one of my peers because I thought she knew me well enough that she wouldn't ask a bunch of stupid questions. What's there to say when a human being has so bottomed out that he thinks a mental ward commitment is his best alternative?

For a long time she just looked at me. Finally she stood up and sighed. "Of course, Wilson," she said. "It's a brave thing you're doing. Just let me get dressed and make sure the kids are ready for school."

I cringe now at the things I asked that poor woman to do. Years later I would return to thank her, assure her it wasn't all for naught. But that morning I waited until she was safely inside the house before I hurried over to the bathhouse bar, pulled out a couple beers and worked them down.

Sobriety could wait another few hours.

One of the things I enjoyed about the Town & Country Hotel, as I had at The Burlingame, was that they didn't clean your room for you but simply gave you new sheets when you brought in your old ones. (Which I did once a month so they wouldn't get suspicious.) This meant the maids stayed out of my room and I was able to live in a style commensurate to my station, i.e., with debris all around.

I'd like to say the empties were there to remind me of my sordid state in life but I don't know ... I think I was just too lazy to pick them up. What's more I had this idea that – drunk that I was – I was doing a lot better than I had when I ended up at Herrick. So I left my hotel key with Carrie when she dropped me off at Agnews and had Big Mac retrieve it from her later, figuring he'd quickly dispense with whatever was left in the room.

Instead it took he and Ted Grantham an entire afternoon to clean up: they hauled out forty-eight empty whiskey bottles and over two hundred crushed beer cans. Apparently I belonged in Agnews after all.

I know I preferred it to Herrick. For openers it was a grim, gray, bare bones place with sprawling grounds and just the right touch of despair to it. I was assigned to an Addicts Ward this time, holed up with alkies, soapers, smackers and speed freaks instead of schizoids and shock cases. I was still the youngest guy by a good twenty years but now I had some cagey veterans I could *learn* from.

And the first thing I discovered, as I had in AA, was that none of the alkies drank in the morning. They'd get loaded the night before, pass out, wake to a stinking shit and self-hatred and go out to meet the day. This was unfathomable to me: if they didn't hallucinate, if they didn't need hair of the dog just to sit up in bed, much less put one foot in front of the other ... what the hell were they doing at Agnews? They seemed as abashed by the loss of real things (jobs, families and friends) as I was by hallucinations.

Well, some of them, anyway; the next thing I discovered is what many of those rummies *were* doing there. They were drunks, all right, but the functional type, the kind that could put in a quarter year or two at high-paying jobs, get some disability and unemployment benefits locked in, then blow the pay they'd earned on a giant bender. When it was over and everything was gone they'd commit themselves for 30- to 90-day detox stays at a state ward, where they'd enjoy a warm bed, three squares and $80- to $120-a-week in disability pay.

Which they'd gamble in the no-limit poker games. There were a dozen of them who'd been doing this for years, at different times, up and down the state. They called themselves The Sandbag Circuit and had honed institutionalism to an art.

I was welcomed aboard immediately. Not only had I been raised on the game of poker but there was also the drug factor. The standard issue for alkies at the time was, oddly enough, a new upper/downer called *Sinequan*. I guess the shrinks assumed that because we were drunks we were all somehow manic-depressive, so they gave us double doses of the blue and red pills three times a day. This was supposed to counteract up and down emotions but instead only seemed to induce them. So you'd swallow your load, get a sudden euphoric rush, leap up and lose yourself in a task only to slump dejectedly – sulking and morose – a half hour later.

Which meant the poker games constituted a game within a game within a game. It wasn't enough to know the "tells" of guys who'd been playing poker twice as long as I'd been alive: I also had to figure out, when one of them was betting, whether he was riding the *Sinequan* up-or-down cycle, and if he was (and wasn't bluffing that he was), what that meant about his cards.

It might have been the moment I made other people's highs my hobby, actually honed the skills that have served me well in pot judgings, but the longer I played with those characters the more I won.

And we played a lot. We would have done nothing else but there were: (1) the perfunctory group meetings with shrinks everyday, feeble humanist types with Frederick Perls posters on the wall; and (2) the biggest difference between state hospitals and private ones, namely the fact that once they sobered up, drunks were the loony bin factotums.

I was big and young so they assigned me to Building 10, the Violent Ward. Twisted, musclebound plowboys with overactive thyroids that liked to mix it up with anyone available. Fortunately they were all pounded with harpoons of *Thorazine* every morning so they shuffled around the ward with drool swinging from their lips and their skin purplish, almost blue from the capillary-squeezing narcotic. It was a nightmarish scene straight out of George Romero (particularly with the soft rock music playing in the background), and mostly I just stood at a distance observing. I chain-smoked cigarettes and tapped my foot when the *Sinequan* jacked me, felt like those psychos looked when the big slide came.

Everything considered it was pretty easy duty. Then one afternoon my second week there the music stopped and the head nurse's voice broke in over the loudspeaker:

"ATTENTION ALL ATTENDANTS! ATTENTION ALL ATTENDANTS! ACID AL HAS DISAPPEARED!

Fuck Acid Al, I thought, *they probably strapped him down somewhere and forgot about it.* He was a pimply, fat thirty-year-old who'd eaten too much LSD, then tried to vampire his own mother in the neck. I let the other guys look under couches and beds while I wandered down the closest hallway and lit another Camel. Leaned against a linen closet door and fantasized about fucking one of the occupational therapy nurses I'd met. On a *Sinequan* rush I could just about convince myself that she'd be interested in a fat, alcoholic loser like me.

Then I dropped the cigarette butt onto the linoleum. Went to squash it and saw it had landed in the blood oozing between my feet.

Was I hallucinating? No, the cigarette had definitely sizzled before going out. And when I lifted my left boot there was blood on the sole. I turned slowly, stepped away from the linen closet and opened the door.

Inside, wedged between the towels, was Acid Al. He was holding his right wrist with his left hand while he cannibalized his own forearm. Big, wrenching bites that covered his teeth and face with flakes of flesh and blood. I looked at him, mouth working, eyes rolling in his head, blood pumping from the severed veins in his arm, and cleared my throat:

"So ... eh ... hey, Acid Al," I squeaked, "how's it going?"

"ARRRRARAGH!" Pink foam blew from his lips as he leapt to his feet and lunged at me. I might have avoided him altogether but slipped in his blood so the two of us went down in a heap and for just a moment there – until he passed out from lack of blood – his mouth was close enough to my neck that I thought he was going to bite me, too.

Confronting Acid Al instead of calling for help got me demoted from the Violent Ward to the Senility Ward. It was the same silly duty really – everyone around me moving in a daze – and between this non-work, the dope, the minimal psychiatric obligations and the poker, I found myself getting pretty comfortable with the Agnews routine. I'd gone there to dry out while I learned how to stay sober and, if I hadn't made a lot of progress in the latter department, I thought I might over time.

So after three weeks inside I went to Doug Loder, the head of staff, and told him I wanted to sign on for another sixty days.

He laughed in my face. "I bet you would, High," he said bitterly. "Except Governor Reagan's throwing all of you out three days from now."

"What!?"

"That's right. He's shuttering mental health facilities across the state, says they're a waste of the taxpayer's money."

"So what happens to all the crazies? He's just releasing 'em on the streets?"

"Of course," laughed Loder again. "This is California … what's the difference?"

There was something to that. This summary ejection into the real world left *me* in something of a bind, though. I had over $400 in poker winnings but no job, no clothes but the mental ward denims and nowhere in particular to go.

So the next day, out of the blue, I get a phone call from Carl Sampson. He'd heard I was back in a mental ward and was offering me a place to stay when I left.

"It's not another garage or commune, is it?" I said.

"Well," he said, "not exactly. I'm living in a big house in the Sierra Madre Canyon with a dozen other freaks. Or maybe a few more than that, actually … they come and go a lot."

"Girls?"

"Lots of them."

"Jesus."

"Now Wilson, you *are* going to stay sober, aren't you?"

"You know me, Carl."

"That's why I'm asking. There's a chemist with a lab here and he's been making bongo in the basement. We gotta keep things very low-key."

Bongo? That was our code word for LSD.

"Give me directions," I said. "I'll be on the road tomorrow."

I was in the Portland Airport at six in the morning a couple of weeks ago, waiting in a long line at a security checkpoint, and the two guys behind me were drunk. I would have known this from the stench of bourbon – much less their unshaven, dissolute appearance and Las Vegas T-shirts – but as oiled up as they were it was natural they'd be discussing the only thing that mattered:

"Do ya think they serve alcohol on the plane this early in the morning?"

"They must."

"What if they don't, though?"

"Well … it's only an hour flight, Johnny."

"I can't make it that long, Tom!"

They were the shakiest clowns in the airport and they reminded me of myself. Not the young me, but the one now. I can no longer drink or tolerate much of anything except marijuana, but I would if I could and I was sure as hell stoned on an *Indigo Blue* bomber that morning. It was an excellent reminder that the only thing that keeps me sane is the threat of madness. Otherwise I'd be just like old Johnny boy there, hearing the wings before I was even airborne.

Or dead. My friend Tim Hayden, a dentist who lives on the Olympic Peninsula in Washington, called last night to tell me about a college reunion he's organizing. He named a couple people I hadn't seen in 30 years, said he'd spoken to them on the phone.

"And this is the truth, High … you know what they both said when I mentioned you and I are still friends?"

"Let me guess," I said. "'Holy shit! That asshole's still *alive!*'"

Tim paused. "That's exactly right, man," he said. "How'd you know that?"

"Come on, Hayden … I've heard it so many times I feel like *Topper.*"

We both had a good laugh over that but later I thought, *Geez, my brothers wanted to make a mark in the world, and I enjoy people thinking I'm dead. What's that about?*

The Sierra Madre Canyon was in the foothills of Pasadena in a small, woodsy nook just past the city itself. Sampson was living on the top floor of a long, two-story ranch house that backed up against the canyon and I arrived there on a Tuesday afternoon in June 1970. I was feeling pretty good after a month of sobriety and had taken a Greyhound bus to Pasadena, then a taxi to Carl's place. There were stairs on the outside of the house, and I'd no sooner paid the cabbie and started across the lawn than Sampson came out and waved to me from the second floor.

"Hey, High!" he yelled. "Good to see you, man!"

I returned his wave and started up the stairs with my suitcase. "Good to see you too, old buddy," I replied. "It's been a year at least."

"What the fuck are you wearing, Wilson? Is that some kind of prison uniform?"

"No no, just the denims they issued me at Agnews."

"Yeah? And was it better than Herrick?"

"Much better. Better prescription drugs, lots of high stakes poker. I left with over four hundred in winnings."

"No, no," he said, "I meant the alcohol part. Did you learn anything that'll help you stay sober?"

"Oh that." I was almost to the top of the stairs and *Damn!* that suitcase was heavier than it looked … it kept banging against my leg as I climbed. "Well, man," I puffed, "I haven't had a drink in a month."

Then I reached the landing and leaned against the bannister to catch my weak alkie breath. As I did Sampson reached over and grabbed the suitcase.

"What the hell's that clinking noise, Wilson?" he asked. " I heard it all the way up the stairs."

"Oh, you know," I said, "just essentials …"

He gave me a suspicious look, bent down on one knee and flipped the suitcase open. Out rolled a half-dozen whiskey bottles, part of the cache of ten I'd stashed inside.

"Hey careful!" I yelled, scooping up the errant bottles. "You'll break 'em!"

"Fuck, High!" said Carl. *"This* is how you stay sober!?"

"Well," I said, carefully replacing the bottles in their underwear padding, "one of the other alkies gave me this suitcase, and I didn't have anything to put in it, of course, and then I was walking by Ernie's Liquors when I got to Burlingame and they were selling *Black Label* for two bucks a bottle and I thought, *Hey! Serendipity! I'll fill the suitcase with whiskey just* in case *I need it later!"*

Sampson simply stared at me.

"Okay okay," I said, "I thought maybe I'd have … a drink or two soon. But there's plenty for the other people here."

"High, I told you on the phone," sighed Carl, "this is Hippie Central. There's maybe a dozen people who crash here, along with the chemist making LSD downstairs … and *none* of them drink. Most of them are tripping at night, in fact, so I don't want them freaked out by some weird juicer!"

"All right, then … what if *I'm* tripping, too? You know I drink less when I'm doing psychedelics."

"I do? I thought you drank more."

"Oh right … that's downers I was thinking of. But Agnews gave me some of those, too."

Carl shook his head, bent over and picked up the suitcase. "Just be cool, Wilson, okay?" he said. " You think you can handle that?"

I didn't commit myself. And I think it would have been one thing if I was staying in a bedroom, but Sampson (like DeBola with the Bat Cave) put me on the tarpapered porch outside. It overlooked the canyon below and there was an old couch out there so what the hell … it was summer in Southern California, at least I wouldn't be rained on.

Carl introduced me around later that night but I was never exactly sure who the other inhabitants of the house were. For openers they all looked alike with their long blonde hair and bland surfer/hippie mien, and if they weren't interchangeable they at least didn't stay long: every time I glanced inside there seemed to be a different bunch partying in there.

But except for an occasional sandwich, shit or shower I rarely left the couch to find out. Sampson had given me a little jar with thirty hits of "Windowpane" acid in it and it proved to be an excellent complement to the whiskey. I'd sit on the couch – turned to face away from the house and over the canyon, not because I preferred the view but to afford a little privacy – and spend my days in idle reverie. This was a vaguely new tact on my part, trying to enjoy who I'd become instead of worrying about what it was costing me. Once in awhile I'd get a Sympathy Suck from stoner chicks who wanted to do a guy in a mental ward uniform, and for a week there I had a relationship with a dark Mexican girl named Rosemary.

Then she was caught in a raid at work and deported and that was okay, I didn't like people around in the morning, anyway. I'd be up with the sun and The Dread was right there with me, its edge sharpened by all the windowpane and alcohol. I'd have to squeeze it back inside with carefully modulated sips of whiskey and it was difficult maintaining the dead sailor cover while I did so.

Mostly I was thinking ... *this is a wrap, High. I either drop dead out here, or jump or fall into the canyon, or find a way to quit drinking.* Those were my peers, my generation interacting in the house behind me, and there I was staring into the dark, eyes wide and bulging like a madman's, big acid rushes jerking my bloated boozer's body. It was all right but it couldn't go on. Not only would I run out of cash but I didn't have the stamina for it anymore, my weary brain was sick of threats.

Still I made it five weeks out there. I'd discovered a liquor store that delivered, so every couple days I'd place an order, then wait for the little honk at the foot of the stairs. I'd have the driver bring some jerky and hot sticks, too, so I could skip going into the house for meals. All this time I saw Carl maybe once or twice a day. He was working construction in town and, to hear him tell it, sleeping with a string of hot surfer girls.

Then one morning I woke with my face stuck to the tarpaper. It was barely dawn and someone was shaking my shoulder.

"Hey, man!" some girl was saying. "Hey High, wake up!"

I extricated my face, reached up and picked at the pebbles stuck to my cheeks. Rolled over to see one of the blonde hippies that lived there.

"Ehh, Janie ... is that it?" I mumbled.

"Genoa, High," she said, stepping back and falling onto the couch. "The name is Genoa."

"Ahhh." Probably from Santa Barbara. I rose to my knees, slapped the rocks and dirt off the front of my denims, then crawled over to the other end of the couch and settled myself. Found a quarter full bottle of *Ancient Age*, grimaced as I took a pull.

"Holy shit!" she said. "You really *do* drink in the morning!"

I looked over at her. Took a pack of squashed Camels from my pocket, tapped one out and lit it. "What is it, Genoa?" I croaked finally.

"Why'd you wake me up?"

She shook her head and laughed. "Jesus," she said. "You don't remember earlier this morning at all, do you?"

Oh. I thought about it, reached up my tongue and tasted my mustache. No, I hadn't eaten any pussy the night before. I remembered the liquor truck delivering around two in the afternoon, but then what?

Nothing, I guess.

"The cops? The FBI agents?" she asked. "It's all a total blank?"

As I watched her the skin on her face dissolved to reveal the worms beneath. I tipped back the *Ancient Age*, took another gulp. Coughed up some phlegm and spit into the canyon.

"Feel better now?" she said.

"Oh much," I gasped. "Now what was it you wanted to tell me."

It seems the house had been rousted at three in the morning by a squad of G-men and narcs. They'd arrested the chemist and dismantled his acid factory downstairs, then climbed to the second floor and lined everyone up against the wall.

"Sampson, too?" I asked.

"Sure," said Genoa. "All nine of us."

"And I was …?"

"Passed out on the porch. The pigs had us spread-eagled against the wall, and this one FBI prick, he kept saying, 'Where's the dogs, where's the dogs, I hear a couple dogs!' Carl finally shut the guy up by saying, 'That isn't dogs, you asshole, that's my pal Wilson High snoring!'"

"I snore?"

"You kidding me!? It's the worst fuckin' thing I ever heard … it sounds like someone being tortured!"

"Yeah?"

"Yeah. So anyway, a bunch of the narcs came out on the porch here, found you sawing logs on the couch. They shook you, slapped your face, poured cold water over your head from the bird bath but

379

nothing! Not only didn't you wake up, but you snored *louder!* The FBI guy in charge couldn't believe it. 'He's faking,' he said, 'that's no natural human sound!' And to prove it he had two of the bigger agents drag you to the edge of the porch. Then they grabbed your ankles and swung you over the canyon."

"What!?"

"Yeah, like you were a giant sack of potatoes or something. The Feds figured if you were faking, the threat of that 100-foot drop would wake you fast."

"Did it?"

"No, you even snored upside down! It was amazing. They finally just gave up and left you on the porch. 'What the hell,' they said, 'he's just a fat drunk!'"

My epitaph. Genoa droned on about how the others would be making bail later that morning as I took another gulp of the whiskey, walked over to the edge of the porch and looked down.

I could see my next stop clearly, and it wasn't the canyon floor.

Crazy Ray Alturo was a kid my age from Burlingame. He'd been a classmate of DeBola's at Humboldt State, a wild, dark Italian guy who'd earned the "Crazy" moniker with a series of fearless stunts (the first time I saw him he was leaping from the top of a three-story building onto a telephone pole), and I came to know him that summer of '68 when I stayed with Tony. We were fast friends immediately, of course, me being as careless as he was when I drank (though infinitely clumsier), and Crazy was the one who'd run onto the bus with a bottle when I left Arcata that fall.

It was the last time I saw him. A couple months later he took a hit of acid and the delicate psychological teeter-totter in his head turned on him. He went rabid, stole a couple of cars and ended up doing a stretch in Atascadero, the State Hospital for the Criminally Insane. When they released him after eighteen months on *Thorazine* he went to the local high school, ran one lap on the track and died of a heart attack. He was twenty-two years old.

I'd heard about it in my travels and felt terrible, of course, Crazy may have loved risk but he didn't have a mean bone in his body. I mention it here because after leaving the Sierra Madre house that morning I took a Greyhound to San Mateo and went to the same doctor who'd admitted me to Agnews. He waggled me a bed at the Crystal Springs Rehabilitation Center this time. It was a county detox ward as opposed to a state one so was still open for business in Reagan's California. I received a check-in time the next morning and rented a room at The Burlingame Hotel to wait it out. I'd drank just enough to keep me from seizing up on the bus but I brought nothing to that room but my bloated, alkie carcass. I took off my shoes, undid my belt buckle and laid back on the bed to see what kind of withdrawal five weeks of whiskey and LSD would conjure up.

As if there were much doubt: it was the night from the other side of hell, an experience so frightening that words fail me. If I hadn't spent my last five bucks on that room I'd have been out the door for a bottle in the first half hour. It seemed like my blood had turned to sludge and I could only get it to circulate if I hung my head and arms off the side of the bed. But when I did that I couldn't breathe so I'd jerk back up, get dizzy, go back down then up again as the sweat flew off me and my senses were assaulted by sights, smells and sounds that had me sobbing in terror.

Even at its worst, though, when I might be pawing my face because I was sure my skull was a jar of eyeballs ... I always kept the little monitor there, the tiny part of me that hid in back of the tempest.

Otherwise I wouldn't have heard the knock on the door four hours later. At first I thought it was just my heart pounding, then maybe someone down the hall because no one knew I was in town. When the *tap! tap! tap!* came again and it was definitely outside my door I decided it had to be hotel management, that I'd been raving and screaming too loudly.

Or maybe it was The Grim Reaper come to collect my sorry, swinish soul? That's the notion that got me up and moving. *Come on fucker,* I thought, *come on and punch my ticket, I've had enough!* I duck walked, shivering, to the door and swung it open.

It was Ernie Alturo, Crazy Ray's father. I'd met him once but I'd seen him often because he was a longtime local garbage man. He was short and wiry like Crazy, maybe 5'6" or so, with a halo of gray hair and an old hat he was kneading in his hands.

"Wilson?" he said. "Do you remember me? Ray's dad?"

As I watched he morphed into a toad, then a coiled snake and finally a chittering cricket. I did the blink-and-shake, cleared my throat and stuck out my hand.

"Of course I remember you, Ernie," I croaked, trying not to jump when he clasped my hand. "But what are you, eh ... doing *here?*"

"I'm sorry to bother you," he said, "but I heard you lived in this hotel and Ray always spoke so highly of you and well, since he died I've meant to come and speak to you about him. I didn't know any of his other friends, and damn, Wilson, it's really hard ... I still get choked up."

Crazy had died almost a year before; it had been eighteen months since I'd stayed in that hotel. I come through for one night all that time later – to sweat out the d.t.'s, no less – and that's the night his father shows up for a heart-to-heart?

Either he was an apparition or it was meant to be; and his hand had felt solid so it must be the latter. But what was I supposed to do? I was going through withdrawal and lapsing into periods of delirium ... company was the last thing I wanted, much less *tragic* company. And I couldn't tell old, sweet, hardworking Ernie I was going through the d.t.'s, that the only connection he had to his son was a punk drunk.

Anymore than I could turn him away. I stepped back, swung open the door. "Come on in, Ernie," I said. "I'm feeling a little under the weather here … nothing contagious or anything, just a kind of jungle fever I got in L.A., you know … so ignore me if I seem a little sweaty and jerky."

I sat him on the chair at the end of the bed and laid back down on the pillows. For the next two hours he talked about Crazy Ray as I gave it up to the dead sailor. Basically I had to calmly look at Ernie (as he morphed into one hideous hallucination after another and sweat from my sodden scalp ran into my eyes), pretend not to smell him (though he had the garbage-man reek of kitty litter and rotting fruit), while listening attentively to words that turned into gibberish the instant my attention wavered.

Even as what I yearned to do was leap up and scream at the fathomless Dread in my head, the voice telling me that trying to *act* sane is the very thing that would drive me mad.

Crazy would have appreciated the sheer absurdity of the scene, not to mention the tears. Ernie and I must have broken into sobs a dozen times and – inasmuch as I was crying for my own sorry ass, too – I was weepier than he was. The best I could offer him were the few feeble tales of Crazy I trusted myself to censor, like the time he climbed a 6'8" redneck who was threatening me, swung his legs over the giant's shoulders and twisted his jughead ears.

"Oh my God," said Ernie, "what did the big guy do then?"

"He scooped Ray up like a cat, threw him against a wall!"

"Did it hurt him?"

"Nah, you know Ray, he bounced right off." (It knocked him cold.)

"And then you took care of the big asshole, right?" said Ernie.

"Oh yeah." (He hit me so hard I thought he'd killed me.)

We went back and forth like that until Ernie stood up to leave. We hugged and said our good-byes, then I closed the door and slid to the floor, thinking, *Well, I'm pretty tan from my stay in Southern California, maybe Ernie believed the flu stuff.*

Or maybe, as a garbage man, I was just something he saw everyday.

In my mind I always think of the Crystal Springs stint as the end of my boozing days even though it quite obviously wasn't: not only did I drink for another six years, but judging by volume alone the d.t.'s had barely begun.

What actually ended was my hope for outside help, the notion that there was something out there that would make sobriety easier to come by. It turns out I was fully equipped already and what the hell, it's not like I went to Crystal Springs expecting anything but cards and drugs and disability checks. Several of the Sandbag Circuit characters were already there, in fact, keeping a seat at the table warm for me.

"Oh yeah, Stretch," they said. "We're *real* surprised to see you."

Once I'd settled into the dorm I was given a thorough physical exam. When he was done I asked the doctor what he thought and instead of answering he beckoned me to follow him. He took me upstairs to the terminal ward, had me draw close to a comatose old wino dying of cirrhosis. He was jaundiced and bloated, so swollen from liver poisons that when the doctor pulled back his gown the bum's bellybutton jutted up like a second penis.

"This is you, Wilson," said the doctor, pointing to it, "if you don't quit drinking."

That look was worth that last commitment, actually; I damn sure never forgot it. It even inspired me to get my ass to the gym a couple hours a day from there on. I lifted weights, did a little running, tore up the intramural basketball league playing against schizos and drunks.

As for therapy, Crystal Springs had two psychologists on staff. One was Dr. Nancy. She was a tall, attractive, early thirties woman who played piano for the patients, had a smile for everybody and a Snoopy poster ("Happiness Is A Warm Puppy") taped to her door. The other was Dr. Baumgartner, a dry, bitter little gnome with liverwurst lips.

The staff gave me a choice so I went with Baumgartner ... I'd had enough Dr. Nancys at Agnews. We'd meet for a half hour every couple days and it wasn't long before he started pulling out the tests. Word association exercises that I'd do with him, then written exams like the Minnesota Multiphasic Personality Test. After a week of it I showed up for my regular session to find him staring out his window.

"Ah, Wilson," he said, "please sit down."

I took my customary seat across from his desk as he began pulling out the different exams and carefully explaining the results. It was gibberish that didn't mean anything to me and when we got to the Minnesota Multiphasic and he pointed to the red line diving off the graph I stopped him.

"Cut to the chase, Doc," I said. "What's it all mean?"

"Wilson," he said, "based on our sessions and these results I'm afraid I have to consider you a severe manic-depressive personality with dangerous self-destructive tendencies."

I looked at him. "And?" I said finally.

"Well, we don't have the facilities here to treat a condition like yours. I'd like to transfer you to either Atascadero State or Mendocino."

"You've got to be kidding me. Do you need my permission to do that?"

"Of course."

"Fuck off then." I left his office and went back to the poker game. I was on an alkies only ward but we all received different medications so it was different than the *Sinequan* games in Agnews. I remember I got on a streak and had won several hands in a row when Dr. Nancy rushed into the room.

"Oh Wilson," she said, "I need to speak to you right away!"

I looked at my first three cards in a seven card stud deal: buried kings with an ace up. "Maybe some other time, Nancy," I said.

She grabbed me by the collar, damn near dragged me into the hallway. "All right," I said, "Jesus!"

"Wilson," she gasped, backing me up against a wall, "I just wanted to assure you that you're a *very* good person."

"Huh?"

"You're a wonderful man. I heard what happened with you and Dr. Baumgartner and I don't want you worrying about those tests."

"Why would I worry about them?"

"Well, with what the results indicated and all."

"Doc," I laughed, "every shrink I go to tells me something different. It's all horseshit ... no insult intended."

"None taken," said Nancy. "And what *this* shrink thinks ... after getting to know you around here ... is that you're someone with limitless potential. Remember that, Wilson, okay?"

"Sure," I said. "And thanks."

I returned to the game but the magic was gone and I lost my winnings back. The next day I was lying on the veranda, body slathered with suntan oil, shades over the eyes and a glass of iced tea in my lap, when Dr. Nancy appeared again.

"I'm leaving, Wilson," she said, "but before I go I wanted to give you this."

It was a page of bond with a carefully lettered poem on it, "Not

388

Man Apart" by Robinson Jeffers.

"This is beautiful," I said. "Did you do the calligraphy yourself?"

"Yes, last night. And I want you to keep that poem, Wilson, and read it whenever you're low, the way I have over the years. Especially this part." She pointed to a section of prose, read out loud over my shoulder:

> "... the greatest beauty is
> Organic wholeness, the wholeness of
>   life and things,
> the divine beauty of the universe.
>   Love that, not man
>
> Apart from that, or else you will share man's
>   pitiful confusions
> or drown in despair when his days darken."

Whoa ... pretty bleak stuff for bubbly Nancy; she wasn't halfway through when she started sobbing.

"Well, yes," I said at the end, "it's very moving, Nancy, thank you."

"Love that, not man apart from that," she repeated, then hurried away without a backward glance. When I got to the dining hall the next morning the first thing I did was sit down across from old Brad, the wino who slept in the bed next to me.

"Say, Brad," I said, "isn't this the day you see Dr. Nancy?"

"Usually," he said, slurping his porridge.

"Well, how about you let me go in your place this morning. You don't give a shit and I'd like to talk to her."

He looked at me and shook his head. "You can have my place," he cackled, "but she won't have much to say."

"Why's that?"

389

"Dr. Nancy's a goner."

"Huh?"

"Dead. Finito. Bye-bye."

"Come on, I just saw her yesterday."

"When was that?"

"I don't know … four, four-thirty in the afternoon, maybe."

"You might have been the last one to see her alive. She took a header off the Golden Gate Bridge around six."

"What!?"

"If you didn't go to bed so early you woulda heard about it last night."

"But why'd she kill herself!?"

Ben laughed. "I don't know," he said. "Guess you'd have to ask *a shrink!*"

So much for Robinson Jeffers and Snoopy. I heard later that a boyfriend leaving her was the impetus but what, in the end, was there to say about an act that desperate … life's an ephemeral, precious gift and I was in that mental ward trying to salvage mine, trying to step back from my own fascination with the flame. Would I make it? Was I smart enough, tough enough, lucky enough to see my thirties, much less all the sober years beyond?

Only if my personal aversion therapy worked. In the meanwhile I still had it in the back of my mind to finish college so the second week of September I said good-bye to the other drunks, put my typer under my arm and walked to the highway.

The first step in staying sober was breaking familiar patterns, but I loved those tuition and fee waivers in Longview, Washington.

"A friend whose older brother is an indoor grower in Mendocino County came by yesterday to tell me his brother had been busted and jailed last week. Then I pick up the paper this morning to read that the Portland police broke into the home of an amputee (who also suffers from diabetes, arthritis and kidney failure) and threw her from the couch at gunpoint. The charge? Selling a dime bag of pot to an informant. A lousy gram of marijuana. The cops kept her on the floor while they confiscated everything of value she owned, including her wheelchair!

"It's why I laugh when starry-eyed friends talk about marijuana being legalized, as if they or anybody they know is going to live that long: we have Calvinism so far up our ass in this country that we twitch around like finger puppets. Instead of taxing pot and collecting billions we've spent twice that much making it more valuable than gold, even as we've constructed 1,000 new prisons in the last twenty years and filled them to the rafters with drug offenders. (Which means we now incarcerate more people than any nation on earth.) Decriminalization will happen at the same time as: (a) government bureaucrats come to their senses; and (b) the coffers of the prison building and drug testing

industries are full. No time soon, in other words.

"Four centuries ago the Puritans landed here while England shipped its convicts to Australia.

"We was robbed."

I wrote and illustrated the above in the late 90s for a comic I called "How to Enjoy a Rewarding Career in Cannabis Cultivation." A lot has changed in the decade since, including the remote chance that marijuana would be legalized in my lifetime. Now I think it's all but a done deal, particularly when you consider that California has *de facto* legalization already.

And it only makes sense that the state farthest removed from the Puritan stain would lead the way: once its citizens passed a medical marijuana initiative the bud was out of the bag and other western states toppled like dominoes. I'm a medical marijuana grower myself now with six patients depending on me. It means I can have a pound and a half of loose marijuana around and, more importantly, if I'm popped for growing violations the law can't take my house.

So I'm finally safe from the narcs. That seems like a reasonable trade-off for the weakening of a drug war that provided me with so much illicit gain over the years. Plus I managed to operate a criminal enterprise for three decades without getting busted once.

That's as close to success as this old reprobate is gonna get.

Next came the college years. I suppose it was part of the same institutionalized slant to my nature, all the grants, waivers, loans and work-study jobs being so easy to get. But it was also, I think, a nod to my parents: I hadn't done much to make them proud of me and, though I didn't expect that to change, at least if I had a college degree they might not worry as much. (Unfortunately I can't remember an instance in the interim where my degree has helped me get a job, or that anything I studied in college has been applicable to the work I've done.)

Still there I was, back at LCC under the good graces of Dick Kent. I worked in the student office, lived in a shack behind a bigger shack not far from the old recovery house, got straight A's in my classes and very drunk on the weekends. I had two lovers, one a twenty-year-old local named Jeannie who lived in a trailer with her three-year-old

393

daughter, the other that thirty-five-year-old mother of six who I'd met in a Philosophy of Ethics class the year before. Which one I visited depended upon how much I'd had to drink.

My biggest problem was the same one I'd always experienced in college, namely going two quarters in a row. I was in the middle of the winter term and wondering how I'd get through it – much less find a four-year school for my next stint – when Dick Kent walked into the student office and handed me a catalogue.

"Here," he said. "They've built a college for guys like you."

That's the way I will always think of The Evergreen State College: a school for guys like me. I read that catalogue from cover to cover, then read it again. *How could this be,* I thought, *how could the State of Washington allow this to happen?* It was a new four-year college in Olympia that was stressing diversity, hands on experiences, seminars instead of classes, no grades and individual responsibility. A kind of Antioch West to hear them tell it. I immediately sent off for an application and, when it came in the mail, answered the six essay questions with ruthless honesty and sent them back.

A month later I opened what I assumed would be an acceptance letter. Instead I found a short rejection note:

Dear Mr. High:

Thank you for your thoughtful (and quite extraordinary, I might add) application. However, at this time we will be unable to accept you as a student at The Evergreen State College as we have no mental health facilities on campus. I wish you luck with your continuing education.

Sincerely,

Dr. Joseph Schwinn
Vice President

I was furious. They were a new school taking any warm body available, and they dared to reject *me!?* I fired off an immediate appeal, claimed I'd been penalized for candor and demanded a "sanity hearing."

Not only did Schwinn acquiesce, he did Evergreen's "Always give a weirdo a fair shake" doctrine one better by picking my judges from a select group of professors. I met them in a Quonset hut one week later (the campus was still under construction at the time) and it took only one step inside to know I was home free: they were nothing but a bunch of old hippies. They wouldn't care that I lived on beer can beds.

An hour later I walked out with a tuition-and-fee waiver and a job as Student Director of Financial Aid. Evergreen State, at least in those early years, really was a school for guys like me.

The only real difference in my life before Evergreen State and my life while there is I received college credits for the latter. This was mostly my fuzziness about the future and partly the nature of the school at the time. Evergreen is considered one of the best small colleges in the country now, but in the fall of '71 it was finding its way just as its drug-soaked student body was. At twenty-four I was one of the oldest and stoniest of those students and determined to stay atop a fluid situation.

Did I succeed? Well, a decade ago the school asked its "pioneers," those of us from the original class of a thousand or so, to share our recollections from a quarter century before. This is what I remembered:

I'd waggled a swamper's job that summer in California's hot Sutter Basin. Temperatures regularly exceeded 100 degrees and I worked fourteen hours a day, seven days a week spearing 80-pound bales of straw with hooks, lifting them onto my knee, then tossing them over my head to another swamper on a truck bed. It was three dollars an hour plus room and board, and at the end of the summer I had a thousand in cash and a black 1965 Corvair. It was the car with the engine in the rear that Ralph Nader wrote "Unsafe At Any Speed" about, but it only cost fifty bucks and I figured if it got me to Olympia I'd be ahead of the game.

It made it there all right, and even lasted a couple of weeks after that, but it was a noisy bastard and used way more oil than it should have. One afternoon I was sitting at a West Olympia stop light when I noticed the redneck in the truck beside me. He was motioning to me to roll down my window and when I did he pointed to the back of the Corvair and laughed.

"Hey hippie!" he yelled. "Your fuckin' toy car's on fire!"

I glanced back and sure enough there were flames and smoke curling from beneath the trunk hood. I pulled over to the curb, turned off the engine, grabbed the books and papers on the seat next to me and jumped out. It looked like I was running to a nearby shopping center for help but I was actually just getting away ... I'd had my fill of fires by then.

That was exactly the kind of irresponsible behavior the Olympia townsfolk expected from Evergreen students. Now they embrace having the college in their city but then? Well, imagine you grew up in the redneck capital of a small northwestern state. Then imagine further that – because Governor Dan Evans wanted another cushy job when he left office, i.e., President of Evergreen State (he did himself one better and became a U.S. Senator) – you woke one morning to a thousand furry freaks on your doorstep. You'd be pissed. They were, too.

Which might have been neither here nor there to me except it was my responsibility, as a financial aid assistant, to find off-campus jobs for students. The first week of classes I actually tried to do it. Then after a dozen-odd employers laughed and hung up on me I thought, *Okay, this might work out ... I'm in charge of a department that doesn't exist.* I started steering inquiring students to the plethora of on-campus jobs and readied excuses for the day my boss, the Financial Aid Director, checked up on my progress.

But he never really did. This was Evergreen, where the emphasis was on leaving students to their own devices, and mine had the addict's touch.

I used the extra time on the job to study for whatever obscure seminar I was attending at the moment. This changed almost monthly as I wandered from one program to another, finally settling on something called "Human Development." We would meet individually and collectively with the professors a few times a week and then once a quarter a dozen of us would go on field trips together. I enjoyed the latter immensely, so much that my fellow classmates ditched me (not once but twice) in both Port Angeles, Washington and Vancouver, B.C. It seems their political correctness did not extend to a guy who drank *Mad Dog 20/20* for breakfast.

So when I came back for my senior year in 1972 I had the wherewithal to sign up for an individual writing contract with Jake Harley. He'd been one of the judges at my sanity hearing and was both a literature professor and a world-renowned mountain climber. The deal was I'd meet with him every few weeks in a tavern and we'd go over whatever short story I'd written in the interim. I soon figured out that the more I wrote, the more beers he'd buy, which was as close to incentive as I was going to get.

After college years spent in a whorehouse, a firehouse, a recovery house and assorted dive rooms around Longview, I had it in my mind to live in an on-campus dormitory at Evergreen. It's not something I would have pursued at a regular university (anymore than I was the fraternity type), but the *strange* had a friend in Evergreen … outside of Reed College in Portland, it's hard to imagine a place with more characters per square inch. I was sure I'd get a roommate weirder than I was and the two of us could experience the good ol' college high life together.

So in October, when the dormitories were finally finished, I moved into a two-person studio on the ninth floor of Building A and promptly went through four roommates in six weeks. This was vaguely puzzling to me. The basic room setup was a couple of beds along each wall, opposite a pair of desks and closets, with a bathroom in between connecting you to the next studio. Except these were new rooms so the beds and desks were in pieces and had to be assembled by the occupants.

I never bothered, of course, I'd been sleeping on the ground, typing in my lap and living out of suitcases for so many years that it seemed perfectly natural to me to live on the floor. (I might have slept on the bed or sat at the desk if they'd come preassembled, of course, but other than that they were simply too much trouble.) I assumed any hippie I got for a roommate would – if he didn't have the same sensibilities – at least allow me my space, but instead I had one after another of these odd little prissy boys. They seemed genuinely terrified of either me, my drug and alcohol appetites, or both: a couple of them only made it two nights before they requested transfers. My last roomie, Big Bob, a guy my age who later became, of all things, a prison warden, made it the longest. He lasted three whole weeks before choking me awake one morning.

I woke on my carpet of beer cans with his hands around my throat. "Jesus!" I coughed. "What the fuck's going on!?"

He put a portable tape recorder on my chest and punched the "play" button. "Listen to that, asshole!" he said. "It's what your snoring sounds like."

It was pretty frightening, all right. Ugly grunts, gasps and swallows, followed by long sleep apnea pauses that ended in explosive blubbering and choking. When Big Bob was finished packing he grabbed the recorder from my chest and went off to play the tape for Jerry Kirk, the Director of Housing.

Jerry called me at the Financial Aid office later.

"You know, High," he said, "I should really eighty-six you from the dorms, but you happen to be a staff person, too."

"Sort of," I said.

"Well, here's the deal: if you promise never to stay in on-campus facilities again, I'll let you have that two-person studio to yourself for the rest of the year. I don't know how I'd find anyone to room with you, anyway."

"Done."

I might have flopped with roommates but I actually made a lot of friends at Evergreen (many of whom I have to this day). When I look back at those years, though, I feel a *distance* between myself and the other students that's at least partly traceable to dorm life. We shared a community kitchen on the ninth floor and it seems I liked to come in drunk at three or four in the morning and stash beer in the refrigerator. This was okay if I only had a six-pack or two, but when (as was often the case, because I liked to be prepared) I carried a case or more, it meant clearing the fridge of yogurt, goat's milk, vegetables and other hippie perishables to make room for the beer cans.

Then I would go to my room, pass out, wake up to the dark wind of withdrawal at dawn and head to the kitchen for beer. A number of times there was a group of angry students there, waving wilted greens or spoiled cartons in my face as I made my way to the refrigerator. I wasn't physically threatened by them (in my memory they're no bigger than hobbits), but their squeaky voices were so strident I'd promise them anything for a little peace.

Then I'd reach the refrigerator, swing open the door, grab two beers to take back to the room while I drank a third on the spot.

Which would get the whole chorus started again, because how could you trust a guy who bottoms up beers for breakfast?

It was an incident on that very ninth floor, in fact, that summed up my Evergreen experience. By the late spring of '72 I'd been in that studio for six months. The room was L-shaped, with those ostensible chairs and desks on one end and the beds on the other. One of the beds had been assembled by my first roommate, but it had long disappeared beneath a mountain of beer cans that started at the bathroom door and

400

rose eight feet to a spot on the far wall. That's where I lived, in a space maybe three feet high and three feet wide, with my typewriter, books, psychedelics, cigarettes, bags of weed and cold packs of beer. It seems like a pretty freakish scene in retrospect (because the mountain wasn't made solely of beer cans, of course, there were plenty of fast food wrappers, newspapers and empty wine and liquor bottles in there, too), but I was reasonably comfortable and not the type to encourage visitors.

I know none of my ninth floor neighbors had been past my door. They must have had their suspicions, of course, and it's even possible that curiosity was the reason they elected a delegate to approach me one afternoon. I'd just stepped off the elevator when I spotted John Bucknell (I'd played some intramural basketball with him) standing by the kitchen door.

"Wilson," he said, stepping forward and speaking in hushed tones, "I've been asked to speak to you by the other students on the floor."

"Hey, John," I said, waving a cold pack of *Olympia* in his face, "I haven't even used the fridge lately."

"No no," he said, "this is about your television. You do own one, don't you?"

I had an old TV with coat hanger rabbit ears. It sat at the foot of the beer mountain. "Yeah," I said. "What about it?"

"Well, you're the only guy on the floor who has one, and on Friday night Don McClean is appearing on the Johnny Carson show. You know who he is, don't you? He wrote that song 'American Pie?'"

"Uh huh."

"It's an amazing anthem, isn't it? We've all been trying to figure out what it means! And we thought you might let a group of us come to your room and watch McClean when he's on Friday night."

"You mean *late* on Friday night? Eleven-thirty or twelve, that kind of thing?"

"Uh huh. There'd be about ten of us. Is that too many, would we all be able to fit in there?"

"Oh yeah," I laughed. "There's even stadium seating."

"Huh?"

"Never mind."

"So it's okay with you then?"

"You're welcome to come, John, but remember ... it'll be Friday night, so I'm liable to be fucked up."

"Oh don't worry," John whispered, sidling up closer to me. "We're all taking LSD for this."

Shades of The Incredible Hulk incident crept into my mind. I actually thought about cleaning up the room, then decided it would make more sense to create an alcoholic amphitheater. Kind of flatten out rows of cans in a staircase pattern so there actually would be stadium seating. But I kept putting it off and the next thing I knew I was up in my nest on Friday night drinking Peyote Fizzes. These were an odd cocktail developed by a friend on campus, a barely there Vietnam vet who loved the peyote high but couldn't stand the taste of the buds. So he'd grind them into powder, put them in the bottom of a mason jar, fill the jar with beer and drink it.

The result was a foamy, vile green concoction that I thought was worse than chewing the buds. But what could I do? I had plenty of beer and he'd given me a bag of the chalky powder instead of buds. So I'd crack a can of *Heidelberg*, drink half of it down, then pour a stream of peyote into the hole and suck up the result. The biggest problem was quantity control: every time a gusher of green beer spilled onto my beard and shirt I'd figure half the high was wasted and initiate another round of Fizzes.

If drinking by yourself is bad juju, then drinking psychedelics alone is a recipe for madness. And with all those beers and the happy hour cocktails earlier in the day that evening was no Vision Quest. I was raving and sweating and swiping at phantoms in there, working the dark with the lights out, when somebody knocked on the door. I ignored it; I wasn't expecting anybody. Then there was more knocking, followed by the buzzing of voices in the hallway. *Oh shit,* I thought, *it's the Don McClean crowd!*

I sat up, pulled my beer-soaked T-shirt over my gut and made a few passes at wiping the foam from my beard. "Come in!" I croaked finally.

The knob turned and the door pushed open as far as it could, which was about three feet. I saw John Bucknell down there, his red Afro backlit by the hallway. He was trying to widen the gap.

"That's all there is," I said. "You'll have to squeeze through."

He seemed tentative and weird, like he was walking into a trap, and kept glancing around as the others piled up behind him.

"Where are you?" he said. "Why does it sound like you're up on the ceiling?"

"And what's all that smoke?" said a voice behind him. "Is the room on fire!?"

I remembered they were on acid and wondered, just for an instant, if the next few moments would be good for them.

But the sensation passed. "There's a light switch beside the door," I said. "Turn it on and come in."

Bucknell flipped the switch and I heard a collective gasp from the group. I'd been chain smoking joints and cigarettes with the windows closed and had the thermostat set at seventy-five, so for those young stoners it must have seemed like a steamy wino jungle in there. Except it was a dorm studio just like their own.

All of them gasped, and two girls in the back took one glance inside and ran for it.

And they could still barely see me. You had to take a step or two inside, bend down beneath the smoke and let your eyes follow the garbage staircase to the top. John and a girl student tried, then drew back in horror when they spotted my wild, foam-splotched carcass against the ceiling. They scrambled backwards and caucused with the other students as I thought, *Fuck a duck, weirdos, you're only here to watch TV!*

Eventually they agreed. There were four girls and an equal number of guys and John pointed to the television set. "So ... can we turn that on and watch Don McClean?" he asked. "He should be just about on now."

"Sure," I said. "And sit wherever you want."

They moved forward two at a time, eyes averted and lips trembling, as they clambered over the cans and positioned themselves in rows above the television. John got it working but it was hard to see the screen with the glare from the overhead light.

"You'll have to turn the light off," I told him.

This was cause for still another caucus and the room was so thick with tension you could hardly breathe in there. (Well, I suppose you could hardly breathe in there, anyway.) And there must have been some pretty primal smells happening, especially on LSD. After the light went out the eight of them sat as rigid as statues as McClean came on and started chatting with Johnny. I sank down in my nest to get more comfortable and rattled some cans in the process. Which made the couple in front of me jump straight in the air. They glanced at me nervously before settling back, their heads on a swivel in case I moved again.

Finally McClean took the stage and started singing his "Chevy to the levee" ballad. Or was it the one about Vincent Van Gogh? I know that when two of the girls started singing along I thought their voices were terrible. Then I realized they weren't singing but whimpering, little moans and gasps of terror.

"I'm freaking out!" I heard one of them whisper. "This is hell ... we're sitting in fuckin' hell!"

"And that High guy's a total psycho!"

"Shhhhh, he'll hear you."

Then there'd be quiet for a moment – this was Don McClean after all, this was why they'd dumped the lump in the first place – then:

"Oh my God ... something just moved beneath me! I think there's rats in here!"

"It's only the cans shifting. Listen to the music."

The longer the song went on the more the tension mounted until I couldn't tell whether it was the peyote rush or the situation but my body felt ready to explode.

Then I realized it was simply stomach distress. I tried to fart surreptitiously, but let go a good long loud one instead, blasting the room with gas.

It turned into a bugle call:

"THAT'S IT I CAN'T STAND IT LET ME OUT! LET ME OUT!"

"ME TOO FUCK DON MCCLEAN GET OUT OF MY WAY!"

"AHHHHHHHHHHHH! MOVE MOVE MOVE!"

It was startling ... they all seemed to jump and lunge for the door at the same time. So of course they couldn't get a foothold in those beer cans and once the ones on top had careened into the group on the bottom the bunch of them rolled down the mountain and into the TV, knocking it backwards into the bathroom.

Where it exploded with a loud *Pop!* on the tile floor, sizzling in the dark as my fellow students writhed and screamed. I laid back on the cans and cracked another *Heidelberg*.

Turns out I wasn't the dorm type after all.

When I came back for my senior year, after another summer of bucking hay bales in the Sutter Basin, I was driving a gold, '63 Caddy with only 10,000 miles on it. (The boss' mom had owned it and when she died he sold it to me for 1,500 dollars.) I rented a small room above a Korean grocery downtown and drove the El Dorado back and forth to campus until one night I left the lights on and killed the battery. I meant to charge it but in the meanwhile it was easier to hitchhike or bum rides with friends. I remember parking tickets piling up on the windshield but hadn't noticed the car was gone until one morning I was hitching to campus and a middle-aged guy in a Cadillac stopped to pick me up. I hopped inside and chatted with him for awhile before I realized he was driving *my* car.

"Say, man," I said, "nice Caddy you got here."

"No shit, pal," he laughed. "The clown who owned it got a dead battery and left it parked on the street for months. The cops finally towed it away and I bought it at auction for two hundred bucks! Can you believe it! What a pathetic fuck that guy must be."

"Yeah," I laughed, "you got that right."

In the early 70s cocaine was hard to find and prohibitively expensive when you did ($100 to $120 a gram). This is what made Kevin Kleindale such a center of attention on campus. Not only was he the only guy at Evergreen with that overpriced bauble for sale, he had LOTS of it. And if you were willing to hang out and pretend to be his buddy, you could snort all you wanted for free.

This was easier said than done. Cocaine Kevin was a pale, skinny, bug-eyed creep who looked like a fish and chittered like a cricket: the first thing you thought when you met him is that he ate his own boogers and fondled children. I nicknamed him "Golem" and, inasmuch as he'd never read *The Lord of the Rings* (or any other fiction, for that matter), he took it as a compliment.

Still he taught me two of the most important things I learned at Evergreen. The first was that I'd do pretty much anything for a drug I wanted. I can't list the number of times over the years that one person or another has shown up at my door – all their own weed gone – because they know I'll get them high. When I feel like telling them to fuck off, or find myself sneering inwardly at the way they'll demean themselves for a hit … I think "Cocaine Kevin" and flick the Bic.

Because I was easily as big a loser as the other guys who crowded

Kleindale's house on weekends. The setup was simple. Kevin liked to play Monopoly, and if you wanted to hang around and snort his coke you had to play it with him. Except there'd often be fifteen or twenty of us there and not everyone could play at once so you'd wait your turn with the other coke whores in the living room. All of whom were doing monstrous quantities of blow and drinking hard liquor straight from the bottle. We'd sit around, gesticulating wildly and babbling like baboons, while Jimi Hendrix tapes played over and over in the background and different guys (as I learned later) scurried to the back bedroom to fuck Kevin's wife.

All I knew is that when you needed more coke you had to go into the kitchen to get it. That's where Kevin had a glistening white mound of the powder smack in the middle of the game board. The unspoken rule was that it was gauche to just lean in, make yourself a couple fat lines and snort them up. No, first you had to pretend to take an interest in the game itself. Who was winning, who was losing, how Kevin was doing and did he need encouragement or consolation. What's more you'd often have to get *in line* to do this, waiting like wobbly retainers for the moment Kevin inclined his head towards the coke mound.

"More coke? Oh really, Kev, do you think so? Well shit, thanks, man. Maybe just a couple (scrape scrape, honnnnnnnnnnnnnnnnk honnnnnnnnnnnnnnnk) lines here ..."

Every time I slunk back to that house I hated myself more than the time before. After a month of such weekends I was glad I didn't own a gun. Then one Saturday night the regular bathroom was backed up so I found the guest facilities and sat down on the toilet to relieve my numbing constipation. I picked up a magazine, felt too jittery and irritable to read and tossed it across the room. Reached over to a knee-high cabinet, slid back the door and fumbled inside. I wasn't looking for anything in particular, just killing time until my bowels moved, so was only mildly curious when my fingers closed on a cold, heavy package.

407

I dragged it into view, found myself staring at a huge bag of cocaine. The scrawled label on the front read "One lb./cut twice." My first inclination was to simply bury my face in it. Then I thought, *Hey, wait a minute ... I could take some of this and Cocaine Kevin would never know the difference.* And even if he did what could he do about it? Everyone who attended his Monopoly marathons was a potential suspect. Delirious, wretched hippy characters working their jaws like washing machines. I looked each of them over as I walked back through the living room, my dump forgotten and rationalizations rumbling through my head. *I wouldn't have to hang out with these characters anymore,* I thought, *or demean myself toadying up to Kevin.* Plus you really couldn't call what I was considering *theft,* not when it's coke I'd be snorting if I stuck around, anyway. Hell, I was just facilitating the process for everybody!

Even as my Jiminy Cricket consciousness whispered in the background that stealing was stealing and I was a pathetic piece of shit who WOULD do anything for a drug. I drowned it out with a long draught of tequila, considered my options. What was needed here was some stealth and patience and I had little of either; this left me with the Gumbo Approach, a move so bold and obvious that no one would believe it later.

So I walked straight up to Kevin and asked him for a baggie. He was squabbling with another freak over the rent on Park Place and hardly looked up, pointing across the kitchen to a drawer. I hurried over, drew out a sandwich bag. Grabbed a plastic drinking cup from the sink and returned to the guest bathroom. The coke was right where I'd left it and I opened the top, filled the plastic cup with powder and poured it into the baggie. It turned out to be a bit more than I'd planned on taking (just under an ounce, actually, or $3,000 worth), but I told myself there was no sense doing a regrettable thing halfway. I put the pound back in the cabinet, the baggie in my jacket pocket and walked out of Cocaine Kevin's for the last time.

It was late winter of my senior year and I was living in a deserted ranch house with no heat or electricity. I'd rented the place in January with two other students but when a snowstorm froze the pipes in the ceiling the whole roof collapsed. The only room left intact was mine. I'd spent my grant check insulating it with cases of cheap, 11-oz *Lucky Lager* cases, and since they were stacked five high against the walls and were, in effect, already *in* an icebox … I simply stuck around with them. I dressed in layers of clothes and cut arm and face holes from a sleeping bag I wore. I was trying to write short stories on my portable typer but it'd been pretty slow going until I stole that coke. Then the pages piled up in bunches. I had lines of blow on one side of me, sixers of *Lucky* on the other, and between them, the chain smoking and the typer I bobbed back and forth for days on end, circumventing the d.t.'s and cocaine blues by never coming down long enough to confront them.

When I finally did I was half blind, my bloody sinuses were swollen shut and everything I'd written was gibberish. This was my second lesson courtesy of Kevin, i.e., cocaine was a worthless drug. It promised much, delivered little and wasn't good for anything but doing more of it.

For this I'd traded my serotonin and integrity? I tossed what was left of the baggie in the snow outside and didn't breathe right for a month. Years later, when many of my friends were bankrupting themselves over coke, I stuck to psychedelics.

A true 'Greener, I used my experience from the inaugural year to land a job the following fall as weekend manager of the activities building. It was newly constructed and featured a cafeteria, a pool room, a swimming pool and a gym … none of which anybody used, particularly on weekends. (Which was hardly surprising and the main reason I took the job: I was more or less the closest thing to a jock the school had and you could bet none of my hippie classmates were swimming laps or pumping weights.)

I was supposed to be on site from 8:00 a.m. to 8:00 p.m. on Saturdays and Sundays and after a couple weekends of it, during which I might see one or two students the entire day, I called my freshman assistant Denny into the office.

"Denny," I said, "I want you to know I won't be coming in anymore."

"You're quitting?" he said.

"No, I just won't be coming in. There's nobody here on weekends, and no reason for two of us to waste our time. You can have this office, run the show yourself. If there's a problem … give me a call."

"But wait! You don't have a phone."

"That's better yet. You've a ready-made excuse if anything happens."

"I don't know," he said. "Isn't this … against the rules or something?"

"No, no," I said. "This is *Evergreen State*, pal. We make 'em up as we go along."

I had some vague guilt picking up my monthly checks the rest of the school year but it would pass when I'd run into Denny and he'd assure me the building was still comfortably empty on weekends. When the Activities Director finally caught on it was nearly May and what could he say? He was the head of recreation at Hippie U … he had less to do than I did.

I graduated in the spring of 1973 with a B.A. in Philosophy. Looking back I was grateful to Evergreen for affording me the best (if not the only) chance I had for earning a degree.

Though it didn't keep me from using my diploma as a bar coaster later.

After finishing college and another summer in the hay fields I began another novel called *Blue Yonder.* I worked on it off and on over the next three-and-a-half years while I drifted up and down the West Coast, following whim and circumstance through a series of towns and jobs. I was employed at a couple casinos in Nevada, a furniture store in Lacey, Washington, a roofing outfit in Petaluma, California, a restaurant in Seattle, the water department for the City of San Mateo and a horse ranch in Half Moon Bay, California. In between were a slew of part-time jobs, unemployment checks and friends who'd stash me in back rooms while I wrote. I will always love them dearly for that, particularly the ones who sheltered me while I was still drinking.

The boozing stopped, for all intents and purposes, in January of 1975. I was back at the Burlingame Hotel at the time, imbibing sporadically and living off the money I'd made working a warehouse demolition job in San Francisco, and the end – when it came – kind of surprised me. It had taken more and more booze to get over the withdrawal hump over the years but I was merely a weekend drunk by then so wasn't counting. Then one Sunday morning I woke in my seedy little room, manuscript and garbage all over the floor, and the d.t.'s were coming, they were always coming, I could feel that old alkie aura clanging like a cowbell. I had a pint of whiskey in the nightstand for just such emergencies but resisted reaching for it because I didn't actually *like* drinking in the morning.

But that dawn's Dread wore me down and I finally took a good long swig of the bourbon. Drank some water, lay back down, waited for the edges to soften. Nothing ... the d.t.'s got worse. I took another greedy gulp, then another, and the mental savagery only increased. Finally I finished the goddamned bottle and it was like I'd never picked it up ... *hair of the dog didn't work anymore!*

The end of the antidote was the end of my drinking days. Oh, I tried another half-dozen times over the next year or so, eventually reaching the point where one beer would give me the shakes the next morning and I had no way of combating it (other than with tranquilizers, of course, which I truly despised). Every cell in my body was telling me that the next time I drank I'd die and – thirty-five years later – they're still screaming it.

This personal aversion therapy proved so effective, in fact, that I later shared its tenets in a short-lived, alcoholic counselor career, suggesting to fellow drunks that perhaps they weren't drinking *enough*, that without some serious consequences they'd be weekend beer boys forever.

But they'd probably need a childhood rewiring of their brains first and it's not like there were no consequences for me. I severely damaged my liver and for twenty years after my last drink I was still subject to fearsome "d.t. flashbacks" – vicious, hallucinatory panic attacks that struck without warning and reminded me of the high price I paid for sobriety.

It's been a long time since the last episode, however, and I comfort myself with the idea that brain damaged is better than brain dead. As for being around other boozers in the three decades since, well, it's mostly just irritating. The upside of the drinking experience is that once you've been scared sober, the rest of life is infinitely easier.

The d.t.'s build character ... if you live.

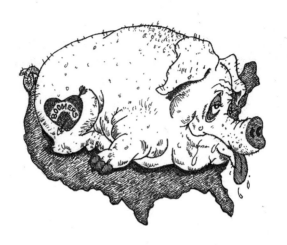

I'm sixty-four years old today. Being another year older is generally a mixed blessing at this age but what never changes is how lucky I was to be born in 1947. Every ten years I get up at those high school reunions to remind my classmates of that, how as part of America's "pig through the python" crowd (1946 – 62) we've had the best of everything all our lives.

Just the other day, for example, I was driving Brian, the twenty-five-year-old son of a friend of mine, to see his father. He's a husky, bright, good-looking kid who works in a warehouse, and I asked him how things were going.

"Not so great," he said. "Every woman I meet, the first thing they want to know is what I do for a living and how much money I make."

"You're kidding me."

"No. It's all about *greed* now!"

"You know," I said, "when your father and I were your age, the bigger the loser you were, the more likely you were to get laid. We looked *down* on guys with jobs."

Brian pulled a pack of cigarettes from his pocket and tapped one out.

"And those?" I said. "They were twenty-five cents a pack."

He lit up, blew some smoke in my face. "Fuckin' baby boomers," he said. "Someday we're coming for the lot of you, dude, and it won't be pretty."

I don't blame 'em a bit.

I went to a pot expo in San Francisco last April and bought a Volcano Vaporizer for five hundred cash. They're considered the Ferrari of vaporizers, with a patented technology that closely monitors the cylinder temperature and fills the "Easy Valve" bags quickly.

I bought it for my customers. I first tried the Volcano at a Tokers Bowl six years ago and didn't like the effect. It was a "blanket high" to me, a sort of slurred murmur of a load when what I'm looking for from pot is creative energy.

There's no question that vaporizers are easier on the lungs, though, and they're certainly more efficient than burning marijuana. This tracks well with my wheezy boomer customers, who after forty years of smoke are looking for a cheaper, safer way to get high. When they came to buy their ounces this time I plugged in the Volcano, gave them an opportunity to test the vapor effect for themselves.

They seemed to enjoy it but I didn't join them (particularly in the morning or early afternoon) because I haven't changed my mind about the high. What has changed is its relative utility: I now heat up

416

the Volcano late in the evening and suck down three or four bags in succession. Then I pass out, sleep a solid five to six hours and wake up rested. This is a miracle to a lifelong insomniac (and an effect rarely achieved when I smoke before retiring). I've often said that if a genie gave me a choice between "you can drink again" or "you can sleep like a real person," I'd be hard pressed to choose.

Now, in a way, I've tapped into both ... after twenty-odd hits of vapor the effect is similar to drunkenness. I lay on my couch in the dark, slobber on the chin with eyes glazed, and all seems right with the world, I'm back in those long ago alleys, bobbing in my blurry whiskey dreamboat.

Which is pretty much the only place I ever wanted to be. I knew that at nineteen and nothing's changed in the decades since. If anything my longing for a drink has increased, so abstaining as long as I have underscores how powerful my personal aversion therapy has been. Think about it ... thirty-five years have passed and I'm still scared shitless of alcohol.

That's some serious "rehab."
VA-PO-RIZE!

I finished the first draft of *Blue Yonder,* a partly autobiographical, partly fictional ode to a boy coming of age in the Sixties, in the summer of 1976. I was working in another Lake Tahoe casino at the time and living in a small room above a garage. I'd quit drinking the preceding April and had used weightlifting and a Spartan diet to drop fifty pounds in three months. When you threw in the beach volleyball and my dark tan it was probably the best I ever looked.

Once I affixed "The End" to *Blue Yonder* I felt better yet. At least until I reread it a month later. Then I realized that for all the people – friends and strangers alike – who'd read portions of it over the years and professed to like it … it was really just garbage. I wasn't a bad storyteller but so what? That made me an Irishman or a bartender, not a writer.

This wasn't *exactly* a revelation, the longer it had taken to finish the manuscript the more my confidence had waned, but I was still bitterly disappointed in myself. I spent a week or two wondering whether I should give up the dream of writing before I acknowledged that the *idea* of it was all I'd ever had, anyway. It was my excuse, the way to explain away a life of aimless drifting: "Oh yeah, I'm writing a novel."

I felt okay about that then and I still do. I *was* putting words to paper, after all, unlike the early years when I merely claimed to be, and what else was there for me to do with myself, anyway? I was totally devoid of ambition, had no career to postpone and wasn't looking to settle down anywhere.

Then I ran into Patti Carver. I'd taken a leave from the casino in September to be best man at a friend's wedding in Seattle and Patti was one of the guests. She was an ex-lover of the groom's and I'd always been fond of her. She was small and elfin, with a personality so buoyant she seemed to float in the air, and the longer I spoke to her the more she intrigued me.

The attraction was mutual ... we were in her bed four hours later and stayed there for a couple days. A month after that I'd quit my casino job and was living with Patti in an old house in the Fremont district of Seattle. It was the dead of winter and the place was a dump with no heat. I had two hundred bucks to my name while Patti was a part-time waitress who also volunteered at the local Scientology organization (or "Org" as they called it).

It was my idea of a settled time: Patti and I got along famously then and are still good friends now. We probably should have left it that way because Scientology ... I wasn't quite as fond of that. I had this naïve notion that Scientologists wanted to save the world but would somehow ignore me. My plan was to sit in that house and smoke the Thai sticks I'd brought along while trying to figure out whether to give *Blue Yonder* a reworking or start something new.

I made it two weeks. They were an excellent two weeks, at least until I figured out that all of Patti's friends were Scientologists, most of the books on the shelves were Scientology texts, and she and these other people talked some kind of weird Scientologese, making nouns into verbs ("cognition" to "cognate"), calling themselves "Thetans" and throwing around terms like "key-outs" and "floating needles."

Did I mind? Not really. Everything considered, in fact, I *preferred* the company of fringe characters, especially on Thai stick.

The problem began when Patti would leave my side. Then the other Thetans, subtly at first but with increasing emphasis as time went on, made clear to me that not only was it unacceptable for an "Officer" of the Org, like Patti, to be living with a non-Scientologist, but being around someone who used drugs was *completely* verboten.

I was, as far as they were concerned, "PTS," or a "potential trouble source."

Sounded right to me. (And here I was thinking I was a great guy because I didn't drink anymore.) I laughed off these mind police at first but when it became evident that my pot smoking was hurting Patti's relationship with her fellows – she, to her credit, never asked me to quit or join anything – I tried to step back and look at the big picture. Could I stop smoking dope? Except for the sixty days post-Herrick I'd been doing it every chance I got since 1965. And if I did, what would I do with no drug but nicotine in my life? I'd attempted *that* after Herrick and turned into a faraway, grim bastard.

But I'd had no support group then. And wasn't it time, on the cusp of my thirtieth birthday, to find out whether I could cut it in the world as a *totally* sober guy?

I decided to find out. I sold all but one Thai stick, spent a last night with its piquant reality distortion, then headed into Seattle the next day for a different weirdness altogether, joining Patti's Scientology Org.

In the years since I've often been asked to describe my Scientology experience and it was, oddly enough, a generally positive one. Oh, there were plenty of weird, paranoid bastards around and zealotry in general has always given me the creeps, but participating in the organization helped keep me sober – Scientologists are forbidden to use any recreational drugs except caffeine and cigarettes (the latter because L. Ron Hubbard, the founder, chain smoked) – and everything I learned in the classes validated what I'd believed since I was a teenager, i.e., that you're responsible for your own ass in this world.

Unfortunately taking care of mine meant finding a job. I answered a few ads in the paper, finally hired on at a fireplace warehouse in the industrial area. My official title was Pipe Washer, which meant that for $3.50 an hour I stood on a concrete floor in an unventilated room, clothed in a space suit and helmet as I dissolved grease from new pipes by dipping them in acid.

It was actually worse than it sounds, and so dangerous that after I'd been there a month I was rewarded a paltry 25 cent an hour raise. I should have been offended, I suppose, except it all seemed vaguely appropriate, as if dressing as an alien during the day and straggling to the Org as a Pod Person at night were concurrent, even reasonable fates.

The evenings and most of my time with Patti were when the sobriety was easiest. Trying to read, or walk around, or, worst of all, having to act interested in the course of general conversation ... this is when I felt the serious disconnect that has always made me partial to drugs. In a lot of ways that horrible little acid room at the warehouse – that none of the other dozen guys that worked there would even enter because of the fumes – was my sanctuary, the barrier that kept the world away while I struggled with the ennui.

I fight the same battle today with even fewer expectations of success. At least in '77 I still put some hope in reversible brain damage, the notion that after being afloat for so many years my psyche was suffering sea legs. As proof of how muddled I was Patti and I decided – after eight months of living together – to get married and move to Los Angeles.

Sometimes now I'll run across a photograph from the wedding. We had it in August on Fox Island, Washington, where after a Scientology ceremony in a small, rustic church we gathered with forty friends on the waterfront property that Patti's mother owned. No one but my little brother showed up from my family (the rest of them still think I was kidding), and Patti's father, Hartford, who lived in Spain and was long divorced from her mother, flew over to see us a week before the ceremony. He took us to an expensive Seattle restaurant for our first good meal in months and then stayed overnight at the Fremont house. I woke early the next morning, about 5:30, and went to make myself a cup of tea before heading for work. As I entered the living room I heard Hartford talking to Patti's mother on the telephone. He had his back to me and I was halfway past him when he mentioned my name.

"Damn it, Jean," he exclaimed, "we've gotta do something about this Wilson High character!"

Whoa, I thought, *this might be good*, and settled myself onto the couch behind him.

"'What do I mean?'" he said. "Well, how about this for starters. I take the two of them out to dinner and … mind you, these are thirty-year-old college graduates dressed in rags and participating in some fruity church … and I ask Wilson what he does for work. He's marrying my firstborn, right? This is a legitimate concern for a parent. And he says, 'Oh, I wash acid off pipe in a warehouse.' And I say, 'Well, that sounds pretty awful, Wilson. Why do you do it?' 'What the hell's the difference,' he says. *'There's no such thing as a good job!'* Can you believe that!? Huh!?"

I heard something loud on the other end of the line, probably laughter. Patti's mother was a misanthrope who basically didn't like anybody *but* me.

"I'm serious here, Jean! This guy's a bum, an alcoholic, a tumor on society and he's marrying *our daughter!*" On and on he went and the harder he pushed it the harder I imagined Jean yukking it up on the other end. Finally he slammed the phone down, spun around in the ratty office chair to find me slouched on the couch behind him.

He pulled out a cigarette, lit it without offering me one. "Well,

Wilson," he said finally, "how much of that did you hear?"

"All of it," I laughed, jumping up and giving him a slap on the back. "And you know what's even worse … dad?"

"What's that?"

"I agree with everything you said."

To his credit old Hartford kicked in with an all-expenses-paid honeymoon to Victoria, British Columbia, hoping, I guess, that I'd fall off the wagon *and* the ferry.

We moved to Los Angeles in September so Patti could work at an Org in the Hollywood area. I rented us a large one-bedroom apartment on Vermont Street and began scanning the want ads. My first job was selling frozen meat door-to-door in Watts, an experience so grim I barely remember the four days it took me to quit. Then I answered a Western Union advertisement for a teletype operator.

I was hired as a clerk in the money order department instead. This was at the main Western Union headquarters on Flower Street in L.A. and the office was open twenty-four hours a day. There were four cashier windows and we were separated from the customers by foot-thick bulletproof glass. This was partly the large amount of cash we carried and mostly the nature of the business, servicing generally desperate people (including criminals on the lam) and, at least in that office, a lot of angry Mexican guys. Illegal aliens who'd snuck across the border to do the shit jobs Americans didn't want. When they were paid they'd come in with cash to wire to their families back home (if they sent it through the mail it was *sure* to be stolen). Half of such money orders arrived without incident; the other half, though, were appropriated by the Mexican Telegrafica clerks, who deposited them in their own bank accounts to draw the high interest rates, then (six to twenty-four months later) would pass the original sum onto the families.

As if it had just arrived on horseback. In the meanwhile those same families were starving and papa in L.A. blamed Western Union for something we had zero control over. You'd try to explain this to them but they didn't speak English and the one girl in the office who understood Spanish refused to interpret for her countrymen. "Let the bastards learn the English!" she said. "I had to!"

The place was utter chaos and I took to it right away. (The same thing I liked about the casino jobs later, the way crazy things were happening every minute.) I particularly enjoyed processing orders at the counter. To keep boredom at bay I tried never to spend more than three minutes on a transaction. This was tricky because there was always money involved, either incoming or outgoing, and if your sheet didn't balance at the end of the day the difference was subtracted from your paycheck.

The other clerks? Most of them had been there for years and would often take as long as fifteen minutes to process a single order. On my sixth day on the job the District Supervisor, Ted Feeney, called me into his office.

"Well, Wilson," he said, "I've heard glowing reports about your progress."

"Well," I said, "I'm learning, Mr. Feeney."

"You're learning *fast,* son. So fast we've decided to make you a Shift Supervisor."

I remember I actually turned in my chair and looked around, as if he were speaking to someone behind me.

"Excuse me?" I said finally.

"We're going to make you the Alternate Shift Supervisor, Wilson. You'll take over when other supervisors are sick or on vacation, and in the meanwhile will fill in at different times during the week."

"But this is only my sixth day here!"

"You're a natural at this business."

"But I don't know anything yet!"

"You'll pick it up."

"This is nuts! What about the other clerks? You don't think they'll resent my being made their boss when I'm still an operations *trainee?*"

Feeney laughed. "You think I'd be doing this, High, if anybody else in there wanted the responsibility?"

And he was right ... if anything the other clerks felt sorry for me. Not only would I be personally responsible for over $100,000 a day in cash and complaints from dissatisfied customers (if they weren't in the lobby they were on the phone), but I'd have to do it on constantly changing shifts. A good week would be, say, when the Swing Shift Supervisor went on vacation and I'd go in at the same time everyday to fill in for him. That happened about once a month; the rest of the time I'd work a couple days on Day Shift, then a night on Graveyard, then three late afternoons on Swing, then maybe go back to Graveyard for a few nights.

All this as someone who had trouble sleeping in the first place, with the days off few and far between. As time passed and my grip on reality faded I had to hand it to Ted Feeney; it's like he'd been sitting there for years, waiting for some dumb fuck adrenaline junkie to show up.

I rarely saw Patti and was usually trying to sleep when I did. Before I met her I'd never owned furniture and the cohabitation and marriage vows hadn't changed that. The apartment was carpeted so we slept on the bedroom floor under a blanket and, other than an old chair I found in the alleyway behind us, that was all the amenities we had. We didn't even own silverware until she stole a fork from the Org commissary. She'd use it to eat the only food in the house, frozen packages of Eggplant Parmesan that I'd store in the freezer for her.

I ate out when I bothered to eat at all. It seems like a bleak tableau in retrospect but it was pretty much how I'd always lived without the booze and drugs. And I got away with it precisely because I saw so little of Patti.

She never complained, though, and that should have told me something. I thought she was guilty about wanting to move to L.A. so

425

she could work twelve hours a day, seven days a week at a Scientology Org (for zero wages). More likely, though, she just stopped giving a damn. To hear her now my reluctance to have children caused our split but every time she brought the subject up I thought she was kidding: how could anyone who considered me father material be responsible enough to have kids?

Plus I was going through some serious personality disintegration. Between the stress of that job, the long and bizarre hours, the lack of sleep and the sobriety I was watching the color bleed from my life. There was a little closet off the living room where I had my typewriter on a shelf and I liked to drag the kitchen chair in there and sit in the dark. Light one cigarette after another so I could watch the flame jitter in my hands. I was thirty years old and I was living off my own juices instead of a bottle. My marriage was going to hell, there was a locomotive in my head and a pool at the office over when I'd drop from exhaustion ... and I couldn't connect to any of it. Was I having a nervous breakdown, or was this simply what being sober was all about?

A little of both, I think. Patti and I saw less and less of each other and began to quarrel when we did. Just before Christmas I came home to find she'd moved out. This was evident from the note taped to the refrigerator:

Dear Wilson:

I've left. You can keep the TV.

Love,
Patti

We'd been married six months.
We'd never owned a television.

Patti leaving was certainly another low point in the days. Not because it was unexpected or we should have stayed together, but because my whole existence was ashes. There I was in Los Angeles, the place where Western civilization ran out, with a murderous job, a failed six-month marriage, a worthless novel and no prospects. Worse yet, the only thing I'd done right in the last ten years was scaring myself straight with alcohol, so now I couldn't even get drunk.

I did the next best thing and quit the Western Union job. Found a ratty little studio apartment on South Benton Way and spent a couple months living off my savings. It was an odd but instructive time, one when I walked from dawn to dusk and tried to take stock of my life. I kept running into the notion that it was hard to believe I'd failed when I'd never set any goals to begin with. It was also, I think, a source of vindication to me that sobriety was as terrible as I'd imagined.

But that was tough shit, of course, because there'd be no more drinks for me: I'd put a bullet in my head before suffering one more second of withdrawal. What I finally concluded was that if life was going to be all sharp corners for awhile then I needed some art in my days. I'd oil painted as a kid and loved the smell of turpentine and so – in my continued (and ultimately ill-fated) crusade to stay totally sober – I bought myself a set of acrylics and began doing still lifes.

They all came out as cartoons. A painting would only take me a day or two, and sometimes I wouldn't realize it until later, but eventually I'd work through the clutter of canvases and find even the most serious work had an irreverent, comic book quality to it. This was my first hint that the cartoonist mentality I'd grown up with hadn't disappeared over time but was, in fact, *me*.

In the meanwhile I'd hired on at a one-hundred-partner law office in Century City as one of the first of the "word processors." The system we used was called *Compu-Text* and, like the company that designed it, would be defunct in a year or two. In the meanwhile it was easy enough to learn and over the first three months I worked there I realized something even more important, i.e., that the faster I typed the more attorneys paid me.

Then just as summer came around I hit my real low point. I thought I'd developed some weird flu and called in sick at work for a couple days. On the third day, when I had trouble lifting my head, I grabbed a cab to the Kaiser Hospital emergency room. They said they thought I had hepatitis – but maybe mononucleosis – so I should check back with them if my skin or eyes turned yellow.

Two feverish days later I looked in the mirror and sure enough my eyes were yellow and the skin on my face lime green. I went back to Kaiser and was admitted to intensive care with a fever of 105. Apparently I'd eaten a tainted burrito or its equivalent over the past few months because I had a severe case of Hepatitis B. I was hooked up to IVs and remember nothing but delirium and oppressive fever for days, then finally waking to a doctor standing over my bed with an x-ray. They'd shot me full of dye and taken a picture of my liver and that, apparently, was the flaming red watermelon he was pointing at.

"I'm Dr. Emery, a liver specialist, Wilson," he said. "You have to tell me … are you a heavy drinker of alcohol?"

"I was," I croaked. "Nothing for a year or so, though."

"Well, it appears that cirrhotic tissue – or scarring – is why your liver is so swollen from the hepatitis. Do you see it here? It takes up almost the whole side of your body! It should be one-third that size, Wilson! You're in a very serious state here!"

I did a bit of a gag, then passed out again. It is roughly before or after this point, my mother tells me, that she and my father received a call from Emery at their apartment in San Mateo. (I was surprised he even knew where they were, but I must have listed them on an application at work.) It was my mom who answered and Emery introduced himself, detailed the circumstances and asked, in the event of my death, if they wished to claim the body.

"It's that bad?" she asked.

"It's almost total liver failure at this point, Mrs. High," he said. "I'm sorry, but I think it's likely Wilson will expire within the next twenty-four hours."

"Well," my mother responded, "I wouldn't count him out yet. He's fooled you doctors before."

Two days later I woke with a normal temperature. It would take months for the swelling in my liver to subside enough for a biopsy, and in the meanwhile I spent six months on disability. My mother only told me about her conversation with Emery a couple years ago, and I certainly didn't feel like I'd survived a near-death experience at the time. Mostly I was just irritated that I was so exhausted morning, noon and night. I had few friends in Los Angeles so spent my time in that little room reading novels and taking short walks in the neighborhood.

I gave up the painting and haven't picked up a brush since. It was 1979 before I went back to work at the law firm. The booze had almost killed me in more ways than one and, according to Dr. Emery, I wasn't clear of its consequences yet. He called me at the office not long after

I returned to tell me he couldn't figure out the biopsy results.

"What do you mean?" I said.

"Well, it's like they're not even liver cells ... we've never seen anything like them and don't know what we've got here. So I'm sending the results to specialists around the country to see what they think. I'll get back to you."

I was feeling better by then so didn't think much of it. Nearly a year later, though, the week before I left the firm and moved to Seattle, he called back.

"So what's the verdict, Doc?" I asked.

"I'm still not sure," he said.

"Really? What about all those specialists? What did they say?"

"They don't know, either. How are you feeling?"

"Great. I'm moving to Seattle next Monday."

"Well, Wilson, what I do know is that your liver is heavily scarred and full of granulomas."

"What the hell's a *granuloma?*"

"They're distinctive formations characterized by giant cells. They can be one hundred times larger than your normal cells and are surrounded by inflammatory cells. More significant to you is that, well ... they shouldn't be in your liver."

I paused, drew out a Camel and lit it. No sense worrying about cigarettes anymore. "So ... what are you saying? That I'm dying of giant cells?"

"I don't know what to tell you, Wilson. If I had to give a prognosis I'd say that, given the present state of your liver, you may have five, maybe ten years at best. IF you stay off the booze."

So over thirty years later the only time I'm reminded I have a liver problem is when I take a Vitamin B supplement. Then I more or less fall over and spend the next twenty-four to forty-eight hours in bed with mono-like symptoms. I tell this to doctors and they tell me I'm crazy, that my enzyme levels are excellent so my liver must be, too.

Even if the functional part of it is roughly the size of a golf ball.

Before I left Los Angeles there were a couple of things I had to take care of. The first was marijuana. I'd spent two-and-a-half years using no drug other than nicotine and it had been a very negative experience. I'd hoped that the dull emptiness I suffered was merely a drying out period, my sodden brain readjusting to life without booze, but when I was honest with myself, it was simply more of the malaise I'd suffered as a teenager. (I once estimated that I've awakened in a bad mood about 98% of my life.)

Except then I'd been able to stave off the ennui with Herculean tasks: making an athlete of myself, doing elaborate cartoons for anyone who asked, working lunatic jobs, even pretending to be a regular guy. It was like I needed constant risk to function and, failing that, some way to change my mood artificially.

Life ceased to be an experiment to me when I was straight, in other words. I loathed the nothingness of my sober self, the way I felt so dry and hollow inside. What's more it wasn't the alcohol or coke or psychedelics I missed as much as I did good weed. When I'd established (to my own satisfaction, anyway) that it was the only relief available, I bought an ounce of primo bud from a taxi driver buddy. Rolled a joint and took it to the underground garage where I worked so I could smoke it at lunch. I had an old '62 Ford that I drove at the time and after hurriedly shoving a sandwich down I fired up the reefer.

Years later I'd walk into my twenty-year high school reunion and, after not smoking for three years, buy four packs of Camels and two lighters in the hotel gift shop. *No sense in fuckin' around,* I thought, and the same applied when I toked that first joint: I sucked 'til it was gone, then stepped out of the Ford and looked around.

I was back.

The last issue I needed to handle before leaving L.A. was a divorce from Patti. Neither of us had ever submitted the legal paper work and now she was pregnant with her first child and eager to marry the father (another Scientologist, of course). I sure as hell wasn't going to hire a lawyer to do the filing – not with no children, property or acrimony involved – and I was too lazy to do it myself.

Especially when it had been such a tenuous marriage to begin with; an annulment seemed way more appropriate. And then it hit me: why not get a Tijuana divorce? There was some question about their legality but what did I care … for anyone to challenge it there'd have to be someone who cared.

So I took a day off from work and drove to Mexico. When I crossed the border and pulled into Tijuana I saw that all the shabbiest buildings had "Divorce" shingles hanging from their doors. I stopped at the first one I came to, a faded stucco building that looked more like a bunker than an office, and walked inside.

There was a rumpled old Mexican guy asleep on the floor, which only made sense given there wasn't any furniture around. I walked over, nudged him with my shoe.

"Hola, Paco," I said, remembering my one line of Spanish. "Que tal?"

He snorted himself awake, looked up at me and scrambled to his feet. "Oh excuse me, señor," he said. "I must have dozed off somehow."

"No problem," I said. "Are you the attorney? I need a divorce."

He laughed. "Oh no, señor, I am not the attorney, I am his assistant. He will be here soon. Allow me to escort you into his office."

He opened the door behind him and led me into a still smaller room with a desk and two chairs. It must have been 90 degrees in there and the warm air was thick with flies.

"If you wait here," said the assistant, motioning to the chair in front of the desk, "I will see that the esteemed Señor Lopez is with you pronto."

I sat down, opened my shirt collar and lit a cigarette. Only the smoke kept those hungry flies at bay and sweat was streaming down my face and chest by the time Julio Lopez, Esq. arrived. He was nearly as tall as I was and twice as wide. He stormed through the door, flung it closed behind him and walked past me with barely a nod. Slammed his metal briefcase on the desktop and clicked it open. I expected to see some sheaths of paper inside, maybe a couple of law books or a notepad or two.

Instead there was only a single, wadded up *Time* magazine, its top encrusted with squashed insects. The attorney reached in, grabbed the bottom half of it and started whacking flies. *Whap! Whap! Whap!* He was smashing them against the wall, popping them out of the air like raindrops. It was perfect, it felt like the end of the world. I leaned back in my chair, crushed out my cigarette on the floor. Looked over at Señor Lopez's diplomas on the wall and all of a sudden it hits me: college, marriage, writing a novel … they were all the same to me. Not serious endeavors, just stuff I wanted to try before I died.

I sniggered out loud at the sick, twisted irony of it all, making the attorney pause. He lowered the magazine, turned around and looked at me.

"Oh excuse me, señor," he said. "Do you *like* flies?"

THE END

About the Author

Park, a longtime factotum and drifter, now wanders the streets of Portland, Oregon with a dog named Hobo.

UNIVERSITY OF HELL PRESS

CPSIA information can be obtained at www.ICGtesting.com
Printed in the USA
BVOW040949011212

307026BV00001B/9/P